AUDITING
PUBLIC
EDUCATION

AUDITING PUBLIC EDUCATION

Current Status and Future Potential

Peter L. McMickle
Gene Elrod

THE AIDE PROJECT

This publication was financed through funds provided by the Elementary and Secondary Education Act of 1965 (Public Law 89-10, Title V, Section 505) and the State of Alabama. However, the findings, conclusions, and opinions expressed herein are those of the authors and do not necessarily reflect the position or policy of the U.S. Office of Education or the Alabama Department of Education, and no official endorsement should be inferred.

Printed in the United States of America
Library of Congress Catalog Card Number: 74-620040

"AUDITING to IMPROVE DEPARTMENTS of EDUCATION"
— The AIDE Project —
304 Dexter Avenue
Montgomery, Alabama 36104

Project Staff
Peter L. McMickle
Gene Elrod

State Coordinator
W. H. Kimbrough, Director
Division of Administration and Finance
Alabama Department of Education

U. S. Office of Education Coordinators
A. L. White, Division of State Assistance
U. S. Office of Education
Department of Health, Education, and Welfare

Allen King, Division of State Assistance
U. S. Office of Education
Department of Health, Education, and Welfare

Policy Committee
LeRoy Brown, State Superintendent of Education, Alabama
J. W. Edgar, Commissioner of Education, Texas
Lyman Ginger, Superintendent of Public Instruction, Kentucky

Technical Committee
Robert J. Freeman, Professor of Accounting, University of Alabama

Leon R. Graham, Assistant Commissioner for Administration, Texas Education Agency

Lennis M. Knighton, Professor of Accounting and Public Administration, Brigham Young University

James P. Melton, Assistant Superintendent, Division of Administration and Finance, Kentucky Department of Education

Philip S. Shaw, Comptroller, Florida Department of Education

William H. Van Horn, Assistant Deputy Commissioner, Texas Education Agency

Ex-Officio Members:

Mortimer A. Dittenhofer, Assistant Director, Financial and General Management Studies Division, U. S. General Accounting Office

Philip Kropatkin, Deputy Director, HEW Audit Agency

John J. Lordon, Director, Office of Financial Management, U. S. General Services Administration

Acknowledgements

This research study was possible only through the combined efforts and cooperation of a great many individuals and organizations. To list them all would be impossible, but we would like to give a special "thanks" to those to whom we are particularly indebted.

We wish to express our sincere appreciation for the comments, advice, and encouragement received from the members of our Policy and Technical Committees. These distinguished authorities have actively participated in every stage of the project.

The Alabama State Department of Education has administered this project in cooperation with the Texas Education Agency and the Kentucky Department of Education. We wish to thank Dr. LeRoy Brown, Alabama Superintendent of Education; Dr. J. W. Edgar, Texas Commissioner of Education; and Dr. Lyman Ginger, Kentucky Superintendent of Public Instruction and their staffs for giving so generously of their time and assistance.

We owe a special debt of gratitude to Dr. William H. Kimbrough, Director of the Division of Administration and Finance, Alabama State Department of Education, who has served as State Coordinator of the project. We would also like to acknowledge the contribution of Dr. Edward M. Lindbloom, former Project Director, who, for reasons of health, was unable to continue with the Project.

We gratefully recognize the assistance of the U.S. Office of Education. We would particularly like to thank Dr. A. L. White and Mr. Allen King, our USOE Coordinators, who have worked closely with the Project and have contributed a great deal of time and effort toward the accomplishment of this study. We also thank the HEW Audit Agency and the U.S. General Accounting Office for their cooperation.

Our technical consultants, Dr. Robert J. Freeman and Dr. Lennis M. Knighton, are nationally recognized authorities in the field of governmental accounting and auditing. The Project and the Project Staff have truly profited from their assistance and close association.

We would also like to acknowledge the assistance of the Brigham Young Survey Research Center in the tabulation and analysis of our questionnaire data.

We deeply appreciate all the assistance, encouragement, and late hour help we have received from our editorial consultants, Gail McMickle and Ed Nivert. Thanks also to our secretary/typist, Mrs. Suzette Allen, who had to decipher our handwritten drafts. Finally, we would like to thank the State Education Agency and State Audit Agency personnel throughout the nation who have contributed so much to this study. The response to our questionnaires and the many courtesies extended during our interviews made this an especially rewarding and pleasant experience.

Pete McMickle
Gene Elrod
April 1, 1974

PREFACE

In early 1970, the U.S. Office of Education became interested in the possibility of sponsoring interstate research projects that dealt with auditing and accountability of public education programs. This interest had developed as a result of a number of factors and events.

. . There was concern over the increasing number and severity of audit exceptions associated with Federal elementary and secondary education programs.

. . It was felt that current audit procedures and reports were not fully oriented to the program needs of educational managers.

. . There had been a recent surge of interest at the national level concerning the accountability of educational management and the potential of performance auditing as an accountability technique.

The Office of Education was aware that the General Accounting Office was sponsoring a study of governmental auditing standards which later resulted in the publication *Standards for Audit of Governmental Organizations, Programs, Activities and Functions.* An informal liaison was established between the Office of Education's Division of State Agency Cooperation and the Audit Standards Working Group. As a result, the Office of Education decided to give priority status to auditing and accountability as potential areas of research for ESEA Title V, Section 505 Projects. This program authorizes special research projects which have the potential of making ". . . a substantial contribution to the solution of problems common to the State Educational Agencies of all or several states."

Subsequently, the Office of Education approved a proposal for an interstate project submitted by the State of Alabama in cooperation with the States of Texas and Kentucky. The objective of this project was to: investigate auditing of, by, and involving State Education Agencies for the purpose of making auditing more beneficial for State Education Agency management. The original title of the project was "Accountability in Educational Management: The Use of the Audit Process to Improve the Management of Federally Assisted Educational Programs." The title was later changed to "The AIDE Project" — AIDE standing for *Auditing to Improve Departments of Education.*

The AIDE Project began in June of 1970. The Project Staff initiated the study by consulting with leading authorities in the fields of Auditing and Education. They then assembled what was to become one of the nation's most comprehensive libraries on auditing, public education, and accountability. By means of a cross-index, the data collected proved to be beneficial in all phases of the Project research. After an in-depth analysis of this material, a conceptual framework of auditing was developed for use in the examination and evaluation of the SEA audit environment.

The Project Staff commenced their field studies with a series of visits and interviews with U.S. Office of Education managers and with auditors from the General Accounting Office and HEW Audit Agency. These interviews were followed by visits to nine State Education Agencies.

Alabama

California	Florida
Kentucky	Maryland
Massachusetts	Ohio
Texas	Washington

In conjunction with these visits the AIDE Staff also called upon State Audit Agencies, and Regional OE, HEW Audit Agency, and GAO Offices.

In order to gain a more comprehensive view of State Education Agency/Local Education Agency Auditing, a detailed questionnaire (See Appendix A) was mailed to the remaining 41 State Education Agencies. Response was excellent, with 90% of the State Education Agencies returning a completed and usable questionnaire. The Project Staff analyzed this data with the assistance of the Brigham Young University Survey Research Center.

During this period, three interim reports were constructed and presented to the Policy and Technical Committees. These Committees assisted in the development of the project design; provided suggestions, encouragement, and assistance in the implementation of Project research; and evaluated the results of each project stage including a critique of each interim report.

The Project Staff has now concluded their study of educational auditing. The results of their research is reported in the following pages of this publication. Currently, the AIDE Project is conducting seminars for the purpose of further disseminating the research findings. The Project Staff is also developing SEA auditor training courses and professional development courses on auditing for State Education Agency managers which will be pilot tested in at least three States.

TABLE OF CONTENTS

APPENDIXES

LIST OF TABLES

LIST OF ILLUSTRATIONS

ACRONYMS AND ABBREVIATIONS

AIDE	The AIDE Project — "Auditing to Improve Departments of Education."
CPA	Certified Public Accountant
CSSO	Chief State School Officer
GAO	U.S. General Accounting Office
HEW	U.S. Department of Health, Education, and Welfare
HEWAA	HEW Audit Agency
LEA	Local Education Agency
OE	U.S. Office of Education
PA	Public Accountant
SAA	State Audit Agency
SEA	State Education Agency

CHAPTER I

INTRODUCTION

This study is about *Auditing Public Education*. The administrative hierarchy of *public education* is the public elementary and secondary school, the School District (Local Education Agency), and the State Department of Education (State Education Agency). In this country there are approximately 16,000 Local Education Agencies and fifty-five State Education Agencies (including Territories). *To delimit and facilitate our discussion, the primary focus of this report is upon auditing at the State Education Agency (SEA) level.* However, auditing at the Local Education Agency (LEA) level is also considered.

This environment of auditing includes (1) Federal audits of the administration of Federal education programs at the State and Local level, (2) State Audit Agency audits of State and Local Education Agencies, (3) State Education Agency internal audits, (4) SEA external audits of Local programs, and (4) several other categories of auditing such as CPA audits of school districts. Some of the significant issues and topics discussed in the following chapters include:

. . The nature, essential characteristics, and fundamental concepts of auditing.
. . How auditing has been changing on a national basis.
. . The current status and future potential of SEA/LEA auditing.
. . Attitudes, concerns, and perceptions of SEA managers and Federal/State auditors.

. . How performance/operational/management audits are conducted.
. . The weaknesses and strengths of the Federal-State-Local audit network.
. . New Federal Audit Standards and what they mean for audits of State and Local Education Agencies.
. . Audit settlement processes including new Federal audit arbitration procedures.
. . The need for and potential usefulness of SEA internal auditing.

This study is prompted, in part, by recent events in the fields of Auditing and Education. In the past few years, auditors — particularly governmental auditors — have been expanding the scope of their audit activities to encompass management or program matters. At the same time, there has been a secondary movement to make auditing more management aid oriented and somewhat less of a policing or oversight technique.

In the field of Education, a related occurrence is the "Accountability in Education" movement. This movement, which started in 1969, emphasizes that Educators must be accountable for results. This has, in turn, stimulated expansion of the scope of educational auditing as an accountability device.

Educators and auditors have responded to these changes in auditing with mixed emotions. Some of their concerns, include:

. . To what extent, if any, can or should auditing concern non-financial, management activities?
. . What authority do auditors have to make broad scope audits?
. . Since most auditors have an accounting background, are they qualified to do more than a financial audit?
. . How can a management audit be logically conducted in areas where no generally accepted standards exist, either for the management activity or the auditor himself?
. . Is it possible for the auditor to be both (1) the critical representative of the audit user, and (2) a valued consultant to auditee management?
. . Is it really possible for auditing to be a significant aid to educational management?

In subsequent chapters, these and many other issues are examined and discussed. However, this report is not intended to represent a comprehensive analysis of all aspects of educational auditing. But this discussion should provide insight into many matters that are of interest to both educators and auditors.

This book is organized into six chapters. The following chapter is an in-depth review of the development of contemporary auditing. This discussion provides a background on how and why auditing has been changing. Chapter III develops a conceptual framework that identifies important audit concepts and discusses proper approaches to the conduct of contemporary auditing. Chapter IV, identifies and discusses the audit agencies that are members of the SEA/LEA Audit network. The findings of The AIDE Project are presented in Chapter V. This chapter is organized around Chapter II's conceptual framework of auditing and compares actual conditions against the "ideal." The final chapter discusses future directions of SEA/LEA auditing including specific recommendations of The AIDE Project.

This book is principally addressed to two user groups: LEA/SEA/OE Managers and Local/State/Federal Auditors. For the educational manager, this report can (1) clarify the changes that are taking place in the field of auditing, (2) show the manager what he can and *should* expect from auditors, and (3) identify ways in which the manager himself can make auditing of educational programs more positive and beneficial. For the educational auditor, this report can (1) help him place his audit activities in perspective, (2) provide suggestions and ideas concerning the proper conduct of contemporary audits, and (3) help him maximize his audit productivity.

Through constructive discussion of problems and issues, possible solutions often become evident. Research studies such as The AIDE Project can serve as the reinforcing element, resource document, and/or connecting thread for new ideas, practices, and procedures. Therefore, the mission of this study is to provide the fertile soil from which ideas may grow for making audits more beneficial for Educational Management.

CHAPTER II

THE EVOLUTION OF
AUDIT CONCEPTS

In this chapter, the evolution of auditing is reviewed in order to provide a framework for interpretation of present concepts. For example, a current and significant auditing controversy concerns extension of the scope of auditing beyond traditional boundaries. This chapter supplies a basis for analysis of such issues.

ANCIENT TO 1500

"Whenever the advance of civilization brought about the necessity of one man being entrusted to some extent with the property of another, the advisability of some kind of check upon the fidelity of the former would become apparent."[1] Thus, many ancient civilizations developed various audit-type procedures.

As far back as 2,000 B.C., the Egyptians employed a type of checking process. Money was unknown at that time and a barter economy existed. This system necessitated a large number of government storehouses for the keeping of the royal treasury. Shipments in and out of the storehouses were carefully controlled. For example, when grain was to be carried to a storehouse, each sack was filled in the sight of an overseer; and noted and recorded by a scribe. When the grain was delivered to the storehouse, a scribe stationed there recorded the amount received. Thus, the activities of one man were checked — and, in a sense audited — by another.[2]

Centuries later, the Greeks instituted a system of verifying public accounts by means of checking-clerks. Every official who had any part in government or administration was subjected to scrutiny at the expiration of his office. According to Aristotle (384-322 B.C.), "No person who had not rendered his account could go abroad, consecrate his property to a god, or even dedicate a sacred offering; nor could he make a will, or be adopted from one family into another."[3]

In China, during the Han dynasty (200 B.C.), all financial officers of different governmental agencies throughout the country were required to go to the national capital to make their annual reports in person. Despite the fact that travel between the capital and the different provinces was quite difficult, this audit-type process was carried out satisfactorily.[4]

Although rudimentary concepts of auditing were developed and used by various ancient civilizations, the lineage of modern auditing stems from the Roman descendents in England and Europe. The word audit is derived from the Latin word *auditus,* meaning a hearing (as is audience, audition, and audio).[5] The term was first used in Roman times when the records of the "Quaestors" (treasurers) were required to be heard upon their leaving office.[6]

The actual basis or foundation of contemporary auditing is found in the audit practices that arose following the dark ages in England and Europe, around the thirteenth and fourteenth centuries. A respected individual or individuals, considered qualified and independent, would examine the accounts of some governmental agency, merchant guild, family business or estate. Frequently, the job of auditor was a temporary position held by a private individual who had been appointed by some higher authority for the term of one audit. The audit consisted of a detailed examination of the accounts for the purpose of detection and prevention of fraud and, secondarily, for the detection of error.

For example, the English Statute 13 Edward I. C. II (A.D. 1285), "Concerning servants, baillifs, Chamberlains, and all manner of Receivers which are bound to yield Accompt," provides

> That when the Masters of such Servants do assign Auditors (*auditores*) to take their Accompt, and they be found in arrearages upon the Accompt, all Things allowed which ought to be allowed, their Bodies shall be arrested, and by the Testimoney of the Auditors of the same Ac-

compt, shall be sent or delivered unto the next Gaol of the King's in those Parts.[7]

In the late thirteenth century accounts of landed estates were carefully audited. A thirteenth century French treatise on estate management recommends that the lord of the manor ought to command that the accounts be heard every year at each manor. The auditors ought to be faithful and prudent, knowing their business. "It is not necessary," states the author of the treatise, "so to speak to the auditor (*acunturs*) about making audit because of their office, for they ought to be so prudent, and so faithful, and so knowing in their business, that they have no need of other teaching about things connected with the account."[8]

City of London records show that the accounts of the Chamberlain were audited in the time of Edward I. In 1298 the Mayor, Aldermen, Sheriffs, and certain others were appointed auditors; and a few years later — in 1310 — "Six good men of the City were elected in the presence of the whole Commonalty."[9]

In Peebles, Scotland, the audit was held before the provost, council, and inhabitants of the Burgh after warning by "Proclamatioun to cum and heir thair thesaurare (storehouse or treasure) to mak his compt as vse is." The records refer to the "awdytouris" under date 17th November 1457, when the "cont" of the Burge of Pebillis was made. Again, in 1458, the names of the auditors (eight in number "with other mony") are given, and it is said that "all thingis contyt that suld be contyt and alowit that suld be lowyt" — a comprehensive, but rather vague certificate.[10]

1500-1840

From the sixteenth century onwards there is ample evidence that the advisability of having accounts audited was widely recognized. Most audits in this period were of governmental activities, but there were also examples of private audits for businessmen or firms. There was no real change in the scope of auditing in this period. The major objective continued to be the detection of fraud with the detection or error of secondary importance.

In 1711 the "Commissioners for Taking, Examining, and Stating the Public Accounts" reported to the English House of Commons on the abuse of public funds by John Churchill, first Duke of Marlborough, and Robert Walpole, first Earl of Oxford. Interestingly, their reports of 1711 (16 pgs.) and 1712 (35 pgs.) also considered such issues as *"mismanagements,"* possible *"savings," "legality"* of governmental activities and expenditures, and proper *"comptrol."*[11]

In Stirling, Scotland, in 1695, steps were taken to make the audit more independent and effective by enacting certain rules for selecting auditors.

> . . . that neither provosts nor bailies should be auditors of the accounts, but that, in addition to the ordinary number of auditors chosen by the town council, two merchants should be chosen by the guildry and two tradesmen by the incorporated trades; that the auditors should have the exclusive power to approve or reject the accounts as they see cause; that the burgesses should be entitled to inspect the accounts and state objections during the auditing; and that members of council should, at their election, be sworn to observe these rules in all time coming.[12]

Auditors in this period were usually respected "Amatures" appointed for a particular audit. In fact, such an appointment was often considered an honor. The professional public auditor was uncommon, though some permanent government audit posts were created.

The earliest record of an American auditor is found in 1748. In this year, Benjamin Franklin sold his interest in Franklin and Hall and asked James Parker to audit the firm's accounts. Mr. Parker did so and presented Mr. Franklin with a report entitled "State of Your Accounts with Mr. Hall."[13] Forty years later, in 1789, the U.S. Congress passed an act which created the Treasury Department and provided for an auditor and comptroller.[14]

This period also saw the rise of double-entry accounting. Pacioli's "Summa" of 1494 was the first book on double-entry. It was followed in the intervening years by hundreds of texts, making very little improvement upon his basic system. Accounting and auditing were not to achieve their prominence until shortly before the 20th Century.

1840-1910

Although auditing and auditors date from a remote period, the professional public auditor is a product of comparatively modern times. The time from 1840-1910 was a period of great expansion with the construction of large railroad systems and the development and growth of huge stock companies. This industrial and economic growth created the need for more sophisticated accounting systems and the development and use of financial statements for credit purposes and disclosure to stockholders. To add credibility to financial statements, professional public accountants were engaged to audit the records and issue a certificate attesting to their "correctness."

England first set the trend in this direction with the passage of the Companies Act of 1862. To quote Richard Brown:

> The Companies Act of 1862 may well be termed the 'accountant's friend,' for it provides him with occupation (and incidentally with remuneration) at the inception, during the progress, and in the liquidation of public companies. The Act did not expressly require audit of the accounts, though the model set of regulations contained in Schedule A had such a provision; it was not till the Amendment Act of 1900 that the accounts of all limited companies were required to be audited, . . .[15]

Seventy years later the United States included similar legislation in the Securities and Exchange Acts of 1933 and 1934.

The primary objective of auditing in this period continued to be the detection and prevention of fraud and, secondarily, the detection of error. Robert Montgomery — auditor, author, and original partner of the firm of Lybrand, Ross Brothers, and Montgomery — stated in his first book on auditing (1909) that the object of an audit was threefold.

1. Detection of fraud.
2. Detection of technical errors.
3. Detection of errors of principle.[16]

He further stated that, "The detection of fraud is a most important portion of the auditor's duties, and there will be no disputing the contention that the auditor who is able to detect fraud is — other things being equal — a better man than the auditor who cannot."[17]

Auditing at this time primarily consisted of a detailed examination of the accounting records. The concepts of reliance upon internal control and testing (rather than 100 per cent examinations) were beginning to develop because of the difficulty and expense of auditing every transaction of large concerns. Robert Montgomery estimated that three-fourths of the audit time was spent in completely verifying footings and postings, whereas experience had shown that three-fourths of the defalcations were hidden by failures to account for income or cash receipts.[18]

American recognition of the public accounting profession began with the passage of legislation in the State of New York in 1896 authorizing the professional designation of "Certified Public Accountant." The primary audit activity of this period was that conducted by professional public accountants. This activity is reflected in the definition of an auditor by the author of the first American auditing book, George Soule' in 1892:

> A person appointed and authorized to audit, *i.e.,* to examine accounts, books and monetary statements of corporations, to compare the charges with the vouchers, and to *attest* with his certificate and signature the accuracy of the financial affairs of the corporation.
>
> An auditor is the critical representative of the stockholders, the reviewer of the work of the financial officers, and the supervisor of the Board of Directors, in case they have neglected their duties or intentionally prepared erroneous Accounts or Statements to be presented to their Stockholders.[19] (emphasis added)

A typical public accountant's certificate would be something like the following.

> We hereby certify that we have thoroughly audited these accounts for the (year) ended (day/month) last, and that the same appear to be correct. We further certify that the above Balance-Sheet is in accordance with the books, and appears to us to be a correct statement of the financial position of the firm, as it appeared on the above shown date.[20]

In 1887, the first organized body of professional accountants in the United States came into existence. This was The American Association of Public Accountants which, after several mergers, became the American Institute of Accountants in 1916 (and, ultimately, the AICPA in 1957).

Around the turn of the century a new dimension was added to the field of auditing with the introduction of internal auditing in some large organizations — particularly in the railroad industry. An accounting text of that period referred to the "permanent company auditor" as an accountant:

> . . . whose duty consists in verifying all the accounting work of a corporation, and preparing the necessary verified statistical statements of the condition of the business. These officers proceed from one branch to another checking the work in detail. They are also responsible for the suitability of the various forms used.[21]

Governmental auditing during this period was in its infancy in the United States. The objective of such auditing was primarily the verification of compliance with government rules, regulations, and procedures with the detection of fraud and error being secondary objectives. (Normanton refers to this as a test of regularity — the lowest common denominator of governmental auditing.)[22] The audit generally consisted of a detailed examination of pertinent accounting documents, the purpose being to approve or disapprove expenditures rather than to form and render a written opinion on financial statements. Federal audit activities were then under the auspices of six audit offices assigned to the Treasury Department. Also, most states and some municipalities had established audit activities.

It should be noted that government auditors of this period were not always highly regarded by their peers. For example, Robert Montgomery (in 1909) commented upon the competency in general of governmental auditors by stating:

> There are, therefore, two reasons at least why official auditors are not so competent as professional auditors, one being the fact that nearly all of the appointments are in payment of political debts, with the consequent result that wholly inexperienced and incompetent men are frequently chosen; and, secondly, even if the places were filled solely upon the basis of merit, it is not to be expected that capable men will be found, in any great number at least, occupying positions of great responsibility but with small salaries attached.[23]

1910-1950

In this era the leadership in accounting and auditing shifted from Great Britain to the United States; therefore, this section emphasizes events taking place in this country. It should be remembered, however, that similar developments in accounting and auditing were taking place throughout the world.

PUBLIC AUDITING

The public accounting profession remained dominant in the field of auditing. During this period all States began the certification of public accountants, large accounting firms were formed, and the accounting profession experienced rapid growth. Primary impetus for this growth came from industrial expansion and the 20th Century innovation of personal and corporate income taxation.

The accounting discipline was coming of age. Accounting techniques had become sophisticated and, frequently, complex. Accounting became a subject of serious study at the university level, and accounting literature in the form of texts and periodicals proliferated. Large professional accounting organizations were organized and developed in this period, including:

The American Institute of Accountants — 1916 (AICPA — 1957);

American Association of University Instructors in Accounting — 1916 (American Accounting Association — 1935);

National Association of Cost Accountants — 1919 (National Association of Accountants — 1956);

Comptrollers' Institute of America — 1931 (Financial Executives Institute — 1963).

The Securities and Exchange Acts of 1933 and 1934 required that listed corporations registering securities for sale provide audited financial statements. Also in this era, major fraud suits were instigated involving firms that had been audited by public accounting firms — in particular, The Ultramares Case and The McKesson-Robbins Case. As a result, public auditors increasingly concerned themselves with refining the wording of their certificates in order to limit their liability for failure to detect fraud.

Fraud detection was no longer considered by the public accounting profession to be the major objective of auditing. Instead, the objectives of public auditing had become: (1) primarily, to ascertain the actual financial condition and earnings of an enterprise and (2) secondly, to detect errors and fraud.[24] Auditing techniques were also changing. Use of statistical sampling became more widespread and greater reliance was placed upon internal controls. The auditor's report was generally two short paragraphs expressing the auditor's opinion concerning the fairness of financial statements prepared by a firm's management.

GOVERNMENTAL AUDITING

Governmental auditing during this period was relatively stagnant. Although public accountants were engaged to conduct some governmental audits, most audits were done by permanent Federal, State, and local audit staffs. A significant development during this period was the creation of the General Accounting Office (GAO) with the passage of the Budgeting and Accounting Act of 1921.

The Act created a General Accounting Office to replace the six audit offices of the Treasury. The GAO was a legislative organization, rather than executive, with the Comptroller appointed by the President for a fifteen year term. The Act authorized and directed that:

The Comptroller General shall investigate, at the seat of government or elsewhere, all matters relating to the receipt, disbursement, and application of public funds, and shall make to the President when requested by him, and to Congress at the beginning of each regular session, a report in writing of the work of the General Accounting Office, containing recommendations concerning the legislation he may deem necessary to facilitate the prompt and accurate rendition and settlement of accounts and concerning such other matters relating to the receipt, disbursement, and application of public funds as he may think advisable. In such regular report, or in special reports at any time when Congress is in session, he shall make recommendations looking to *greater economy or efficiency in public expenditures.*[25] (emphasis added)

Furthermore, Chairman Good, author of the bill, stated that:

It was the intention of the Committee that the Comptroller General should be something more than a book-keeper or accountant, that he should be a *real critic,* and at all times should come to Congress, no matter what the political complexion of Congress or the Executive might be, and *point out inefficiency* if he found that money was being misapplied — which is another term for inefficiency — and that he should bring such facts to the notice of the committees having jurisdiction of appropriations.[26] (emphasis added)

In 1946, the Legislative Reorganization Act reinforced this broad role of the GAO.

The Comptroller General is authorized and directed to make an expenditure analysis of each agency in the executive branch of the Government (including Government corporations), which in the opinion of the Comptroller General, will enable Congress to determine whether public funds have been *economically and efficiently administered and expended.*[27] (emphasis added)

However, it was not until the 1950's that the GAO truly began to live up to its charge of "looking to greater economy or efficiency in public expenditures."

The 1930's saw a confrontation between GAO and the TVA.

Interestingly, one result was an amendment to the TVA Act stipulating that TVA be allowed to review GAO reports prior to their publication. The amendment also required GAO to file with the reports any criticisms or comments made by TVA.[28] GAO's primary activity during this period was the review and approval of Federal Agency expenditure vouchers. This activity was conducted in Washington and consisted of a hundred per cent review — it was not until 1950 that auditing on a sampling basis was introduced.

INTERNAL AUDITING

Internal auditing was developing in industry during this period; however, it was not until the late thirties and early forties that it achieved widespread interest. In 1941, the first significant text on internal auditing was published — Victor Z. Brinks's *Internal Auditing.* This publication served as a catalyst to bring together in that same year the twenty-four founders of the Institute of Internal Auditors.[29] The Institute and the profession grew rapidly due, to a great extent, to the pressing needs of World War II.

Almost from the beginning (of 1941) internal auditors were concerned with more than a financial audit. Big business management realized that the internal auditors "were there," and could perform a greater service than just looking for accounting errors. Thus, internal auditors began focusing upon improving operations. This concept of auditing received management acceptance because the recommendations were more helpful than those typically provided by external auditors; and, significantly, because findings remained internal and were not made public.

Internal auditors adopted the term operations or operational auditing to describe their activity. This term first came to the attention of internal auditors in an article by Arthur H. Kent published in the March, 1949 issue of *The Internal Auditor.* (Kent has been credited with coining the term; however, it had actually been used on occasion by several other authors as far back as 1931.)[30]

Operational auditing evolved from the "back-up" internal financial audit. In these early days, it was usually an extension of the financial audit and generally concerned such things as cost analysis or payroll analysis. Basically, operational auditing was an inductive approach in that it drew from accounting documents, recommendations for change (*i.e.,* moved from the specific or actual to the ideal).

Thus, internal auditors pioneered the concept of operational auditing. However, during this same period a similar concept, called management auditing, was developing in the literature of management.

MANAGEMENT AUDITING

It is believed that T. G. Rose coined the term "management audit" in 1932 in his book of the same name published in London. A. S. Comyns-Carr commented on Mr. Rose's originality by stating that he:

> . . . brings forward an individual idea of an interesting and original kind, the idea that the management of an undertaking might profitably be made subject to periodical expert investigation from outside analogous to the audit of its financial accounts.[31]

Rose's audit was basically a questionnaire type interview designed to analyze functional activities; it was the forerunner of a more comprehensive approach presented in 1940 by the Metropolitan Life Insurance Company in its *Outline for a Management Audit.*[32]

This report presented an approach to management analysis that had been previously developed for policyholder companies. It enlarged upon Rose's early work but pursued a similar outline. This work was followed several years later (in 1948) by Howard G. Benedict's *Yardsticks of Management.*[33] Benedict's questionnaire had nine major divisions and many subdivisions. His system attempted to evaluate management by means of weighted factorial analysis.

These writings represent the earliest attempts to develop an interview type, management audit. It should be noted that they generated as a whole relatively little interest at that time in such an approach. The works — written by managers for managers — would have to be classified as belonging to the field of management rather than auditing. Although internal auditors were developing similar approaches, they do not appear to have relied to any extent upon these earlier attempts.

At this time the "management audit" was different in concept from the "operational audit." The management audit was organized around the functions of management and followed a deductive approach as opposed to the inductive approach of operational auditing. In effect, a general model of an ideal organization was conceptualized. Based on this conceptual model (which was not formally presented), a questionnaire was developed. Then, the organization was tested against the questionnaire; hence, a deductive approach was employed, moving from the general (the model) to the specific (the organization).

In summary, there were two similar but separate concepts developing in this period: the internal auditor's "operational auditing" and management's "management auditing." These early initiatives were the forerunners of today's movement toward extension of the scope of auditing.

1950 to Date

In previous sections auditing has been discussed categorically by fields, *i.e.*, public auditing, governmental auditing, internal auditing, and management auditing. In recent years, audit activities and developments have frequently crossed such boundaries. For example, internal auditing is now a significant activity in government as well as private industry, and internal auditing has influenced public auditing. Similarly, developments in public auditing have had an impact on internal and governmental auditing. In addition, there is a movement of auditors from one area into another, which creates additional dispersion of ideas, thoughts, and concepts.

For these reasons, it is somewhat difficult to discuss recent audit events categorically. Yet, there are definite advantages to doing so since the needs of various areas of auditing are quite distinct. Therefore, the following section is organized into private and governmental auditing, external and internal — even though the classifications are not totally discrete.

PRIVATE EXTERNAL AUDITING

Private external auditing is a descriptive category for the audit work of public accountants. There are now (1974) more than 100,000 Certified Public Accountants in the United States and a great many licensed Public Accountants. Certified Public Accountants and Public Accountants not only perform audits but also render tax services and management services.

Since 1937, The American Institute of Certified Public Accountants has issued over fifty official statements on auditing procedures. The most frequently referred to statement has been Number 33 published in 1961. This statement is a codification of earlier statements including the 1947 publication "A Tentative Statement of Auditing Standards — Their Generally Accepted Significance and Scope."

This report divided audit standards into these categories:

General Standards
    (1) The examination is to be performed by a person or persons having adequate technical training and proficiency as an auditor.

(2) In all matters relating to the assignment, an independence in mental attitude is to be maintained by the auditor or auditors.

(3) Due professional care is to be exercised in the performance of the examination and the preparation of the report.

Standards of Field Work

(1) The work is to be adequately planned and assistants, if any, are to be properly supervised.

(2) There is to be a proper study and evaluation of the existing internal control as a basis for reliance thereon and for the determination of the resultant extent of the tests to which auditing procedures are to be restricted.

(3) Sufficient competent evidential matter is to be obtained through inspection, observation, inquiries, and confirmations to afford a reasonable basis for an opinion regarding the financial statements under examination.

Standards of Reporting

(1) The report shall state whether the financial statements are presented in accordance with generally accepted accounting principles.

(2) The report shall state whether such principles have been consistently observed in the current period in relation to the preceding period.

(3) Informative disclosures in the financial statements are to be regarded as reasonably adequate unless otherwise stated in the report.

Later, in 1954, a fourth standard of reporting was added:

(4) The report shall either contain an expression of opinion regarding the financial statements, taken as a whole, or an assertion to the effect that an opinion cannot be expressed. When an overall opinion cannot be expressed, the reasons therefor should be stated. In all cases where an auditor's name is associated with financial statements, the report should contain a clearcut indication of the character of the auditor's examination, if any, and the degree of responsibility he is taking.

These audit standards were approved by the membership of the AIA at their meeting of September, 1948. Today, they are considered by the public accounting profession to be the cornerstone of their financial audits. (Recently, the Institute incorporated all previous audit statements into one publication — *Statement on Auditing Standards: Codification of Auditing Standards and Procedures Number One.)*

The greatest challenge of this period to public auditing has been the widespread introduction of electronic data processing. To meet this challenge, public auditors have developed special techniques for auditing "around, through, and with" computer systems. Considerable research has also been conducted in the area of statistical sampling in auditing.

Since 1950, however, there has been relatively little change in the public auditor's concept of auditing. Although public auditors conduct many governmental audits, their major effort continues to be the rendering of professional opinions upon the fairness of financial statements prepared by business management.

The public auditor has received comparatively little pressure from the public, the financial community, or business to extend the scope of his audit to include management or operational matters. However, he has received pressure to move in this direction from his governmental clients and from theoreticians considering the proper or future role of public auditing.

At present, questions of extending the scope of auditing that most concern public auditors are in such areas as: opinions upon budgets and forecasts, interim financial statements, financial statistics, and adequacy of financial internal controls.[34] However, some public accounting firms have experimented with operational audits. Recent articles report that two of the "Big Eight" accounting firms have "definite commitments in the operational auditing area."[35]

Contributing to the public auditors qualms about operational or management auditing are a number of factors. These include:

> ... The concept of operational or management auditing is not, as of yet, well-defined.
> ... There are presently no generally accepted standards or procedures for a management audit or for the management activity under review.
> ... Since such audits go beyond financial matters, are they properly considered audits or are they better classified as a management service? Would such audits possibly compromise the auditor's independence?
> ... Should the results of management audits be made public? If so, then there are unanswered questions relating to proper report format, the liability of the auditor, and the nature of acceptable and adequate evidence.

PRIVATE INTERNAL AUDITING

Internal auditing continued to expand in the private sector and during the fifties the concept of operational auditing really began to materialize. Kent had used the term "operations" auditing in 1948. Frederick E. Mint popularized the more generally used term "operational" in 1954 through an article in *The Internal Auditor*.[36] Mr. Mint has since stated:

> My usage of the term was first planned during a brainstorming session which Mr. Kent and I held during the summer of 1953 in preparation for a talk on the subject. We considered a number of alternative titles and decided 'operational' had the most ear-appeal. I have subsequently had some regrets on this choice.[37]

During this same period, the "management auditing" approach which had been developing in the literature of management began to gain interest. In 1950, Jackson Martindell, president of the American Institute of Management, published *The Scientific Appraisal of Management*.[38] He used the term "management audit" to describe his company evaluation that was similar to, but more comprehensive than, the Rose, Metropolitan, and Benedict audits.

During the 1950's the American Institute of Management promoted the concept of management auditing with the publication of over a hundred case examples of management audits of prominent organizations such as Standard Cash Register, Toledo Edison, Statler Hotels, and General Electric. They also published, for a short while, a periodical entitled *Management Audit*.

What is probably the most significant work on management auditing first appeared in 1959. This was William P. Leonard's *The Management Audit: An Appraisal of Management Methods and Performance*. As in the case of previous writings, Leonard's audit took a deductive checklist or questionnaire approach.[39]

Management auditing and operational auditing began to merge in the late 1950's and early 1960's. Internal auditors frequently referred to their audit as a management audit, and many writers stated that the terms were synonymous. At present, both terms refer to an audit that goes beyond traditional financial attestation into the area of managerial economy, efficiency, and effectiveness. Such audits may be either deductive or inductive, internal or external.

In this era there also appeared scattered terms that referred to similar activities such as: efficiency audit, depth audit, substantive audit, functional audit, mission audit, etc. However, in the private sector at least, the terms operational or management audit were by far the most prevalent.

During the 1960's, there were numerous conferences, workshops, and publications devoted to the topics of operational auditing. The Institute of Internal Auditors and the American Management Association sponsored many such activities. The IIA published a major text in 1964 — Bradford Cadmus' *Operational Auditing Handbook*.[40] Despite the widespread literature on the topic, however, relatively little reliable information is available concerning the actual acceptance and utilization of these concepts in practice.

Although many firms report excellent results from these activities, it appears that there may be more discussion and talk than actual practice. In other words, many organizations have successfully experimented with internal operational auditing, and many are putting it to permanent and excellent use. But for private business as a whole, it is still in the formative stage.

GOVERNMENTAL EXTERNAL AUDITING

The external audit agency for the Federal government is the General Accounting Office which has authority to audit all Federal programs and agencies, with some few exceptions. There are other Federal audit agencies, but they are "internal" relative to their organization. These audit agencies may perform audits that are "external" relative to governmental contractors and recipients of Federal grants — for example, HEW Audit Agency audits Federal programs administered by State and local agencies. Nevertheless, these audit agencies are technically internal audit agencies. For example, when HEW Audit Agency audits Federal education programs at the State level, it is technically reviewing the work of its sister HEW agency, the Office of Education.

A similar situation exists at the State level and in some cases at the local level. All States have one or more external State Audit Agency that audits the activities of other State agencies. The State Auditor is considered external to other State agencies. However, some State agencies have their own internal auditors; and some State Audit Agencies have cognizance over audits at the local level. Also, a few local governments have permanent external and/or internal auditors.

As noted earlier, the GAO has grown in posture since 1950. Prior to this period, its main audit activity consisted of a "detailed examination of vouchers"[41] referred to by Normanton as "the old centralized audit of regularity."[42] The late 40's was a period of general interest in improving management for government. In 1947, Congress established the first Hoover Commission, headed by former President

Hoover, for the purpose of studying the overlapping functions of executive departments, agencies, commissions, and bureaus.[43] The Commission report recommended that the GAO adopt on-site, spot-sampling procedures and conduct more comprehensive audits.[44] This recommendation, coupled with the fact that the GAO had been given a broad responsibility originally in 1921 and again in 1945, resulted in the instigation on October 19, 1949, of the "Comprehensive Audit Program."[45]

The Hoover recommendation led directly to the passage of the Budget and Accounting Procedures Act of 1950.[46] This authorized the GAO to apply "selective" auditing procedures and was, in effect, formal endorsement of the comprehensive audit.[47] Thus, this act signaled the beginning of extended audit concepts in the Federal government.

By 1954, the purpose of the "comprehensive audit" was described as:

> To determine to what extent the agency under audit has discharged its financial responsibilities, which imply equally the expenditure of public funds and the utilization of materials and personnel, within the limit of its programs and activities and their execution in an effective, efficient and economical fashion.[48]

Since then, the GAO has continued to promote this concept of broad-scope, far-reaching audits. However, they have learned that generally it is physically impossible for one audit to evaluate all aspects of a program. Thus, the comprehensive audit program is no longer conceived of as necessarily a single, all-encompassing document, but rather as a series of reports examining particular activities and programs.[49]

In June of 1972, the General Accounting Office made a significant contribution toward the advancement of governmental auditing with the publication of *Standards for Audit of Government Organizations, Programs, Activities, and Functions.* These new governmental audit standards build upon the public audit standards of the AICPA with the principal addition being an extension of the scope of governmental auditing to potentially encompass the areas of: financial, compliance, economy, efficiency and effectiveness. Today, the General Accounting Office looks forward to continued efforts in this direction.

In the 1950's, State Audit Agencies began to explore and experiment with expanded audit concepts. The impetus for this movement was similar to that experienced in the Federal government. Many State legislatures began pushing for information on the economy, efficiency, and effectiveness of State operations. Additionally, State Auditors became aware of efforts being made in this direction by the Federal government and the progressive trends of auditing literature. Also, State Audit Agencies began conducting audits of Federal programs administered by State agencies. To comply with Federal auditing standards it became necessary for the State Audit Agency to broaden the scope of its traditional audit.

The first State to move in this direction was Michigan. On April 1, 1963, the citizens of Michigan approved a new constitution which stated in part:

> The legislature . . . shall appoint an auditor general, who . . . shall conduct post audits of financial transactions and accounts of the state and of all branches, departments, offices, boards, commissions, agencies, authorities, and institutions of the state established by this constitution or by law, and performance post audits thereof.[50]

Performance auditing is the term that most State Auditors use to describe State audit activities that go beyond financial and compliance boundaries into the area of operational evaluation. It is quite similar, if not the same, as operational, management, and comprehensive auditing; and can take an inductive or deductive approach, or both.

The concept had been considered in Michigan for a number of years. As a result of the first Hoover Commission report of 1949, a study known as the "Little Hoover Commission" was made in Michigan in 1950 and 1951.[51] This study contained the following comment:

> Because the appropriations process involves the determination of policy, it is necessary that the legislature hold the executive responsible for not only the honest expenditure of all funds but also the efficient use of public money in accordance with policies prescribed by law. This is known as an operational audit or a performance audit, and it too should be undertaken by a staff responsible to the legislature.[52]

> (The Commission then recommended) . . . strengthening the legislature's means for effective control, particularly through establishment of a legislative auditor general to be appointed by and responsible to the legislature (whose responsibility it would be) to undertake performance as well as fiscal audits of all state agencies.[53]

This seems to be the first appearance of the term performance audit, and there are some who feel that it was coined from the term "performance budget" used by the first Hoover Commission in 1949.[54]

In 1967, Lennis M. Knighton reported the emergence of this new concept in State Audits in *The Performance Post Audit in State Government*.[55] Since then several states, including Michigan, have been attempting to introduce this concept into their State Audits. The two national organizations of State Auditors (The National Legislative Conference and The National Association of State Auditors, Comptrollers, and Treasurers) have provided forums for discussion of these concepts both at their national conventions and in their publications.

GOVERNMENTAL INTERNAL AUDITING

The first internal audit organization in a Federal agency was established in 1933 by the Home Owner's Loan Corporation.[56] It was not until after 1949, however, that significant progress was made in this direction. The National Security Act amendments of that year provided for the creation of internal audit organizations in the military departments. In the following year, the Budget and Accounting Procedures Act placed specific responsibility upon the head of each executive agency to develop and maintain effective systems of accounting and internal control including internal auditing.[57]

During the 1950's, internal auditing was developing slowly throughout the Federal government. The greatest strides were made in the defense agencies with the work and publications of the Institute of Internal Auditing significantly influencing the internal audit movement.

In 1957, the General Accounting Office issued a *Statement of Basic Principles and Concepts for Internal Auditing* "to provide guidance to the agencies in developing internal audit organizations and procedures."[58] However, as late as 1963 a House Committee on government operations stated:

> Today, there are internal audit groups sprinkled throughout the agencies and departments of government. The term is well recognized. Unfortunately, recognition of the *need* for effective internal audits has not always been translated into the establishment of such systems. While many exist, there is considerable room for general improvement.[59]

Since 1963, a number of efforts have been made toward improving the quality of Federal internal audit systems. For example, the

GAO has reviewed many Federal audit programs and made recommendations for improvement.

In particular, several audit agencies of the Department of Defense have been frequently cited in articles and seminars for their progressive efforts in the area of operational or management auditing. The Department of Defense has seven internal audit agencies:

The U.S. Army Audit Agency
The Naval Audit Service
The Air Force Audit Agency
The Auditor General, Defense Supply Agency
The Deputy Controller for Internal Audit, Office of the
    Assistant Secretary of Defense
The Defense Contract Audit Agency

Another group that has worked in this direction is the Atomic Energy Commission — Audit Branch. Of particular interest to Education Agency managers is the HEW Audit Agency that reviews the activities of all branches of this mammoth Federal department, including education grants to State and Local Education Agencies. Like most Federal internal audit agencies, HEWAA is relatively new, having been created in 1965 from the consolidation of fifteen separate HEW audit organizations. Since its creation, HEW Audit Agency has continuously upgraded its audit activities and is persistently expanding the scope of its audits.

These are only a few of the many Federal internal audit organizations. They are mentioned here because they are frequently referred to in the literature and elsewhere for their progressive audit efforts. However, to date there is no "hard" quantitative data concerning the extent or status of Federal internal auditing. There are without doubt many efforts being made to extend the scope of auditing into the areas of economy, efficiency, and effectiveness of operations. But contrary to some reports, it appears that these concepts are definitely in the early stages of development. Much has been done, but much more remains to be done — particularly with regard to audit theory and procedures.

Not much can presently be said with reliability relative to the status and extent of internal auditing at the State and Local level. Although internal auditing in State and Local government was practically nonexistent prior to 1950, there are now "a number" of internal staffs in State agencies and perhaps "some" in Local agencies.

From general observation, it appears that modern internal auditing is rather infrequently encountered at the State and Local level of government. Here then appears to be an area of great neglect. Internal auditing has proven its worth in private industry and more recently in the Federal government. State and Local governments should give careful consideration to the benefits that could accrue from the introduction and utilization of the internal operational audit.

SUMMARY AND ANALYSIS

The concept of auditing dates back to the beginning of civilization. Though the primary purpose of auditing through the ages has been the detection of fraud, in recent years the scope of auditing has been changing to include evaluations of management or, in particular, the economy, efficiency, and effectiveness of operations. However, this movement is still evolving and developing. The position from which different individuals view their involvement in auditing and their pragmatic approach to auditing directly influences their reaction to the expanding audit concept. Another identifiable factor that influences this expansion is the environmental constraints of various categories of auditing.

For example, public auditing primarily concerns the expression of an auditor's opinion upon the fairness of presentation of financial statements prepared by business management for the benefit of external parties such as stockholders and creditors. Internal auditing, on the other hand, addresses itself to the needs of — and is for the benefit of — internal management; while auditing in the government sector, both external and internal, finds increasing pressure from both the public and Congress to consider problems relating to the economy, efficiency, and effectiveness of governmental activities.

The public auditor may wonder if management and/or operational audits are more appropriately "management service" activities because (1) they are not necessarily financial, and (2) they could possibly compromise his "independence." This is not a significant problem for private internal auditors or governmental auditors. They do not have management service divisions and are generally less concerned with independence.

Private internal auditors and the governmental auditors receive pressure from top management and the public, respectively, to extend the scope of their audit into operational areas. The public auditor is not presently receiving as much pressure, but it may well be on the horizon.

As in the case of any dynamic and evolving situation, the movement or crossover of audit concepts has created a certain amount of confusion. One result has been a proliferation of terminology that in some cases is confusing and conflicting. A more important problem has been the development of disagreements, often stemming from unrecognized basic differences in the objectives, needs, and pressures exerted on the various fields of auditing.

These environmental differences are often the basis for present-day audit controversies. For instance, the public auditor is concerned with the sensitivity of issues contained in his audit reports which are to be directed to external users. He is most anxious to have firm and specific standards and evidence to support his opinions. On the other hand, the internal auditor does not have to worry about public disclosure or civil suits. Therefore, he is *comparatively* less concerned with sensitivity, standards, and evidence. "Getting the job done." is his main concern, the job being to please management through meaningful operational recommendations.

Thus, auditing can and should mean different things to different people, depending upon the basic objectives of particular audit activities. However, the die is definitely cast — and in the future, auditing of all types will be increasingly concerned with matters of a managerial or operational nature.

FOOTNOTES

Chapter II

[1]Richard Brown, *A History of Accounting and Accountants,* (Edinburgh, Scotland: T. C. and E. C. Jack, 1905), p. 74.

[2]*Ibid.,* p. 21.

[3]*Ibid.,* p. 24.

[4]J. Stephen Nom Lee, "Government Auditing in China," *The Journal of Accountancy,* LXII (September, 1936), p. 190.

[5]*The American Heritage Dictionary of the English Language,* (New York: American Heritage Publishing Co., 1973), p. 86.

[6]Willard E. Stone, "Auditing Management Efficiency," *The Australian Accountant,* XXXVII (March, 1967), p. 155.

[7]Brown, *History,* p. 76.

[8]*Ibid.,* p. 77.

[9]*Ibid.,* p. 77.

[10]*Ibid.,* p. 81.

[11]*The Report of the Commissioners for Taking, Examining, and Stating the Public Accounts of the Kindgom,* (London: 1711). and *The Second Report of the Commissioners for Taking, Examining, and Stating the Public Accounts, Etc.,* (London: 1712). From the collection of P. L. McMickle.

[12]Brown, *History,* p. 89.

[13]James Don Edwards, *History of Public Accounting in the United States,* (East Lansing, Michigan: Bureau of Business and Economic Research, Michigan State University, 1960), p. 43.

[14]W. B. Jencks, *et al.,* "Historical Dates in Accounting," *The Accounting Review,* XXIX (July, 1954), p. 488.

[15]Brown, *History,* p. 318.

[16]Robert H. Montgomery, *Auditing,* (Chicago: American School of Correspondence, 1909), p. 12.

[17]*Ibid.*

[18]*Ibid.,* p. 44.

[19]George Soulé, *Soulé's New Science and Practice of Accounts,* 5th ed., (New Orleans: George Soulé, 1897), p. 560. (Which quotes from *Soulé's Manual on Auditing,* 1892.)

[20]E. H. Beach and W. W. Thorne, *The American Business and Accounting Encyclopaedia,* I (Detroit: The Book-Keeper Publishing Co., 1901), p. 141.

[21]*Ibid.*

[22]E. L. Normanton, *The Accountability and Audit of Governments,* (Manchester, England: The University Press, 1966), p. 57.

[23]Montgomery, *Auditing,* pp. 6-7.

[24]Robert H. Montgomery, *Auditing Theory and Practice,* (New York: The Ronald Press Company, 1912), pp. 10-11.

[25]Darrell Hevenor Smith, *The General Accounting Office: Its History, Activities, and Organization,* (Baltimore, Maryland: The Johns Hopkins Press, 1927), p. 64.

[26]*Ibid.,* p. 63.

[27]Richard E. Brown, *The GAO: Untapped Source of Congressional Power,* (Knoxville, Tennessee: The University of Tennessee Press, 1970), pp. 41-42.

[28]*Ibid.,* p. 20.

[29]Bradford Cadmus, "Operational Auditing," *The Internal Auditor,* XVII (March, 1960), p. 28.

[30]Arthur H. Kent, "Audits of Operations," *The Internal Auditor,* V (March, 1948), p. 12. For earlier examples, see for instance: Edward F. O'Toole, "Office Operations Audits Increase Executive Control," *Office,* XXIII (February, 1946), pp. 36-38; and Frank L. Rowland, "Home Office Operating Audits," *Proceedings of the 1931 Annual Conference of the Life Office Management Association,* (New York: The Association, 1931), pp. 13-24.

[31]T. G. Rose, *The Management Audit,* (London: Gee & Co., 1932), p. vii.

[32]Policyholders Service Bureau, *Outline for a Management Audit,* (New York: Metropolitan Life Insurance Co., 1940).

[33]Howard G. Benedict, *Yardsticks of Management,* (Los Angeles: Management Book Company, 1948).

[34]See: Hugo Nurnberg, "The Independent Auditor's Attest Function: Its Prospects for Extension," *The New York Certified Public Accountant,* XLI (October, 1971), pp. 727-32, 783.

[35]Corine T. Norgaard, "The Professional Accountant's View of Operational Auditing," *The Journal of Accountancy,* CXXVIII (December, 1969), p. 46.

[36]Frederic E. Mints, "Operational Auditing," *The Internal Auditor,* XI (June, 1954).

[37]See Editor's Footnote in: D. E. Pooley, "Nothing New Under the Sun," *The Internal Auditor,* XXII (Summer, 1965), p. 13.

[38]Jackson Martindell, *The Scientific Appraisal of Management,* (New York: Harber and Brothers, 1950).

[39]William P. Leonard, *The Management Audit: An Appraisal of Management Methods and Performance,* (Englewood Cliffs, N.J.: Prentice-Hall, Inc., 1962). An earlier edition appeared in: Victor Lazzaro, ed., *Systems and Procedures: A Handbook for Business and Industry,* (Englewood Cliffs, N.J.: Prentice-Hall, Inc., 1959).

[40]Bradford Cadmus, *Operational Auditing Handbook,* (New York: The Institute of Internal Auditors, 1964).

[41]"New Law Governing Federal Accounting and Auditing," Editorial, *The Journal of Accountancy*, XC (November, 1950), p. 370.

[42]Normanton, *The Accountability and Audit of Governments*, p. 113.

[43]Sol Holt, *Dictionary of American Government*, (New York: Macfadden-Bartell Corp., 1970), p. 143.

[44]Brown, *The GAO*, p. 15.

[45]"The General Accounting Office and Its Functions — A Brief Historical Outline," *The GAO Review*, (Summer, 1971), p. 8.

[46]Brown, *The GAO*, p. 15.

[47]"New Law," p. 370.

[48]Normanton, *Accountability*, p. 113.

[49]Brown, *The GAO*, pp. 27-28.

[50]Lennis M. Knighton, *The Performance Post Audit in State Government*, (East Lansing, Michigan: Bureau of Business and Economic Research, Michigan State University, 1967), p. 1.

[51]*Ibid.*, p. 14.

[52]*Ibid.*

[53]*Ibid.*, pp. 14-15.

[54]*Ibid.*, p. 15.

[55]*Ibid.*

[56]Elmer B. Staats, "The Growing Importance of Internal Auditing in the Federal Government," *The Internal Auditor*, XXV (September-October, 1968), p. 49.

[57]United States General Accounting Office, *Internal Auditing in Federal Agencies*, (Washington: U.S. General Accounting Office, 1968), p. iii.

[58]*Ibid.*

[59]*Ibid.*, p. 20.

A CONCEPTUAL

FRAMEWORK OF

AUDITING

INTRODUCTION

Man lives by concepts. He has concepts of himself and his environment and these concepts form the basis for his everyday decisions and activities. A conceptual framework is a blueprint or organization chart that identifies and structures those key concepts that together form, relate, and surround a certain subject matter.

Not only is a conceptual framework a valuable tool for classroom instruction, but it can also serve as an effective system for communication, the organization of research, and the planning and execution of real world activities. A conceptual framework can also be used to identify problem areas or inconsistencies in current conditions.

This chapter presents a conceptual framework that encompasses, integrates, and clarifies the concepts of auditing. The purpose of this chapter is two-fold: (1) to identify and discuss basic audit concepts, and (2) to present a framework that will be used later to analyze and evaluate the audit environment of public education. The primary objective of this later discussion (Chapter V) is to identify the disparity gap(s) between "where we are now in SEA/LEA auditing and where we aspire to be."[1]

Although the ideal audit environment may never be completely achieved, it is important to know what goals to strive for. The advantage of the conceptual approach is that it integrates the major aspects of a subject — in this case, auditing. In turn, contemporary audit issues and problems can be considered in a more complete context.

In a very practical sense, educational managers can learn through this discussion what they should expect from audits and auditors, and they can become more fully aware of the place of auditing in the management of State and Local Education Agencies. For the auditor, it can serve as a valuable reference not only for the conduct of educational audits, but for audits in all areas of government and business.

THE NATURE OF AUDITING

What is auditing? Surprisingly, this is a difficult question to answer. Even the experts disagree as there is no "generally accepted" definition of the term. Of course, it is a *word* — a word that has been used for over two thousand years to describe a certain type of human activity or process. However, during this long period, this activity — like many other human processes — has slowly evolved and changed. Thus, "auditing" is not precisely the same today as it was 500 years ago, or even twenty years ago.

This evolution, which has accelerated during the past few years, has contributed to the confusion now surrounding the subject. For example, there appears to be a broadening of the scope of auditing. But this broadening is not occurring uniformly, is not recognized by all authorities, and, in any case, is definitely in the formulative stages. Another problem is the complex environment of auditing itself which contributes to variances in approach and philosophy. However, there are certain essential elements that are common to any audit.

In order to identify these elements of auditing, the project staff extensively reviewed the literature of auditing, examined hundreds of audits of different periods and areas, and conferred and worked with leading authorities in the field. As a result, it was determined that for an activity to be properly called an audit, there must be:

1. An auditor, auditee, and audit recipient;
2. An accountability relationship between the auditee (subordinate) and the audit recipient (higher authority);
3. Independence between the auditor and auditee; and
4. An examination and evaluation of certain of the auditee's accountable activities by the auditor for the audit recipient.

Fig. 1   THE ELEMENTS OF AN AUDIT

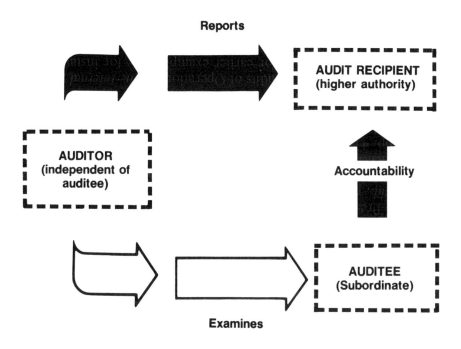

These are *essential* elements or characteristics of an audit. There are also a number of other topics and concepts that relate to auditing, including: audit scope, audit networks, auditor competencies, auditor ethics and standards, behavioral relationships, and specific audit procedures and techniques. The authors found that all of these concepts could be logically organized for discussion and examination around the following conceptual framework.

A CONCEPTUAL FRAMEWORK OF AUDITING

I. Objective   (Why?)
   Accountability
   Management Control

II. Scope   (What?)
   Financial
   Compliance
   Performance

III. Parties   (Who?)
   Auditor
     Independent
     Competent
     Professional
   Auditee
   Audit Recipient

IV. Process   (How?)
   Preparation
   Conduct
   Reporting
   Settlement

This conceptual framework identifies four areas of reference (objective, scope, parties, process) that provide the answers to four frequently asked questions: Why, What, Who, and How? These are questions that every auditor, auditee, and audit recipient should know (or seek) the answers to. The framework may also be expressed in the form of a comprehensive definition of auditing:

> *Auditing is an analytical <u>process</u> consisting of preparation, conduct (examination and evaluation), reporting (communication), and settlement. The basic <u>elements</u> of this process are: an independent, competent, and professional auditor who executes the process upon an auditee for an audit recipient. The <u>scope</u> or area of concern can involve matters of the following nature: financial (accounting error, fraud, financial controls, fairness of financial statements, etc.,), and/or compliance (faithful adherence to administrative and legal requirements, policies, regulations, etc.), and/or performance (economy, efficiency, and/or effectiveness of operational controls, management information systems, programs, etc.). The <u>objective</u> or purpose of auditing can be some combination of accountability and management control.*

This definition of auditing is comprehensive, flexible, and encompassing. It includes the major components of auditing; and for this reason it is more comprehensive (and, therefore useful) than other, less complete definitions. It is flexible in that it may be applied to auditing in both the governmental and private sectors, to internal as well as external auditing. It encompasses audits of various scopes such as financial audits, operational audits, management audits, etc. Thus, it provides an integrated structure in which the major components of auditing may be discussed and related.

THE OBJECTIVE OF AUDITING

The conceptual framework identifies two objectives of auditing: accountability and management control. These two terms appear frequently in the literature of auditing and management. However, their exact definitions are somewhat unsettled. For example, E. S. L. Goodwin states:

> There is no general agreement on the meaning of control and, oddly, no clear-cut disagreements — merely fuzziness about the meaning, a condition of mild schizosemantia, most of whose victims seem happily unaware of their malady.[2]

And Arthur R. Pontarelli, Deputy Director of the Rhode Island SEA, states that:

> Since accountability tends to have variable meanings for different persons the concept is difficult to operationalize. . . .[3]

In order to minimize confusion, we considered choosing other, less ambiguous, terms to describe the objectives of auditing. However, since auditing is so often referred to as an accountability device and a control technique, it appeared advisable to use these familiar terms, but with appropriate clarification. Thus, these terms are stipulatively defined in the following paragraphs.

ACCOUNTABILITY

Most dictionaries define accountability as synonymous with responsibility. Paul Gaddis, author of *Corporate Accountability,* states that accountability is the "responsibility for causing something to happen."[4] But observation of current usage indicates that accountability generally implies a higher or stronger degree of obligation than does the term responsibility. There is also the implication that a person may be responsible for many things — but formally accountable only for certain things. In other words accountability may, in some instances, be more restricted in scope than responsibility even though the degree of obligation is greater. Hence, one may be responsible for doing a satisfactory job — but formally accountable only for safeguarding the assets.

Some authorities go a step further, stating that responsibility must be "specified and measurable" to be accountability.[5] This appears to be a logical requirement, for it seems unfair to hold a person accountable for vague, unclear, and implied responsibilities. Yet, in reality, managers are sometimes held accountable for certain responsibilities that are only implied and/or difficult to measure. Therefore, for purposes of this discussion, accountability is stipulatively defined as: *the state of being accountable — being answerable or formally responsible for certain specified or implied performance.*

The most basic accountability relationship involves two parties, a higher authority and a subordinate. As one author describes this relationship:

> The manager [higher authority] assigns responsibility and transfers all authority necessary to the discharge of the duty as defined. When a man [subordinate] accepts the responsibility, he thereby assumes personally the obligation for carrying out the duty assigned to him and the accountability for doing so.[6]

This basic relationship is quite common and can arise for various reasons. It may evolve naturally, as when one person finds that he needs assistance to accomplish certain objectives that are beyond his physical ability, e.g., his "span of control." Such systems are most often intentionally created and form the foundation for organization theory and management hierarchies in both the governmental and private sectors. This relation can also exist between groups of individuals and organizations. For example, State agencies may be accountable to Federal agencies relative to their management of Federal grant-in-aids.

Thus, the concept of accountability implies the existence of authority and responsibility. There is the further implication that (1) a person or organization is answerable or formally responsible for certain specified or implied performance, (2) the actual performance will be reviewed, and (3) as a result, appropriate action may be taken by the higher authority.

TABLE 1

THE FUNCTIONS OF MANAGEMENT

AUTHOR	THE FUNCTIONS OF MANAGEMENT
Henri Fayol (1st to List Functions)	Planning, Organization, Command, Coordination, Control
Robert N. Anthony	Strategic Planning, Management Control, Operational Control
Paul M. Dauten	Planning, Organizing, Controlling
Ralph C. Davis	Creative Planning, Organizing, Controlling
Peter F. Drucker	Sets Objectives, Organizes, Motivates and Communicates, Measurement
Robert Y. Durand	Planning, Control
Arnold F. Emch	Control
Theo Haimann	Plans, Organizes, Staffs, Directs, Controls
Paul Holden, *et al.*	Planning, Direction, Coordination, Control
T. S. Isaac	Planning, Organizing, Controlling
Harold Koontz	Planning, Control
LeBreton & Henning	Planning, Organizing, Controlling
Ralph F. Lewis	Planning, Control
Joseph L. Massie	Planning, Directing, Organizing, Control
G. E. Milward	Forecasting, Planning, Organization, Command, Coordination, Control
William H. Newman	Planning, Organizing, Assembling Resources, Supervising, Controlling
Alex W. Rathe	Planning, Operations, Control
Norman J. Ream	Planning, Organizing, Assembling Resources, Directing, Controlling
Lyndall F. Urwick	Forecast, Plan, Organize, Direct, Coordinate, Control, Communicate

Data Source: R. N. Anthony, *Planning and Control Systems*, (Boston, Mass.: Graduate School of Business Administration, Harvard University, 1965), pp. 129-47.

MANAGEMENT CONTROL

The first use of the term "control" in a management context was in Henri Fayol's *Administration Industrielle et Générale* published in France in 1916.[7] Fayol felt that management was a series of functions consisting of: planning, organization, command, coordination, and control. Most analysts since Fayol have essentially followed this classification scheme, though some have confused the issue by introducing their own terminology. For instance, one author lists seven functions of management while another combines them all into the one function of control. (See Table 1.)

Fayol intended for control to mean "checking, comparing, or verifying."[8] However, some modern theorists refer to a two-step process of (1) checking or comparing what actually happened against what was planned, and (2) taking action to correct any observed discrepancies.[9] Other authorities use the term synonymously with direction, or even with the all-inclusive "management" itself.[10] To the general public, control may have a more negative connotation, such as — to exercise a regulating influence; to direct, restrain, check, or dominate.[11]

Of these various interpretations of control there are two clear-cut extremes: (1) control used synonymously with management, and (2) control as an inhibiting or restraining influence. The most generally accepted management definition must lie somewhere between these limits. To quote E. S. L. Goodwin:

> If asked which of the two, the steering wheel or the speedometer, is a control mechanism in our car, most of us will unhesitatingly pick the wheel, Yet, *in the management sense,* the *only* correct answer is speedometer.[12]

Therefore, for use in this discussion, management control is stipulatively defined as: *to measure or evaluate performance as an aid to management.*

AUDITING AS AN ACCOUNTABILITY DEVICE

Historically, the term auditing has been used to refer to those reviews conducted by an independent "auditor" (one who audits) for the primary objective of accountability. For example, when a higher authority could not review the performance of a subordinate manager himself (for any of a number of reasons), he frequently appointed an auditor to do it for him. It was necessary that the auditor be independent of the subordinate manager (auditee) and competent to conduct the review so that the higher authority (audit recipient) could rely upon his evaluation.

Usually, auditing is not the only accountability device in such situations. Production reports, information from other managers, and general observations, for example, also contribute to the flow of accountability information. However, auditing is a particularly valuable accountability technique for two reasons: (1) the independence and competence of the auditor add credence to the audit (accountability) report, and (2) auditing can provide an added dimension of information — advice and recommendations.

As noted in the previous chapter, auditing has traditionally been used in situations where the subordinate acted and was accountable in a fiduciary capacity. Hence, the primary purpose of the audit was the detection of fraud and accounting error. For example, in 1931 the AICPA (then AIA) Special Committee on Terminology defined auditing as:

> An examination of the books of account, vouchers and other records of a public body, institution, corporation, firm, or person, or of any person or persons standing in any *fiduciary* capacity, for the purpose of ascertaining the accuracy or inaccuracy of the records and of expressing opinion upon the statements rendered, usually in the form of a certificate.[13] (emphasis added)

However, as was also shown in the previous chapter, the scope of auditing has expanded in recent years to encompass matters of a performance nature. This extension of the scope of auditing has, in many instances, been a direct result of an expansion of the scope of accountability — both implied and specified.

Within the last decade, there has been a broadening of the scope of implied accountability of managers — particularly in the governmental environment. Herman Bevis predicted this movement in 1959:

> Observers of the Washington scene are usually amazed at how little time is devoted to finding out the actual results of what happened under the budgets and appropriations on which so much time was spent.
>
> . . . .
>
> It seems inevitable that there will ultimately be greater emphasis on accountability in the supervision and management of the federal government's operations.[14]

Seven years later, E. L. Normanton commented:

A fresh conception of accountability is, never-the-less, evolving. It implies not merely the possibility of imposing budgetary discipline upon the accountable bodies, or of criticising their errors, but also of contributing towards understanding of the general administrative process.[15]

This broad concept of accountability has now become more widely accepted. For example, the recently published *Standards for Audit of Governmental Organizations, Programs, Activities, and Functions* by the General Accounting Office states quite positively:

> A fundamental tenet of a democratic society holds that governments and agencies entrusted with public resources and the authority for applying them have a responsibility to render a full accounting of their activities. This accountability is inherent in the governmental process and is not always *specifically* identified by legislative provision. This governmental accountability should identify not only the object for which the public resources have been devoted but also the manner and effect of their application.[16] (emphasis added)

The force behind this extension of the scope of accountability in government is an increased awareness on the part of the public, the press, and governmental officials of the need — in fact the necessity — for greater economy, efficiency, and effectiveness of governmental programs and organizations.

In the field of education, this increased scope of implied accountability has been demonstrated by the recent "Accountability in Education" movement. The essence of this movement is a growing awareness in the educational community that educators are increasingly accountable for results. The spearhead of this movement was the Presidential Elementary and Secondary Education Message of 1970, which stated at one point:

> We must stop congratulating ourselves for spending nearly as much money on education as does the entire rest of the world — 65 billion a year on all levels — when we are not getting as much as we should out of the dollar we spend. We have, as a nation, too long avoided thinking of the productivity of the schools. What we have too often been doing is avoiding accountability for our own local performance. Ironic though it is, the avoidance of accountability is the single most serious threat to a continued and even more pluralistic education system.[17]

This extension of the scope of accountability of governmental managers is not only implied, but in some instances is very clearly specified. For example, local education agency recipients of ESEA Title I grant-in-aids for educationally deprived children are specifically directed in the enabling legislation to adopt:

> . . . effective procedures, including . . . appropriate objective measurements of educational achievement, . . . for evaluating at least annually the effectiveness of the program in meeting the special educational needs of educationally deprived children.[18]

By spelling out acceptable performance in legislation, regulations, or guidelines, governmental authorities have in turn forced extension of the scope of auditing of these programs to include evaluations of such performance. Hence, the auditor in some instances must review performance matters, because acceptable minimum standards of performance accountability are spelled out in the law.

Thus, the scope of auditing as an accountability device has been expanding because accountability has been expanding. However, auditing has also received pressure to expand because of its potential as a management control technique.

AUDITING AS A MANAGEMENT CONTROL TECHNIQUE

Management control, like accountability, also implies a review. The main difference is a matter of emphasis. Accountability implies a review for purposes of supervising or evaluating the subordinate manager. Management control, on the other hand, implies a review for purposes of aiding or assisting *both* the higher authority (audit recipient) and the subordinate manager (auditee).

Auditors traditionally have made suggestions to management as a by-product or sub-objective of the usual accountability audit. In recent years, however, the potential of auditing as a management control technique has become increasingly recognized. As a result, a number of auditors have been encouraged both by management and through their own professional activities, to extend the scope of their audits and, at the same time, to de-emphasize accountability and to stress or accentuate management control.

In this context, it may be noted that most contemporary authorities refer to internal auditing as a management control technique. For instance, the Institute of Internal Auditors, in their 1971 *Statement of Responsibilities of the Internal Auditor,* defined internal auditing as:

. . . an independent appraisal activity within an organization for the review of operations as a *service* to management. It is a managerial control which functions by measuring and evaluating the effectiveness of other controls.[19] (emphasis added)

This deliberate de-emphasis of the accountability aspect of internal auditing has definitely made the concept more attractive to management. Obviously, a manager is much more likely to welcome an auditor when he feels that the auditor is there to aid and assist him rather than evaluate his performance for accountability purposes. In fact, there is little question but that this management control emphasis has been a significant factor influencing the high degree of acceptance that internal auditing has gained in many industrial firms.[20]

There has also been a movement to make auditing in the government environment more management control oriented. Some State auditors, both through appropriately worded audit reports and in their own internal audit guides, have emphasized the positive aspect of aiding management and improving future operations rather than criticizing past actions.[21] Some Federal audit agencies have adopted a similar approach to auditing.[22]

The major audit activity of the public accounting profession is attesting to the fairness of financial statements prepared by an organization's management. Since these statements are usually for the benefit of owners, creditors, or regulatory agencies, the principal objective of public auditing is usually accountability. However, some CPA firms are currently generating *two* audit reports: (1) a short form opinion attesting to the fairness of attached financial statements, and (2) an internal, long form, narrative report on administrative controls for the use of management. Corine Norgaard, who in 1969 conducted a survey of operational auditing in the public accounting profession,[23] recently reported that:

. . . some of the techniques of the operational audit are being applied during the course of a financial audit with the result that the audit examination is serving a dual purpose: (1) providing a basis for an opinion to third parties regarding the fairness of the financial statements and (2) providing management with information as to how well both accounting and administrative controls are working.[24]

Thus, auditing is increasingly used as a management control technique, and the scope of such audits is expanding because of a growing acceptance of and desire for this kind of auditing on both the part of management and the auditing profession itself.

AUDITING AS AN INSTRUMENT TO PROMOTE BETTER MANAGEMENT

It has been demonstrated that the scope of auditing in many areas is expanding to encompass matters of a management or performance nature. Recognizing this advance, R. J. Freeman notes that:

> . . . the movement to comprehensive auditing is definitely *evolutionary,* as opposed to revolutionary — all the questions have not been answered as yet nor have all of the problems been solved.[25]

In this regard, a crucial question is: Can improved management be better accomplished through coercion (accountability) or cooperation (management control)? Douglas McGregor recognizes these two diametric approaches to motivation as part of his Theory X and Theory Y of management.

> Man will exercise self-direction and self-control in the service of objectives to which he is committed. This is contrasted with Theory X, that most people must be coerced, controlled, directed, and threatened with punishment to get them to put forth adequate effort toward the achievement of organizational objectives.[26]

McGregor further states,

> The findings which are beginning to emerge from the social sciences challenge the whole set of beliefs about man and human nature and about the task of management. The evidence is far from conclusive, certainly, but it is suggestive. . . . [The suggestion is that] The conventional approach of Theory X is based on mistaken notions of what is cause and what is effect.[27]

McGregor's remarks cause one to wonder just how much *more* good could come from those audits that are broad in scope, but presently are strongly oriented toward accountability. It would seem logical to expect that operational improvements could be more readily accomplished with the encouragement and cooperation, rather than the resistance or passiveness, of the auditee manager. Likewise, it seems logical to assume that the auditee would be more receptive to audit recommendations if the objective of the audit was to aid management rather than evaluate management for accountability purposes.

These logical assumptions have been strongly supported by a recent study of *Behavioral Patterns in Internal Audit Relationships* sponsored by the Institute of Internal Auditors.[28] This significant work offers convincing evidence that a cooperative approach to auditing actually produces better results. In this regard, one of the conclusions of the study is:

RESEARCH HYPOTHESIS NO. 4   *The establishment of participative teamwork relationships between auditors and auditees will help to achieve overall organizational goals.*

This hypothesis was strongly supported by: (1) the results of the laboratory experiments which showed significant differences in the performance of the Style "C" [participative] groups; (2) the considered reactions of the audit managers participating in the field studies that the audit recommendations were accepted and implemented much more readily under the participative approach; and (3) by the gratuitous comments made by the auditees experiencing the participative approach. Accordingly, we conclude that the validity of this hypothesis cannot be rejected from the evidence at hand and therefore accept it as reasonably demonstrated.[29]

It would seem, therefore, that auditing would be a more effective instrument for the improvement of management if the objective of auditing was oriented more toward management control instead of accountability. However, accountability must and will continue to be a cornerstone of organizational systems — particularly those in the governmental environment where public trust is paramount. Also, by its very nature, auditing is irrevocably linked to accountability. Even when an audit report is used primarily for management control at the auditee level, there still exists an environment of accountability — that is, an environment of authority and responsibility. In other words, the auditor reports primarily to the auditee's higher authority. [When an independent examination is (1) for the exclusive benefit of the subordinate manager, (2) solely for management control at the subordinate level, and (3) not associated with accountability, then it is more properly called a management review or service, *not* an audit.]

Thus, it appears that the very nature of auditing hinders the attainment of optimum auditee cooperation. However, even though auditing is basically an accountability device, it has been demonstrated that the accountability aspect of auditing can often be de-emphasized and the more positive aspect of management control or aid emphasized. Thus, the modern objective of auditing can be viewed as a balance between accountability and management aid (see Figure 2). Current thought and recent evidence suggest that this approach will promote greater acceptance and implementation of audit recommendations. And implementation of recommendations that promote better management is, and must be, the ultimate purpose of contemporary auditing.

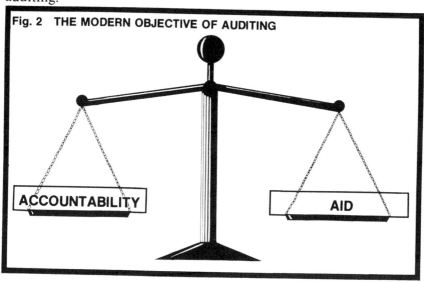

Fig. 2 THE MODERN OBJECTIVE OF AUDITING

THE SCOPE OF AUDITING

As far back as 1953, an editorial in *The Journal of Accountancy* recognized the need to distinguish between audits of differing scope.

There is probably little hope of restricting the use of the term (audit) to describe an examination of accounts and supporting data by independent accountants for the purpose of expressing an opinion of the fairness of financial statements. Perhaps some modifying adjective should be developed to distinguish this type of audit from others.[30]

What actually followed was the introduction of a myriad of modifying adjectives. For example:

Financial Audit	Management Audit
Performance Audit	Program Audit
Depth Audit	Fidelity Audit
Mission Audit	Functional Audit
Fiscal Audit	Responsibility Audit
Operational Audit	Comprehensive Audit
Total Audit	Status Audit
Efficiency Audit	Operations Audit
Substantive Audit	Compliance Audit

This is only a partial list of the many adjectives that have been used in recent years to describe audits of varying scope.

Some of these terms have enhanced the vocabulary of auditing, while others are unnecessary additions to an already overcrowded nomenclature. As far as extended audits are concerned, the most common terms are:

. . *Operational* and/or *management auditing* — which came into widespread use in the early 1950's; principally used by internal auditors and the Institute of Internal Auditors.

. . *Comprehensive auditing* — which has been used for many years (since 1949) by the General Accounting Office to describe their audit activity.

. . *Performance auditing* — which came into widespread use in the mid 1960's; principally used by State Auditors.

Unfortunately, some of these terms have caused more confusion than they have eliminated. For example:

. . What is the difference, if any, between operational, program, comprehensive, or performance audits?

. . What is the exact *scope* of these audits?

. . Specifically, do operational and performance audits include or exclude financial and compliance matters?

At the present time, there are no generally accepted answers to these and similar questions. In fact, much debate and discussion of these issues is taking place. However, there have been several serious attempts to clarify these terms and to describe more clearly and specifically the potential scope of auditing. Some of the more significant efforts in this direction are discussed in the following pages.

NORMANTON

In 1966, the University of Manchester, England published a book written by E. L. Normanton entitled *The Accountability and Audit of Governments.*[31] Normanton's comprehensive study focused upon governmental auditing in the major countries of the western world: England, France, West Germany, the United States, Italy, the Netherlands, Belgium, Norway, Denmark, Austria, and Israel.

As observed earlier, Normanton described governmental auditing as being traditionally limited in scope to matters of "regularity." However, he noted that in recent years the scope of auditing had in many western countries extended beyond regularity to consider such things as: waste, extravagance, unsound projects, complicated policies, and administrative efficiency. In his concluding chapter, he asks and answers the following question.

> *What are the potential new functions and attributes of a state audit body?*
>
> The traditional "regularity" audit, concerned with the *minutiae* of accounts, was the lowest common denominator. All the older audit departments started from that level, and most of them have by their own efforts achieved a discretionary audit, which means they now can take a critical interest in the major financial activities of governments. The newer audit bodies were founded by statute at about this improved level. Some audit departments, both old and new, have advanced beyond that level and have begun to learn the difficult but increasingly important profession of the efficiency auditor.[32]

Hence, Normanton's framework of governmental auditing has three parts:

1. Regularity audit
2. Discretionary audit
3. Efficiency audit

KNIGHTON

Lennis M. Knighton's *The Performance Post Audit in State Government* was published by Michigan State University in 1967.[33] Since then, Knighton has contributed extensively to the literature of governmental auditing and accounting. In 1970, he presented a paper to the National Legislative Conference entitled *An Intergrated Framework for Conceptualizing Alternative Approaches to State Audit Programs* which was later published in *The Federal Accountant.*[34] In this paper, he described the "comprehensive audit and its various parts" as follows:

> COMPREHENSIVE AUDIT: an all-inclusive, umbrella-like concept, encompassing all audit policies and programs, and including both financial audits as well as performance audits, as outlined below.
>
> FINANCIAL AUDIT: an examination restricted essentially to financial records and controls, for the purpose of determining that funds are legally and honestly spent,

that receipts are properly recorded and controlled, and that financial reports and statements are complete and reliable.

PERFORMANCE AUDIT: an examination of records and other evidence to support an appraisal or evaluation of the efficiency of government operations, the effectiveness of government programs, and the faithfulness of responsible administrators to adhere to juridical requirements and administrative policies pertaining to their programs and organizations.

COMPLIANCE AUDIT: that portion of the performance audit which pertains to the faithfulness of administrative adherence to juridical requirements and administrative policies.

OPERATIONAL AUDIT: that portion of the performance audit which pertains to the efficiency of operations — focusing primarily on operating policies, procedures, practices, and controls; including the utilization and control of non-financial resources, such as property, equipment, personnel, supplies, etc.

PROGRAM AUDIT: that portion of the performance audit which pertains to the effectiveness of government programs — focusing essentially on the management control system and the reliability of data contained in performance reports that purport to disclose the results of operations in terms of program accomplishment.[35]

THE GAO

The U. S. General Accounting Office has developed a conceptual framework of the scope of governmental auditing somewhat similar to Normanton's and Knighton's frameworks. This framework has been presented in several articles and discussed in speeches presented by high-ranking members of the GAO. In particular, this framework is embodied as the first general standard of the recently issued *Standards for Audit of Governmental Organization, Programs, Activities, and Functions.*[36]

The full scope of an audit of a governmental program function, activity, or organization should encompass:

a. An examination of financial transactions, accounts, and reports, including an evaluation of compliance with applicable laws and regulations.

b. A review of efficiency and economy in the use of

resources.

c. A review to determine whether desired results are effectively achieved.

In determining the scope for a particular audit, responsible officials should give consideration to the needs of the potential users of the results of that audit.[37]

This framework was also included as part of the recommendations proposed by Controller General Elmer B. Staats and adopted by the 7th International Congress of Supreme Audit Institutions in September 1971.

That a full or complete concept for independent auditing of governmental programs, agencies, or activities include recognition of the following elements.

— Fiscal accountability, which should include fiscal integrity, full disclosure, and compliance with applicable laws and regulations.

— Managerial accountability, which should be concerned with efficiency and economy in the use of public funds, property, personnel, and other resources.

— Program accountability, which should be concerned with whether government programs and activities are achieving the objectives established for them with due regard to both costs and results.[38]

INTERNAL AUDITING

The Institute of Internal Auditing has been for many years concerned with the scope and nature of internal auditing. Its *Statement of Responsibility of the Internal Auditor,* originally issued in 1947 and revised in 1957 and 1971, provides a conceptual framework for the potential scope of internal auditing.

OBJECTIVE AND SCOPE

The objective of internal auditing is to assist all members of management in the effective discharge of their responsibilities, by furnishing them with analyses, appraisals, recommendations, and pertinent comments concerning the activities reviewed. The internal auditor is concerned with any phase of business activity where he can be of service to management. This involves going beyond the accounting and financial records to obtain a full understanding of the operations under review. The attainment of this overall objective involves such activities as:

— Reviewing and appraising the soundness, adequacy, and application of accounting, financial, and other operating controls, and promoting effective control at reasonable cost.

— Ascertaining the extent of compliance with established policies, plans, and procedures.

— Ascertaining the extent to which company assets are accounted for and safeguarded from losses of all kinds.

— Ascertaining the reliability of management data developed within the organization.

— Appraising the quality of performance in carrying out assigned responsibilities.

— Recommending operating improvements.[39]

CPA AUDITING

In 1953, the American Institute of Certified Public Accountants, (then American Institute of Accountants) Committee on Terminology published a definition of (financial) auditing, which remains the most authoritative Institute definition of the term.[40]

In general, an examination of an accounting document and of supporting evidence for the purpose of reaching an informed opinion concerning its propriety. Specifically:

(1) An examination of a claim for payment or credit and of supporting evidence for the purpose of determining whether the expenditure is properly authorized, has been or should be duly made, and how it should be treated in the accounts of the payor — hence, *audited voucher.*

(2) An examination of similar character and purpose of an account purporting to deal with actual transactions only, such as receipts and payments.

(3) By extension, an examination of accounts which purport to reflect not only actual transactions but valuations, estimates, and opinions, for the purpose of determining whether the accounts are properly stated and fairly reflect the matters with which they purport to deal.

(4) An examination intended to serve as a basis for an ex-

pression of opinion regarding the fairness, consistency, and conformity with accepted accounting principles, of statements prepared by a corporation or other entity for submission to the public or to other interested parties.[41]

Of particular interest to this study, however, is a 1972 report prepared by the AICPA's Committee on Auditing for Federal Agencies.[42] This report includes a section on the Scope of Auditor (CPA) Services, which reads in part:

> Although the purposes of federal assistance programs, as well as the means for carrying them out, are highly diverse, the services provided by CPAs can be categorized as follows:
>
> 1. Financial audits.
> 2. Systems surveys (accounting systems and systems of internal control) — usually prior to or early in the period of grant or contract performance but separate from financial audit.
> 3. Compliance reporting (financial and program) — usually incident to financial audit, with or without an extension of audit procedures.
> 4. Other services — in some instances where federal agencies may decide to request other services from CPAs beyond those described above. Such other services may fall within the variety of descriptive terms currently found in the literature, such as operational auditing, management auditing, and performance evaluation, but for which no generally accepted definitions currently exist. Consequently, common definitions of scope for such emerging areas of service have not yet evolved, nor are standards available for either their performance or evaluation.[43]

AIDE PROJECT FRAMEWORK

The preceding frameworks generally reflect the historic extension of auditing — first into financial and compliance matters, then into the area of performance. On the other hand, these are *conceptual* frameworks of the *potential* scope of auditing. They do not reflect the scope of all audits. In addition, many of the descriptions are somewhat vague. For example, what are the precise meanings of such terms as economy, efficiency, and effectiveness?

TABLE 2
CONCEPTUAL FRAMEWORKS OF THE SCOPE OF AUDITING

AIDE PROJECT	Governmental		(1971) GAO	Internal (1971) IIA	CPA (1972) AICPA
	(1966) Normanton	(1970) Knighton			
I. Financial	Regularity Audit	Financial Audit	Fiscal Accountability	Financial and Other Operating Controls	Financial Audits Systems Surveys
II. Compliance	"	Performance: Compliance Audit	"	Compliance	Compliance Reporting
III. Performance	Discretionary Audit Efficiency Audit —	Performance: Operational Audit Performance: Program Audit	Managerial Accountability Program Accountability	Assets Accounted and Safeguarded Management Data Reliability Responsibility Performance Operating Improvements "	Other Services "

For use in our interviews and questionnaires, the project adopted the scope framework shown below.

Fig. 3　AIDE PROJECT SCOPE FRAMEWORK

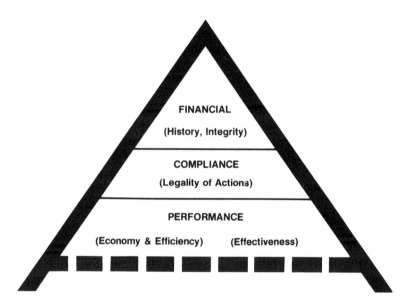

Figure 3 demonstrates the expanding accountability of managers and the corresponding expansion of the scope of contemporary auditing. The dotted line at the bottom of the triangle indicates that neither accountability nor auditing will ever completely encompass the total spectrum of managerial responsibility.

This framework was adopted for purposes of clarity. SEA managers had experienced audits of financial and compliance scopes. Therefore, these terms were meaningful to them. The term performance was chosen because it was felt that:

(1) SEAs, being State Agencies, had been more frequently exposed to the term performance audit, which is commonly used by State Auditors, than to other terms such as operational audit or management audit.

(2) The use of further detail to describe extended audits by using such terms as managerial, operational, or program, would not be sufficiently clear, or consistently interpreted by SEA managers.

FINANCIAL AUDITING

Financial auditing concerns the accuracy, integrity, and fair presentation of financial accounts, documents, and statements. This includes such matters as accounting problems and errors, fraud, financial control weakness, and/or financial position or condition. Historically, auditing has been closely linked with accounting. In fact, most people think of an auditor as an accountant who receives or inspects financial records and accounts.

Although reliable statistics are not available, it is believed that more CPA audits are conducted in this country than any other category, and currently most CPA audits (even in the governmental environment) are principally of a financial nature. The CPA profession has evolved a specialized type of audit and audit report whereby the auditor "attests" to the fairness of financial statements prepared by an organization's management. The CPA first conducts an extensive review and test of the accounting records in order to verify the figures in the financial statements. Rather than discuss in the audit report any errors discovered, the auditor usually confers with management and any necessary corrections are made prior to issuance of the statements. As a result, the CPA audit report is generally a short one or two paragraph opinion (short form report) attached to the published financial statements. In the great majority of cases this opinion is an "unqualified" attestation. Though in some instances the auditor is unable to give an unqualified opinion and instead issues a qualified or adverse opinion, or disclaims an opinion altogether.[44]

CPAs may also issue long-form reports. These are longer, narrative type reports that discuss accounting problems, internal control weaknesses, and other observations the auditor made during the course of his review. These reports, almost always for *internal* use only, are frequently issued as a by-product of the regular financial audit in the form of a separate report or management letter.

As noted earlier, financial auditing has traditionally been concerned with the detection of fraud perpetrated through the manipulation of accounting records and/or the bypass of internal accounting controls. However, since the 1930's the public accounting profession has emphasized that fraud detection is not the principal objective of the CPA audit. This is due in part to legal liability problems that may arise if fraud exists but is not detected. CPAs are not "guarantors" of the correctness of financial statements of the absence of fraud.[45] They are obligated to conduct a competent review with professional due care. However, fraud of a relatively minor nature may not be uncovered; furthermore, fraud on a larger scale may not be discovered where there is extensive collusion by auditee personnel.

Financial auditing also forms the *basis* for most internal and governmental auditing. Some internal and governmental auditors issue short-form opinions similar to those rendered by CPAs. However, most issue the long-form, narrative type, audit report. These reports usually include discussions of accounting errors and other problems discovered during the course of the audit. However, the scope of many internal and governmental audits may also extend into compliance and performance areas.

COMPLIANCE AUDITING

Compliance auditing concerns legality, adherence, and conformity with laws, regulations, policies, and procedures both internal and external to the organization. Compliance is usually of greater concern and pertinence in governmental auditing than in private sector auditing. This is because the governmental manager operates in a strict, legal environment due to his position of public trust. This is not to say that compliance is ignored in the private sector. In fact, the Institute of Internal Auditors has included compliance with organizational policies, plans, and procedures as part of the scope of internal auditing.[46]

Generally, a compliance audit refers to a review to determine if management has complied with applicable legislation, rules, regulations, and other requirements of an *administrative* nature — such as meeting legal deadlines, filing forms properly, and the like. However, *financial* requirements are often a matter of law, and increasingly, the law may spell out *performance* criteria (such as Title I target school selection).

What this means is that, relative to the scope framework, the concept of compliance may overlap financial and performance aspects. Thus, the term compliance can encompass subjects of a financial, administrative, and/or performance nature.

Fig. 4 COMPLIANCE OVERLAP

Compliance → Financial
Administrative
Performance

This overlap may cause the scope framework to be difficult to operationalize. For instance, Federal legislation, regulations, and guidelines may be so explicit with regard to a grant-in-aid as to encompass many aspects of the management process. Thus, some audits that consider performance matters may actually be compliance audits because acceptable performance is spelled out in the "law." For the most part, however, applicable laws and regulations — particularly in State government — deal with administrative matters. Those audits that go beyond administrative concerns would usually be classified as performance audits.

PERFORMANCE AUDITING

Performance auditing was stipulatively defined for purposes of our interviews as going "beyond the traditional financial and compliance audit." In referring to audits of performance, many authorities use the terms economy, efficiency, and effectiveness (often called the "3 E's" of good management).

Audits of economy and efficiency (frequently called operational or management auditing) focus upon the acquisition, control, and utilization of personnel, facilities, materials, and resources (both actual and potential). Audits of effectiveness (often called program auditing) concern the progress, success, and impact of programs, projects, and activities (both actual and potential).

In referring to these concepts, the GAO states that:

A review of efficiency and economy shall include inquiry into whether, in carrying out its responsibilities, the audited entity is giving due consideration to conservation of its resources and minimum expenditure of effort. Examples of uneconomical practices or inefficiencies the auditor should be alert to include:

a. Procedures, whether officially prescribed or merely followed, which are ineffective or more costly than justified.
b. Duplication of effort by employees or between organizational units.
c. Performance of work which serves little or no useful purposes.
d. Inefficient or uneconomical use of equipment.
e. Overstaffing in relation to work to be done.
f. Faulty buying practices and accumulation of un-

needed or excess quantities of property, materials, or supplies.

g. Wasteful use of resources.

. . . .

A review of the results of programs or activities [effectiveness] shall include inquiry into the results or benefits achieved and whether the programs or activities are meeting established objectives. The auditor should consider:

a. The relevance and validity of the criteria used by the audited entity to judge effectiveness in achieving program results.

b. The appropriateness of the methods followed by the entity to evaluate effectiveness in achieving program results.

c. The accuracy of the data accumulated.

d. The reliability of the results obtained.[47]

SUMMARY: THE EXPANDING SCOPE OF AUDITING

Auditing has traditionally been considered a review of financial matters by an independent, competent accountant. This is still an accurate description of many — if not a majority — of today's audits. However, as shown in the last chapter and in the objectives section, auditors in all fields are beginning to broaden the scope of their audits for several reasons: (1) both implied and specified accountability of managers — particularly governmental managers — is expanding, hence the scope of auditing as an accountability device is expanding; (2) managers at all levels are recognizing the contribution that broad-scope auditing can make as a management control technique; and (3) the "self-determination" of auditors themselves in realizing that auditing can make its greatest contribution to business and government as a tool to promote greater economy, efficiency and effectiveness.

However, this extension of audit scope is difficult to measure and describe explicitly. For example, there have been many adjectives used in recent years to describe extended scope audits, such as: management, operational, program, performance, and comprehensive. Still, the exact definitions of these terms are unclear and unsettled. There have also been several attempts to develop frameworks that more clearly explain and delineate these terms and the potential scope of auditing. These frameworks — including the framework used in this project — represent steps in the right direction; but are still imperfect and difficult to operationalize. Hopefully, these efforts will stimulate thought and encourage future research in this area.

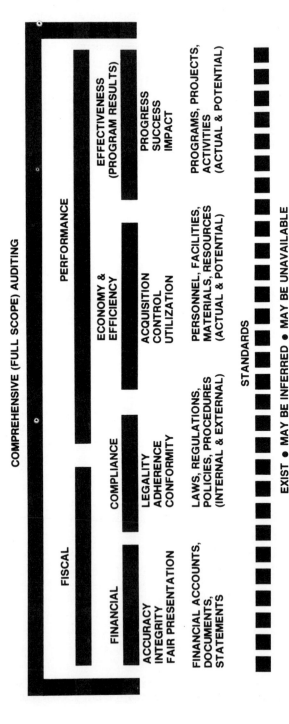

Fig. 5   POTENTIAL SCOPE OF AUDITING

This Figure is based in part on concepts developed by R. J. Freeman and L. N. Knighton (See Footnotes 25 and 34).

The "Potential Scope of Auditing" is illustrated in Figure 5. Starting from the top of the diagram, comprehensive auditing is represented as an all-inclusive, umbrella concept encompassing all possible audit activities — including both fiscal and performance auditing. Fiscal auditing is shown to include both financial and compliance components. However, as discussed earlier, compliance can also overlap into the area of performance with the major focus of performance auditing being upon economy, efficiency, and effectiveness.

Financial auditing concerns the accuracy, integrity, and fair presentation of financial accounts, documents, and statements. Compliance auditing concerns legality, adherence, and conformity with laws, regulations, policies, and procedures (both internal and external to the organization). Audits of economy and efficiency (frequently called operational or management auditing) focus upon the acquisition, control and utilization of personnel, facilities, materials, and resources (both actual and potential). Audits of effectiveness (often called program auditing) concern the progress, success, and impact of programs, projects, and activities (both actual and potential).

Standards of excellence or acceptability generally exist for financial affairs but for audits of compliance and performance matters such standards may have to be inferred and/or they may be unavailable. Fiscal audits are usually attestations of past actions. Performance audits, on the other hand, are generally more suggestive in nature with their emphasis being upon future improvement.

Most authorities feel that broad or comprehensive scope auditing is the "best" kind of auditing and is the way of the future. Past and current experience indicates that, with appropriate caution, this generally is true. However, not all audits should be management audits; nor should all audits comprehensively encompass financial, compliance, and performance matters. Recognizing this, the GAO states:

> These standards provide for a scope of audit that includes not only financial and compliance auditing but also auditing for economy, efficiency, and achievement of desired results. Provision for such a scope of audit is not intended to imply that all audits are presently being conducted this way or that such an extensive scope is always desirable. However, an audit that would include provision for the interests of all potential users of government audits would ordinarily include provision for auditing all the above elements of the accountability of the responsible officials.[48]

Thus, the scope of any audit must depend upon the *needs* and *desires* of the audit recipient relative to the ability (time, competency, cost, etc.)

of the auditor and the nature, size, and willingness of the auditee.

THE PARTIES TO AN AUDIT

The basic parties to an audit are the auditor, the auditee, and the audit recipient. Diagrammatically, the audit recipient is the higher authority, and the auditee is the subordinate (as discussed in the objectives section). The auditor is independent of the auditee and reports to the audit recipient (see Figure 1).

The auditee is accountable, hence answerable, to the audit recipient for the proper discharge of certain specified and/or implied responsibilities. After conducting an examination, the auditor communicates a reliable report of the status of the auditee's activities to the audit recipient. The audit report may be used to evaluate the auditee (accountability) and/or as an instrument to aid both the auditee and the audit recipient in the conduct of the operation (management control). In either case, auditing acts as a tool to encourage proper or optimum performance — be this the presentation of a reliable financial statement, compliance with applicable laws, or economical, efficient, and effective operations.

THE AUDIT NETWORK

It is not uncommon for an organization to be comprised of thousands of "subordinates" and "higher authorities" with many levels of management. Also, an organization may be a member of a system of organizations bound together by accountability relationships. Thus, relative to the organization, there are two basic kinds of organizational systems: Internal and External.

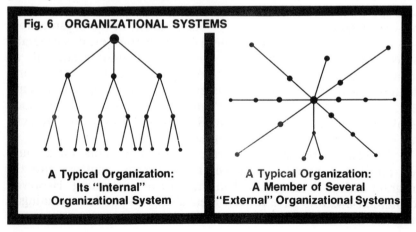

Fig. 6 ORGANIZATIONAL SYSTEMS

A Typical Organization:
Its "Internal"
Organizational System

A Typical Organization:
A Member of Several
"External" Organizational Systems

The size and complexity of organizational systems often create a need for auditing because ultimate authority is often far removed from front-line (action) management. Theoretically, auditing may impinge at any point in the total accountability system, generally with the next higher authority being the primary audit recipient. Realistically, for auditing to impinge at every point would be uneconomical, impractical and would result in much duplication of effort. However, for many complex, integrated organizational systems it is necessary to have several levels of auditing at strategic points in order to have satisfactory and manageable audit coverage. Such auditing frameworks or structures are generally referred to as audit networks. And, as in the case of organizational systems, the basic audit network has both internal and external elements.

INTERNAL AUDITING

Internal auditing refers to those audits in which:

1. The auditor is an employee of the organization in which the audit is conducted.
2. The auditee or subject matter of the audit is within the organizational structure.
3. The primary audit recipient is within the organizational structure.

For example, a review of a Local Education Agency by a State Education Agency auditor would not be an internal audit because the second condition is violated. Nor would a review of SEA activities by a State Auditor or CPA be an internal audit, regardless of the audit recipient, because the first condition is violated. Clearly, internal auditing is an appraisal activity that is conducted by an organization, concerns that organization, and is for the primary benefit of the organization.

Except in the case of large multi-based operations, it is generally unnecessary to have more than one internal audit branch in an organization. In some instances, there may be two groups that perform an audit function with different names and/or audit scopes. For example, an organization may have an "Internal Audit Staff" that conducts fiscal audits only and a "Program Review and Evaluation Branch" that conducts performance or program audits.

The usual rationale for separate audit groups is that the accountant-auditor is poorly qualified in "program" matters and the program-auditor is unqualified in the area of accounting. However, accountant-auditors have proven their ability to conduct meaningful program audits on thousands of occasions during the past twenty years. In many instances, they have been able to make significant contributions in operational areas because of their analytical background; and a team approach of accountants and specialists has proven to be particularly effective. Thus, many organizations have found that one centralized internal audit group (1) maximizes auditor productivity, (2) minimizes audit duplication, and (3) optimizes audit coordination.

The trend in modern internal auditing is decidedly toward audits that encompass performance aspects. Most internal auditors refer to these as operational audits. Financial matters are not overlooked, but primary reliance is placed upon the establishment and periodic review of adequate financial controls. A common belief in this regard is that far more is lost (or not gained) through inefficient and uneconomical operations and programs than from accounting error and fraud.

The primary objective of modern internal auditing is the improvement of management control, rather than accountability. Because the audit report is intended to aid management, and because most reports are confidential and/or remain internal to the organization, the auditee manager is often quite receptive to auditor recommendations. In fact, several organizations with well-established operational audit staffs report that requests for audits far exceed presently available manpower.[49]

Internal auditing is potentially a greater management tool than is external auditing. Not only is the internal audit staff highly management oriented, but it can devote 100% of its attention to the organization. On the other hand, external auditors usually conduct audits of many different organizations. They may audit a particular organization only once a year and, in some instances, there may be a break of several years between audits. Also, external auditors usually report to audit recipients outside of the organization. For this reason, the external audit may be oriented more to the needs of the outside recipient than to the needs of the auditee organization. For example, Federal auditors may audit an SEA only once every several years. Usually their audit is strictly limited to Federal programs, is based upon U.S. Office of Education Regulations, and is primarily directed to USOE for settlement. This is not to say that Federal audits *should* be oriented differently, rather it demonstrates that internal auditing is potentially of greater use to SEA management than external auditing.

In order to insure necessary and adequate independence, objectivity, and coverage the internal audit staff must report and be responsible to the very top of the organization. Stated differently, the lower in the organization that the audit function is placed, the more restricted is the potential audit coverage and benefit.

Fig. 7   HYPOTHETICAL AUDIT PLACEMENT

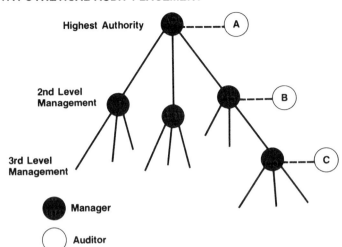

In the preceding illustration, Auditor C reports to a third level manager and has implied authority to review only a small part of the organization, while Auditor A reports directly to the highest authority and feels free to review any area of the organization. Even Auditor B, who reports directly to a second level manager (such as a Controller or Division Director), may be effectively limited to only 1/3 of the organization. Thus, if at all possible, the internal audit staff or director should report to the highest authority in the organization.

Internal auditing is now widely recognized as an important and necessary management tool in medium to large size organizations. Internal auditing may also serve as a meaningful management aid in some small organizations where activities are complex or control is especially important. The Institute of Internal Auditors has often referred to internal auditors as the "eyes and ears of management." However, internal auditors are *not* managers. Their function is to analyze and recommend. Decisions concerning the nature and type of action to be taken, if any, and the implementation of such action must be made by management.

Internal auditors can and should work closely with an organization's external auditors. In many instances the work of the internal auditor can be coordinated with that of the external auditor in order to minimize duplication and maximize audit effort.

EXTERNAL AUDITING

The other half of the basic audit network is the external auditor.

An organization may be accountable to outside owners, creditors, other organizations, and/or the public. These "higher authorities" may authorize audits of the "subordinate" organization for purposes of accountability, management control, or some combination thereof. The auditor should be both external and independent relative to the subordinate organization (auditee), and should report directly to the higher authority (audit recipient).

The external auditor may be an employee of the higher authority. For example, HEW auditors are employees of HEW. On the other hand, the external auditor may be an independent contractor. For instance, CPAs and public accountants are not employees per se of the audit recipient, though they may be engaged by the auditee for the benefit of the higher authority. CPAs who audit corporations for the benefit of the corporation's stockholders are often engaged by the auditee's Board of Directors or Audit Committee.

The external auditor may rely to some degree upon the work of an organization's internal auditor. The extent of such reliance depends largely upon the scope and reliability of the internal auditor's reviews. CPAs often find that the work of an internal auditor is helpful in their evaluation of internal financial controls, a basic step in the financial audit. Governmental auditors may also rely upon the work of internal auditors.

The external auditor can potentially review all matters that his audit recipient has authority over (as can the internal auditor). For example, Federal auditors may review all aspects of State and Local use of Federal Funds. Primary legal authority to do this comes from the Intergovernmental Cooperation Act of 1968 (Public Law 90-577) which states in Section 202:

> All Federal grant-in-aid funds available to the States shall be properly accounted for as Federal funds, in the accounts of the State. In each case the State agency concerned shall render regular authenticated reports to the appropriate Federal agency covering the status and applications for the funds, the liabilities and obligations on hand, and such other facts as may be required by said Federal agency. The head of the Federal Agency and the Comptroller General of the United States or any of their duly authorized representatives shall have access for the purpose of audit and examination to any books, documents, papers, and records that are pertinent to the grant-in-aid received by the States.

Here the key seems to lie in the definition of the word "audit". Both the HEW Audit Agency and the General Accounting Office consider the modern definition of auditing to extend beyond financial stewardship into the areas of compliance and management performance. In practice, however, auditee resistance may effectively limit the scope of the audit and, possibly, preclude auditor entry into some levels of the operation. For example, Federal auditors have been restricted by some States from reviewing Federal programs at the Local Education Agency level. Perhaps, a shift in audit emphasis from accountability to aiding management could eventually eliminate such barriers.

Most external auditors review a number of different auditees each year. For instance, HEW Audit Agency is responsible for reviewing (as of 1969) some 250 programs conducted in more than 1,000 Department installations, 545 State Agencies, 20,000 local units of government, 4,000 universities and other private organizations, 137 insurance companies and other intermediaries, 11,500 hospitals and entended care facilities, and 1,600 home health agencies.[50] Thus, the amount of attention that an external auditor can devote to a single auditee is necessarily limited. Complete, full time audit coverage is therefore best achieved through a combination of both internal and external auditing.

It is not uncommon for an organization to be audited by several external auditors representing several different higher authorities. This often happens in the private sector in the case of large conglomerates and holding companies. In the governmental sector, the most common multiple audit situation is the Federal-State-Local audit network. Federal grants to Local Governments usually pass through State administration. Thus, these programs may be audited by Federal, State, and Local auditors.

HEW Audit Agency, in particular, has encouraged and promoted the Federal-State-Local audit network concept. HEWAA has:

. . . made available to State audit staffs copies of all HEW Audit Agency reports on Federally-funded programs administered by State Agencies.

. . . initiated a number of Federal-State audit demonstration projects designed to foster cooperative auditing of Federal-State programs at all levels.

. . . made Federal audit guides available to numerous State and internal auditors. By this means they have been reasonably successful in keeping State personnel informed regarding the intent and purposes of audits of Federally funded programs.[51]

From all indications, this audit network concept is gaining momentum. However, we are not yet close to achieving a working, integrated audit network. A major reason for this is that most State and Local audit agencies utilize all of the time and other resources presently available to them in attempting to satisfy State and Local needs. Before these agencies will accept responsibility, even jointly, for reviewing Federal-State-Local programs along Federal guidelines and standards, they will no doubt want to know what benefits will accrue to them and what assistance will be forthcoming.

The ultimate goal has been referred to as "the single audit concept." Ideally, through cooperation and coordination, a "single audit" should be able to satisfy the needs of all potential audit users. Achievement of this worthwhile goal will take time, patience, and financial aid.

CHARACTERISTICS OF THE AUDITOR

To conduct an audit — a good audit — requires special skills and attributes. The most essential of these may be categorized under the headings of independence, competency, and professionalism.

INDEPENDENCE

Independence is defined by Webster as the "state or quality of being not subject to bias or influence."[52] Similarly, the *American Heritage Dictionary* describes independence as "free from the influence, guidance, or control of others."[53] For the auditor, independence is both a state of mind as well as a material fact.

This dual aspect of independence was recognized by the Council of the American Institute of CPAs which defined independence as "an attitude of mind, much deeper than the surface display of visible standards."[54] Likewise, John L. Carey and William O. Doherty, writing about the ethics of the CPA, stated:

> Of crucial importance is the statement that independence is not susceptible of precise definition, but is an expression of the professional integrity of the individual. ('Integrity' here is used in the sense of uprightness of character, probity, honesty.) The reason that independence cannot be defined with precision is that it is primarily a condition of the mind and character.[55]

Thomas G. Higgins, former Chairman of the Institute's Committee on Professional Ethics, carried the concept of independence a step further.

> There are actually two kinds of independence which a

CPA must have — independence *in fact* and independence *in appearance.* The former refers to a CPA's objectivity, to the quality of not being influenced by regard to personal advantage. The latter means his freedom from *potential* conflicts of interest which might tend to shake public confidence in his independence *in fact.*[56]

Complete independence is an idealistic goal that in practice may never be reached, but must always be strived for. Employment by the auditee (his client) may compromise the CPA's independence somewhat — at least in appearance. Although the governmental auditor is usually not employed by the auditee, at least directly, he does operate in a political environment and may be subjected to political pressure. The internal auditor is an employee of the organization and may not be deemed independent by external report users. But if the auditor is highly placed in the organization, and if top management is the audit recipient, the internal auditor should not be subject to significant control or influence by lower echelon auditees.

Personal prejudices, pre-conceived notions, friendships or animosities, the "informal organization," and social and economic pressures could hinder an auditor's independence. The auditor has an obligation to recognize such possibilities and to continually strive for objectivity and self-determination.

Independence is an essential characteristic of auditing. Without it, the evaluation ceases to be an audit. This is not to say that an evaluation must be conducted by an independent party to be truthful, significant, and enlightening. Useful evaluations are frequently made by individuals closely associated with the subject of the review. But an audit, both by definition and custom, must be performed by a person who is independent in mind, in fact, and in appearance.

COMPETENCY

Competency implies two things — that the auditor is qualified and that he conducts his examination in a qualified, professional manner (due care). In other words, an auditor may be technically proficient but not competent. (He may not perform at the level of his qualifications.) Hence, it is necessary that the auditor both be and act qualified, i.e., competent.

The nature and extent of acceptable, minimum qualifications for an auditor is a function of the scope of the audit. Simply stated, "the auditor must know what he is doing." This does not mean that he must be a CPA to conduct a financial audit, a lawyer to conduct a compliance audit, or a management analyst to conduct a performance audit. Although such qualifications would certainly be of value, it is unlikely that many auditors could (or should) achieve such a broad background. Rather, a satisfactory level of excellence may be achieved by means of a balanced audit staff of diverse backgrounds and strengths.

Thus, the audit staff as a whole — or through the use of experts in special situations — should be qualified in all areas they may be called upon to evaluate. This pool of talent may be used to provide, as needed, an auditor or audit team suitable to the circumstances and objectives of a particular audit.

The individual auditor obtains his "knowledge" in three basic ways: formal education, special training, and experience. Though most well-rounded auditors will have a respectable amount of each, there is room for flexibility. For example, strong experience may in some instances compensate for the lack of college training.

In recent years, a number of audit agencies have experimented with hiring individuals whose college education was in a field other than accounting, such as political science, engineering, or management. By and large, these agencies report that such individuals have been a welcome addition to the audit staff. However, the backbone of contemporary auditing, continues to be accounting expertise despite the movement toward performance auditing and it is unlikely that auditing will reach a point where accounting is no longer a necessary requisite.

Thus, accounting is generally recognized as a basic background for a career in auditing. Accountants can often make meaningful management recommendations in technical areas without special training through the use of analytical techniques, intelligence, and hard work. In highly technical fields, they can often measure against standards prepared by experts and/or follow pre-developed audit programs and checklists.

In 1969, the Committee on Education and Experience Requirements for CPA's of the American Institute of Certified Public Accountants recommended a model program of college preparation for a career in accounting.[57] This program was based upon the Common Body of Knowledge for CPAs published in 1967 in *Horizons for a Profession* by Roy and McNeil.[58] The committee concluded that the best way to obtain the conceptual knowledge delineated in *Horizons* was through college study. The purpose of this report was to provide more specific guidance for accounting curriculums planners.

The committee felt that by 1975 a five-year program (a masters degree or its equivalent) should be the formal education requisite of the CPA certificate. For those with the recommended five years of study,

TABLE 3

MODEL ACCOUNTING CURRICULUM AS RECOMMENDED BY THE AICPA COMMITTEE ON EDUCATION AND EXPERIENCE REQUIREMENTS FOR CPAs

Subjects	Five-Year	Four-Year
General Education:		
Communications	6-9	6-9
Behavioral Sciences	6	6
Economics	6	6
Elementary Accounting	3-6	3-6
Introduction to the Computer	2-3	2-3
Mathematics, Statistics and Probability	12	12
Other General Education	18-25	18-25
General Business:		
Economics	6	6
Social Environment of Business	6	3
Business Law	6	4
Production or Operational Systems	3	2
Marketing	3	2
Finance	6	4
Organization, Group and Individual Behavior	9	6
Quantitative Applications in Business	9	6
Written Communication	3	2
Business Policy	3	3
Accounting:		
Financial Accounting	9	6
Cost Accounting	6	3
Taxation	3	3
Auditing	6	3
Computers and Information Systems	6	4
Electives	6	3
Total	150	120

Source: *Report of the Committee on Education and Experience Requirements for CPAs,* (New York: AICPA, 1969), Appendix D.

no qualifying experience would be necessary. The report further recommended that "the institute neither specify in terms of courses or course hours how this education should be attained nor encourage such criteria to be made a matter of law or regulation."[59] Their recommended program is shown in Table 3.

This program is designated a "model program" to distinguish it from actual programs. The captions are generic terms rather than course titles, and the semester hours are provided only to indicate relative weight of the various subject areas. Similar suggested or model curricula have been developed by the Federal Government Accountants Association and the Institute of Internal Auditors.

The education of an auditor does not end with his college program. It is just beginning and will continue throughout his professional career. It is essential that any auditor keep abreast of the times and continually strive to further his education. This may be accomplished through reading and contributing to professional literature, participation in professional conferences and meetings, participation in professional societies, special courses and training, on-the-job training experiences, and post-graduate study.

The auditor has a personal responsibility for his continuing self-development. The audit agency also has a responsibility to foster and promote continuing education through active encouragement, sponsorship of special training activities, provision of financial assistance, and by furnishing special working arrangements and experiences.

For the professional auditor, education is a lifelong proposition. However, it should be recognized that there are no universally accepted minimum standards for auditor competency. In fact, many authorities believe the most important qualification of a professional auditor is that innate ability often referred to as "good common sense."

PROFESSIONALISM

Writing in 1915, Abraham Flexner offered six criteria of a profession: (1) intellectual operations coupled with large individual responsibilities, (2) raw materials drawn from science and learning, (3) practical application, (4) an educationally communicable technique, (5) tendency toward self-organization, and (6) increasingly altruistic motivation.[60] Auditing certainly satisfies these requirements. The ethical responsibilities of a professional are implied in the first, fifth, and sixth requirements; professional standards would relate to the second, third, and fourth criteria.

PROFESSIONAL ETHICS

Professional ethics refer to the responsibility and conduct of a professional man. An auditor's ethical responsibilities include the obligations to remain independent, to be satisfactorily competent, and to abide by auditing standards. He should also strive to be honest, moral, prudent, discrete, respectful of confidences, and careful to avoid conflicts of interest. An auditor is obligated to practice such behavior not only in his dealings with audit recipients, but also with *auditees,* other *auditors,* and anyone with whom he comes in contact.

In discussing professional ethics, Mautz and Sharaf state that the professional man:

. . . has an obligation to understand the ideals and functions of his profession. . . . an obligation to consider the possible outcome of any proposed action . . . (and) an obligation to refrain from those activities which detract from the healthy survival of the profession.[61]

Both the American Institute of Certified Public Accountants and the Institute of Internal Auditors have adopted Codes of Professional Ethics. The AICPA Code presently contains 21 rules of conduct divided into five sections: (1) Relations with Clients and Public, (2) Technical Standards, (3) Promotional Practices, (4) Operating Practices, and (5) Relations with Fellow Members.[62] The Institute of Internal Auditor's Code of Ethics contains eight articles and is reproduced on the following page.[63] Both the sizeable body of literature on auditing ethics and the fact that two professional auditing organizations have taken the time and effort to develop rules of professional conduct provides evidence to the fact that auditors in all fields have special obligations and responsibilities as members of the profession of auditing.

THE CODE OF ETHICS
of
The Institute of Internal Auditors

ARTICLES:

I. A member shall have an obligation to exercise honesty, objectivity and diligence in the performance of his duties and responsibilities.

II. A member, in holding the trust of his employer, shall exhibit loyalty in all matters pertaining to the affairs of the employer or to whomever he may be rendering a service. However, a member shall not knowingly be a party to any illegal or improper activity.

III. A member shall refrain from entering into any activity which may be in conflict with the interest of his employer or which would prejudice his ability to carry out objectively his duties and responsibilities.

IV. A member shall not accept a fee or a gift from an employee, a client, a customer or a business associate of his employer, without the knowledge and consent of his senior management.

V. A member shall be prudent in the use of information acquired in the course of his duties. He shall not use confidential information for any personal gain or in a manner which would be detrimental to the welfare of his employer.

VI. A member, in expressing an opinion, shall use all reasonable care to obtain sufficient factual evidence to warrant such expression. In his reporting, a member shall reveal such material facts known to him which, if not revealed, could either distort the report of the results of operations under review or conceal unlawful practice.

VII. A member shall continually strive for improvement in the proficiency and effectiveness of his service.

VIII. A member shall abide by the Bylaws and uphold the objectives of the Institute of Internal Auditors, Inc. In the practice of his profession, he shall be ever mindful of his obligation to maintain the high standard of competence, morality and dignity which the Institute of Internal Auditors, Inc. and its members have established.

AUDITING STANDARDS

Auditing standards are closely related to the subject of professional ethics and also pertain to the general topic of professionalism. A standard is a criterion of excellence or correctness — something to measure against. The most familiar standards are the weight, length, and the time measurements of the U.S. Bureau of Standards. Auditing standards are criterions of excellence or correctness for the field of auditing.

The most widely used and accepted standards for all fields of auditing are those developed by the AICPA (see Chapter 3). However, some authorities have argued in recent years that these standards are not entirely satisfactory for operational or performance auditing and, particularly, for auditing in the governmental environment. In fact, many Federal auditors for the past several years have been abiding by a set of unwritten, almost intuitive, auditing standards — somewhat different from those of the AICPA. The fact that these standards were neither stated nor even generally agreed upon definitely retarded the development of a viable Federal-State-Local audit network.

During the Congressional hearings for the proposed Intergovernmental Cooperation Act of 1970, Comptroller General Elmer B. Staats commented upon the need for the Federal Government to develop auditing standards that could be agreed upon as applicable to all Federal grant programs. At that time the committee chairman, Congressman L. H. Fountain of North Carolina, asked whether GAO could help to "upgrade the quality of post-auditing in the States by setting standards that would enable Federal agencies to place greater reliance upon State efforts."[64]

Following these hearings, the Comptroller General organized an interagency working group (in February of 1970) to develop a body of governmental auditing standards. This significant effort was completed in June of 1972 and issued as an official publication of the General Accounting Office under the signature of the Comptroller General.[65] These new standards provide that governmental auditing should be broad in scope and cooperative in tone. These landmark standards which will certainly be of increasing importance in the governmental audit environment, are reproduced on the following pages.

GOVERNMENTAL AUDITING STANDARDS
The General Accounting Office

General Standards

1. The full scope of an audit of a governmental program, function, activity, or organization should encompass:

    a. An examination of financial transactions, accounts, and reports, including an evaluation of compliance with applicable laws and regulations.

    b. A review of efficiency and economy in the use of resources.

    c. A review to determine whether desired results are effectively achieved.

    In determining the scope for a particular audit, responsible officials should give consideration to the needs of the potential users of the results of that audit.

2. The auditors assigned to perform the audit must collectively possess adequate professional proficiency for the tasks required.

3. In all matters relating to the audit work, the audit organization and the individual auditors shall maintain an independent attitude.

4. Due professional care is to be used in conducting the audit and in preparing related reports.

Examination and Evaluation Standards

1. Work is to be adequately planned.
2. Assistants are to be properly supervised.
3. A review is to be made of compliance with legal and regulatory requirements.
4. An evaluation is to be made of the system of internal control to assess the extent it can be relied upon to ensure accurate information, to ensure compliance with laws and regulations, and to provide for efficient and effective operations.
5. Sufficient, competent, and relevant evidence is to be obtained to afford a reasonable basis for the auditor's opinions, judgments, conclusions, and recommendations.

Reporting Standards

1. Written audit reports are to be submitted to the appropriate officials of the organizations requiring or arranging for the audits. Copies of the reports should be sent to other officials who may be responsible for taking action on audit findings and recommendations and to others responsible or authorized to receive such reports. Copies should also be made available for public inspection.
2. Reports are to be issued on or before the dates specified by law, regulation, or other arrangement and, in any event, as promptly as possible so as to make the information available for timely use by management and by legislative officials.
3. Each report shall:
   a. Be as concise as possible but, at the same time, clear and complete enough to be understood by the users.
   b. Present factual matter accurately, completely, and fairly.
   c. Present findings and conclusions objectively and in language as clear and simple as the subject matter permits.
   d. Include only factual information, findings, and conclusions that are adequately supported by enough evidence in the auditor's working papers to demonstrate or prove, when called upon, the basis for the matters reported and their correctness and reasonableness. Detailed supporting information should be included in the report to the extent necessary to make a convincing presentation.

e. Include, when possible, the auditor's recommendations for actions to effect improvements in problem areas noted in his audit and to otherwise make improvements in operations. Information on underlying causes of problems reported should be included to assist in implementing or devising corrective actions.

f. Place primary emphasis on improvement rather than on criticism of the past; critical comments should be presented in balanced perspective, recognizing any unusual difficulties or circumstances faced by the operating officials concerned.

g. Identify and explain issues and questions needing further study and consideration by the auditor or others.

h. Include recognition of noteworthy accomplishments, particularly when management improvements in one program or activity may be applicable elsewhere.

i. Include recognition of the views of responsible officials of the organization, program, function, or activity audited on the auditor's findings, conclusions, and recommendations. Except where the possibility of fraud or other compelling reason may require different treatment, the auditor's tentative findings and conclusions should be reviewed with such officials. When possible, without undue delay, their views should be obtained in writing and objectively considered and presented in preparing the final report.

j. Clearly explain the scope and objectives of the audit.

k. State whether any significant pertinent information has been omitted because it is deemed privileged or confidential. The nature of such information should be described, and the law or other basis under which it is withheld should be stated.

4.* Each audit report containing financial reports shall:

a. Contain an expression of the auditor's opinion as to whether the information in the financial reports is presented fairly in conformity with generally accepted accounting principles or with other specified accounting principles applicable to the organization, program, function or activity audited, applied on a basis consistent with that of the preceding reporting period. If the auditor cannot express such an opinion, the reasons should be stated in the audit report.

b. Contain appropriate supplementary explanatory information about the contents of the financial reports as may be necessary for full and informative disclosure about the financial operations of the organization, program, function, or activity audited. Material changes in accounting policies and procedures, their effect on the financial reports, and violations of legal or other regulatory requirements, including instances of noncompliance, shall be explained in the audit report.

* Reflects recent changes requested by AICPA.

BEHAVIORAL CONSIDERATIONS

The topic of human relations in auditing has recently begun to appear in the literature with some frequency. Unfortunately, there has been little "definitive" research in this area. Most authorities have written from an intuitive approach based upon their own observations. However, two respectable studies have been conducted, both in the field of internal auditing.[66]

Most authorities who have written in this area believe that auditor-auditee relationships, in general, could be greatly improved. For example, Comptroller General Staats once remarked that:

Auditors are credited as being people with 20-20 hindsight, as people who simply get in the way of others who try to carry out programs or capture headlines by pointing out errors and mismanagement.[67]

Federic E. Mints examined the relationship problem in his study entitled *Behavioral Patterns in Internal Audit Relasionships.*

. . . a great many audit managers are aware of, or at least suspect, some problems in auditor-auditee relationships. If only 26% of the responding audit managers believe that a majority of their accounting managers hold favorable opinions about auditors (and only 29% believe that a majority of other managers are favorably disposed) then there is considerable support for our original premise that greater efforts must be made to improve these relationships.[68]

Apparently, auditor-auditee relationships are not, in general, as good as they could or should be. However, in all fairness it should be noted that "in general" is not "always." Some auditors and auditees have excellent relationships, and it is these good examples that should be studied in order to improve the poorer situations.

What then are the causes of this relationship problem? Edgar H. Schein of M.I.T. expresses his views on the causes as follows:

1. Auditors often feel primary loyalty to the auditing group

rather than the company as a whole; they tend, at times, to feel themselves outside of the organization. Managers, on the other hand, feel primary loyalty to the organization.

2. Auditors are typically rewarded for finding things wrong, less so for helping people get their work done. Managers, on the other hand, are rewarded for getting the job done, whether things were wrong or not.

3. Auditors tend to be (a) *perfectionists,* and (b) focus on *particular* problems in depth. Managers on the other hand, tend to be (a) *"satisfiers"* rather than maximizers (they tend to look for workable rather than perfect or ideal solutions), and (b) *generalists* focusing on getting many imperfect things to work together toward getting a job done, rather than perfecting any one part of the job.

4. The auditor's job tempts him to *evaluate* the line operation and to propose solutions. The manager, on the other hand, wants *descriptive* (non-evaluative) feedback and to design his own solutions.[69]

An analysis of Schein's remarks discloses two basic, underlying causes of auditor-auditee relationship problems: (1) the nature or objective of auditing (point No. 2), and (2) personal traits of the auditor and auditee (points No. 1, 3, and 4).

We have shown in earlier sections that the objective of auditing has traditionally been accountability or policing. Churchill and Cooper give substance to this statement in their study of auditee attitudes, with the question:

TABLE 4
WHOM IS THE INTERNAL AUDITOR MOST LIKE?

Responses	Number	Percentage
Teacher	3	11%
Policeman	15	58
Attorney	6	23
Mixed	2	8
Total	26	100%

Source: Neil C. Churchill and William W. Cooper, "A Field Study of Internal Auditing," *The Accounting Review,* XL (October, 1965), p. 775.

Similar views have also been expressed by various authorities. O. E. Raffensperger states:

We know, however, that auditors are not always received with open arms. People by-in-large do not like to be audited and secondly do not like to have a written report made on the type and quality of work they or their group are doing.[70]

And Archie McGhee, Managing Director of the Institute of Internal Auditors, says:

> The very act of internal auditing, the examination of the work done by another, often creates within the individual subject to scrutiny a feeling of insecurity or one of defensiveness. He feels threatened because he cannot be sure the auditor will really understand his position or reasoning.[71]

Hence, it appears that unless the basic objective of auditing is moderated to some extent — that is, moved more closely to management control or aid, inferior relations between auditor and auditees will probably continue.

The other fundamental cause of poor relations is the personality and attitudes of the auditors and auditees themselves. Many writers place the blame in this regard upon the auditor. They feel that auditees are "reacting" to the auditors attitude and personality. The auditor is a professional, and these writers seem to feel that it is primarily his responsibility to take the initiative in improving relations.

Some possible ways of doing this, are:

1. Have frequent meetings with the auditee.
2. Show a sincere interest in his job and its problems.
3. Try to look at things from the auditee's perspective.
4. Convey the impression that you want to "help" rather than "police." Prove it by your actions.
5. Avoid being secretive — learn to communicate.
6. Try not to carry pre-conceived notions and attitudes.
7. Do not argue — be a professional.
8. Give praise when it is warranted.
9. Do not present findings as criticisms, but as problems needing solutions.
10. *Learn to listen.*

Mints summarizes this situation and makes a particularly noteworthy observation: that "being nice" is not enough.

1. Although many auditors believe they follow practices of good human relations, many auditees still harbor feelings of dislike and distrust toward the auditors.
2. Where these feelings of dislike and distrust exist, the

auditor fights an uphill battle to obtain information, communicate findings, and have his recommendations adopted.

3. The "Be Nice" approach is not enough. Of course, the absence of proffered friendliness is sure to create antagonism. But its presence is no guarantee of the sought for relationship with the auditee.

4. The auditor's own behavior is, of course, significant. But the auditor-auditee relationship is also affected by the attitudes of higher management, the natural resentment of criticism, and the fear of change — factors that need more than a "Be Nice" attitude to combat.

5. The enlightened audit manager is sometimes frustrated in his attempt to develop harmonious relations with auditees — a frustration born of the ingrained behavior patterns of his auditors, patterns that the auditors themselves may not be aware of.

6. The participative approach — the teamwork approach — the problem-solving partnership may well be the light at the end of a dreary tunnel. Our goals should be the auditor and auditee working together to improve conditions; not the critic telling the doer how to do his job better.[72]

THE AUDIT PROCESS

A process is a system of operations or a series of actions or functions. This section examines the process of auditing which consists of five basic operations: Authorization, Examination, Evaluation, Communication, and Reconciliation.

Authorization (1) is the act of requesting an audit and giving the auditor authority to conduct it. Theoretically, the audit recipient requests and authorizes each audit. In practice, however, this is not usually the case. For example, in the private sector, the CPA is usually hired by the auditee firm which, technically, is acting in the capacity of a representative or agent of the audit recipient. Also, most governmental audit agencies and many internal audit departments are given general authority at their inception rather than for each engagement.

Once authorized, the auditor proceeds to conduct his examination (2) of the auditee. The purpose of this operation is to gather "evidence" upon which to base his evaluation (3) of the auditee's activity. Upon completion of his examination and evaluation, the auditor communicates (4) his findings to the audit recipient, usually in the form of a written or oral report.

The audit recipient may then, if necessary, seek to reconcile (5)

Fig. 8   THE AUDIT PROCESS

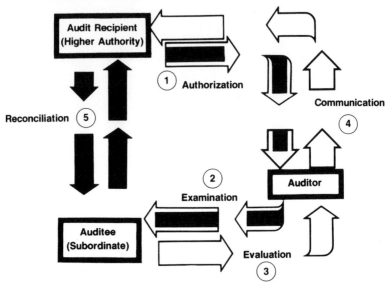

in cooperation with the auditee any pertinent findings and suggestions contained in the audit report. Some authorities would not include reconciliation as part of the audit process because it takes place after communication of the report and does not actively involve the auditor, though he may act in a consultative capacity. We include reconciliation because, in our opinion, it is a very important part of the audit process. The best executed audit is worthless if it is not used; auditors must realize that communication of their report does not complete the audit process.

The five operations of the audit process are more commonly organized into four stages: Preparation, Conduct, Reporting, and Settlement.

TABLE 5
THE STAGES OF AN AUDIT

Technical Designation (Operations)	Common Designation (Stages)
(1) Authorization	(a) Preparation
(2) Examination	
	(b) Conduct
(3) Evaluation	
	(c) Reporting
(4) Communication	
(5) Reconciliation	(d) Settlement

Preparation includes audit authorization and the initial steps of the audit examination. Conduct covers the major part of examination and part of evaluation. Since evaluation is a continuous function, it is included both in conduct and in reporting. Reporting concludes with transmittal or communication of the audit report. Settlement is synonymous with reconciliation.

The remainder of this section will discuss each of these stages in more detail. Each stage will be divided into a series of steps or action categories. Though the discussion is primarily written from the standpoint of external governmental auditing, many of the concepts are equally applicable to internal audits and external audits conducted by CPAs.

However, specific approaches to auditing can vary for a number of reasons, such as differences in audit scope and objectives. Therefore, the following steps are suggestive only. But failure to include one or more of these steps in the audit process should be intentional rather than accidental.

SUGGESTED STEPS IN THE AUDIT PROCESS

Preparation
- I. Decision to Make the Audit
- II. Selection of the Audit Team
- III. Pre-engagement Contact
- IV. Auditor Familiarization
- V. First Draft of the Audit Plan
- VI. The Audit Entrance Conference
- VII. The Walk-Through
- VIII. Revision of the Audit Plan

Conduct
- I. The Preliminary Survey
- II. Examination and Evaluation

Reporting
- I. Continuous Reporting to the Auditee
- II. Flash Reports to the Audit Recipient
- III. The Draft Report
- IV. The Audit Exit Conference
- V. The Final Audit Report
- VI. Distribution of the Audit Report

Settlement
- I. Evaluation of Audit Findings and Recommendations
- II. Joint Agreement on a Plan of Action
- III. Audit Recipient Review of Corrective Action
- IV. Audit Agency Follow-Up

PREPARATION

The success of an audit, particularly a performance audit, is highly dependent upon adequate auditor preparation. Of course, an auditor may get off to a poor start, then back up and make needed corrections in the conduct stage; but an unnecessary impression of incompetency may be left with the auditee.

I. Decision to Make the Audit

Generally, the decision to conduct an audit is made by an internal or external audit agency, division, or staff (hereafter referred to as "audit agency") which has previously been given general authority by the audit recipient to conduct audits. In some cases, however, the auditee requests and authorizes an audit — such as CPA audits which are authorized by the auditee for the benefit of the audit recipient.

The decision to make an audit should not be haphazard or arbitrary. The audit agency should prepare a continuously updated schedule of audits to be conducted — preferably a year or more in advance. The audit schedule should include enough on-the-job time for adequate auditor preparation for *each* audit. Some of the factors that one internal audit group uses to prepare its audit schedule are:

1. Large dollar expenditures.
2. Low return on assets used.
3. Critical function to the organization's success.
4. New function never audited before.
5. New division or section.
6. Specific requests from the division managers.
7. Talents, backgrounds, and experience of the audit staff.
8. Rotation of the staff members.
9. Problem areas spotted during a current audit.
10. Follow-up audit or recycling of previous audits.[73]

The audit agency should also prepare both general audit guides and special guides for programs or operations regularly audited. With regard to audit preparation, these guides should prescribe specific preparatory audit steps, but be general enough to allow auditor interpretation and initiative. The completion of these preparatory steps should be formally documented in the auditor's work papers.

The objective of an audit should be in line with the stated audit philosophy of the audit agency. The general purpose, objective, and need for each audit should be clearly determined before any steps are taken to initiate it.

OTHER LOCAL AUDIT ACTIVITIES

Local Education Agencies may also be audited by local governmental auditors, municipal accountants, management consulting firms, and educational program auditors.

Five States report that certain of their LEAs are audited by local governmental auditors. This occurs almost exclusively in Districts located in large metropolitan areas. Local governmental audits are principally financial in scope with some compliance coverage. However, performance auditing is beginning to reach even the local levels of governmental auditing. For instance, the County Auditor of King County, Washington (Seattle) is directed to:

> . . . report matters concerning the effectiveness and efficiency of the programs and operation of the County.
>
> . . . .
>
> This step involves not only an examination of the financial statements and of the legality of expenditures but also of the prudence of expenditures and the efficiency of the use of all resources including the elimination of wasteful practices.[10]

LEAs in at least two States, Kansas and New Jersey, may be audited by a special category of auditor called a Licensed or Registered Municipal Accountant. This is an accountant licensed by the State as competent to conduct municipal audits and perform other municipal accounting services.

Sometimes a management consulting firm may be engaged to make a special examination of a Local Education Agency. Such evaluations are often quasi-audits particularly when the consulting firm is hired by the School Board or local governmental unit. Although the actual incidence of such examinations is relatively low, several have been worthy of write-ups in professional publications.[11]

Since 1969, the U.S. Office of Education has promoted the concept of educational program auditing (also called independent accomplishment auditing). In particular, educational program auditing has been tried experimentally in certain ESEA Titles III, VII, and VIII Projects.

Basically, these projects, which are administered by Local Education Agencies, must have as a minimum staff: a Director and an Evaluator. The Evaluator develops testing and evaluation procedures to measure the accomplishments of the project. An outside Educational Program Auditor (EPA), also an educator, reviews the Evaluator's reports and procedures and attests to their adequacy.

The objective of educational program auditing is to assist school

1. When I were taken on a tour of one of our factories There was nothing unusual about this After the tour was over, I asked the what they had seen When the auditors would like to begin the on-site work.

6. When the were pretty old; I in many several forks lift trucks like to were the most to descrip had of Boards fire extinguishers and had not been checked in over two years.

8. A and big place!

9. Which of these two tasks the division and with whom the auditors progress, and findings. (Also, arrangements should be made for an appointment with this contact official on the first day of the audit.)

10. A request that a formal entrance conference be called as early as possible (preferably the first day) to discuss the audit with all involved and interested parties.

VIII. Revision of the Audit Plan

After the walk-through and the review and analysis of the preliminary material supplied by the auditee, the audit team should be prepared to update their tentative audit plan and timetable. The objectives should now be reassessed and any necessary adjustments made. The team should then be ready to begin the conduct stage of the audit with the organization to be reviewed. It may be desirable to consult a library and technical journals dealing with the specific types of operation. Sources that deal with proper organization, procedures, activities would generally apply to most audits, regardless of the specific operation. Appropriate legislation, regulations, guidelines, and rules should be reviewed. A permanent file should be established to retain pertinent information for future use.

Old audit files should be examined for information on past audits and recommendations should be noted, however, that although reviews should be planned. Both current and old audit guides may be consulted separately. organizations operating under the old rules and/or part of the current audit may cover prior years. The prospective audit should also be discussed with any other auditors that may have had valuable previous experiences.

I. The Preliminary Survey

The first step in an audit is the preliminary survey. The preliminary survey may be viewed as a gathering of information preparatory to a formal verification and search for evidence. (and, possibly, the audit manager) should develop a preliminary audit plan and timetable. Overall audit objectives and possible areas of investigation should be considered. Preliminary job assignments, audit steps should be developed

A. Financial Auditing

VI. Selection of the Audit Team

The auditor or auditors who are to conduct a particular audit should be selected well in advance by the appropriate audit agency manager or managers. Many audits will require an audit team, though one auditor may suffice on small assignments.

Auditors who have had experience in auditing this auditee, or similar operations, should be included on the audit team. Where certain categories of audits recur each year, or repetitiously, it may be advisable to develop appropriate specialists in the agency or by assigning selected staff members to these audits each time.

The selected team should have objectives and who is responsible for this particular team and who makes on-site job assignments and decisions. As a minimum, the position of audit leader should require experience — preferably as audit team leader.

If the engagement is to be an operational or performance audit in a technical or semi-technical area, technical experts may need to be assigned to the audit team. Possibly members of the auditee's own staff could be temporarily assigned to the audit. In any case, the audit team should possess the necessary competencies to adequately accomplish the objectives of the audit. An underqualified team should never be allowed to begin an assignment. If the audit team is not adequate, the audit should be postponed until individuals with the proper qualifications can be assembled.

III. Pre-Engagement Contact

Before any audit preparation for an audit can begin, the auditee must be contacted. It may be that the start of the audit will need to be delayed or rescheduled because of auditee conflicts or because records need to be made ready for the audit. However, the element of surprise may be essential in some instances — such as those audits requiring cash counts and in cases where fraud is suspected.

The initial contact can be made by letter, telephone call, or short visit. A good approach is both a letter and a follow-up phone call. Generally, organizational protocol should be observed and the highest authority in that organization or division should be contacted first.

VII. The Walk-Through

The audit team should arrange for an escorted tour of the operations (preferably with the contact official). As the auditors walk through the organization, they can observe general working conditions and begin to acquire a working knowledge of the organization itself. In order to insure a better understanding of the operations, they may begin some of their inquiries at this time, with such questions as: "What is this machine used for?" "What does this section do?" At the same time, they should avoid one that will be working with the auditors during the audit. In those instances, the contact official or director may be acquainted with the auditors; perhaps they will make the initial contact and possibly perform the walk-through. In any case, at that time important observations and clues for later investigation can be made during the walk-through. To cite an example by Roger Carolus of Honeywell:

lized the services of management consultants and/or been examined by special study commissions. In a number of instances, such reviews are in fact performance audits. This would prove to be the case if the primary recipient of the recommendations was the SEA's higher authority (such as the State Board of Education, the Governor's Office, or the State Legislature) and if the SEA was expected to abide by the recommendations or show cause.

LOCAL AUDIT ACTIVITIES

CERTIFIED PUBLIC ACCOUNTANTS

The largest category of local audits of LEAs is that performed by Certified Public Accountants. Local Education Agencies in thirty-eight States are audited on a regular basis by CPAs (five other States report occasional CPA audits). In at least four States, however, only certain categories of LEAs—such as city districts—have CPA audits.

CPA audits may either supplement or supplant State Audit Agency audits. In all, fifteen States have both State audits and CPA audits of LEAs, thirteen States give the option of either State or CPA audits, twelve States have principally State Audits, and ten States have primarily CPA audits. In thirty-one States, public accountants (PAs) may on occasion be used instead of Certified Public Accountants (CPAs).

The CPA is usually hired by and is primarily responsible to the LEAs next higher authority which is the School Board or local governmental unit. In a majority of cases, their audit reports are also transmitted to the State Education Agency and in a few cases (13 States) to a State Audit Agency.

In most instances, the CPA audit is strictly financial in scope. A small percentage may also consider compliance matters. There is, however, a discernable trend toward increased compliance evaluations particularly with regard to Federal programs (such audits are now required by Federal regulations). On the other hand, performance audits by CPAs are quite rare. As mentioned earlier, CPAs are slowly moving into performance auditing but are hampered by many things including (1) lack of firm or absolute performance standards, (2) possible conflicts of interest (independence), and (3) fear of possible legal liabilities. CPAs may in some cases submit an internal management letter that comments on observed weaknesses in internal controls and many CPA firms offer management "reviews" as a separate service.

CHAPTER V

SUMMARY AND ANALYSIS OF CONTEMPORARY SEA/LEA AUDIT PRACTICES AND PERCEPTIONS

INTRODUCTION

The previous chapter identified the audit agencies that are members of the SEA/LEA audit network. In this chapter the educational audit activities of these agencies are analyzed. The conceptual framework of auditing, developed in Chapter III, is used to structure this discussion and to identify significant concepts and relationships.

This chapter provides factual information for educational managers and auditors so they may compare and evaluate their own audit activities and experiences. It also provides a basis for recommendations directed toward strengthening the SEA/LEA audit process and, in particular, enhancing the potential of auditing as a significant aid to SEA/LEA management. The information contained in this chapter is based upon:

C. Performance Auditing

lines of communication, and that the interviewee should feel free to convey suggestions or comments to them at any time.

In this stage, the audit team should gather evidence concerning operational control weaknesses indicated during the preliminary stages of the audit. Also, additional and associated problems should be determined and the team should attempt to identify the underlying causes.

Some remarks on interviewing from Bingham and Moore's *How to Interview* should prove useful at this point.

1. Ask only one question at a time.
2. Keep on the subject.
3. Avoid the role of teacher.
4. Be straightforward and frank, rather than shrewd or clever.
5. Give the interviewee a full opportunity to answer the question.
6. Record all data at once, or at the very earliest opportunity.
7. Practice separating facts from inferences.
8. Use interviews discriminately.

There are two basic approaches to the conduct of a performance audit: inductive and deductive. A deductive approach, moving from the general to the specific, can be accomplished by the use of a management control checklist that in effect represents a model of the ideal (the general) which is applied as a yardstick against the organization (the specific). An inductive approach, moving from the specific to the general, can be accomplished by means of a "black box" or systems study that determines organizational and departmental inputs, processes, and outputs.

II. Examination and Evaluation

This is the point in the audit where the analysis is to be gathered to support the earlier observations and to bring the organization closer to the ideal, and evaluated. (Evaluation should, of course, be a continuous, on-going activity.)

A. Financial Auditing

1. The Deductive Checklist Approach

Over the years, auditors and management specialists have designed detailed checklists for both general and specific stages of detailed examination. Many of the accounting and procedures have established the necessity to establish and maintain a variety of checklist and review figures in financial statements. Through the controls of general through individual review, other audit interviews, the audit team should determine the status of each point listed in the checklist. They should also supplement the checklist with their own knowledge of model control procedures, as listed can never cover every conceivable situation.

When checklists are properly available for a particular activity the audit team reviews the audit's significance and develops its own checklists through review of technical literature, discussions with specialists, and reported logic. Indicated weaknesses reported about the organization's management controls and/or procedures should be examined in more detail. Below are some actual examples of control reminders, each taken from a different checklist.

The examination and evaluation should be accomplished through tests of the accounting records, observation of procedures, and outside documentation. Test checks based upon statistical sampling, special files to inexpensive cases for transfer to central storage and/or important accounts, and department where they should be held for a certain period. Also, certain areas needing special attention will have already been identified. Have definite and clear-cut responsibilities been assigned to each employee and department?

The audit team should generally follow a detailed and lengthy audit plan which includes numerous and various kinds of test checks.

...are internal accounting controls and internal checks. Internal accounting controls are those procedures that insure accurate and proper recording and summarization of all authorized financial transactions. Internal checks are those procedures designed to safeguard the assets against defalcation or similar irregularities.

This preliminary evaluation may be conducted by means of a questionnaire which is completed by the responsible manager(s). Often the questionnaire can be divided into sections according to the audit team job assignments, and each auditor can then seek the answers relevant to his particular assignment. Most large CPA firms have developed detailed and lengthy internal control questionnaires. (One of the "Big Eight" CPA Firms uses a 152-page questionnaire.) Weaknesses discovered should be pointed out to the contact official and appropriate supplementary audit steps should be added to the audit plan.

1. Some transactions should be followed from beginning to end.
2. The various aspects of the total accounting system can be test checked by introducing into the system a series of test transactions, particularly if the system is computerized.
3. Supporting documentation should be sampled for proper authorization, nature of transactions, etc.
4. Outside confirmations should be made of transactions, receivables, payables, bank balances, and the like.
5. The taking of inventory should be observed.
6. Arithmetic accuracy should be tested.
7. Major data categories should be cross tabulated.
8. Accounting procedures, forms, and techniques should be sampled and evaluated.
9. Any unclear or questionable areas should be examined in depth.

B. Compliance Auditing

Throughout this stage of the audit (as well as in the other stages) a questioning attitude of reasonableness and an open-eye approach should be maintained by the auditors.

For a compliance audit, the audit team should conduct preliminary surveys in order to make an *initial* determination (before verification) of auditee compliance with pertinent laws, regulations, rules, etc. Here the emphasis should also be upon the existence and effective operation of management controls that insure satisfactory compliance. Weaknesses discovered should be reported to management and appropriate modifications of the audit plan should be made.

The leader of the audit team should see that weaknesses in compliance controls indicated by the preliminary survey are examined in detail by the audit team. Also, the existence of necessary controls for major compliance categories should be verified and their functioning evaluated. The audit team should already have determined which major compliance categories are to be test checked. For example, HEW Auditors of ESEA Title I Programs usually examine a sample of local school districts to determine satisfactory compliance in:

1. The continued targeting and concentration of Title I funds.
2. Design and evaluation of projects.
3. Supplanting and uses of funds and services.
4. What types of performance materials are used in this section or division.
5. Policy activities in private schools.
6. What problems and breakdowns the interviewee has observed in the operations and controls.

C. Performance Auditing

Performance auditors should also conduct preliminary interviews with division and sectional managers. Quite often, they can use interview guides which are not as detailed as questionnaires to structure these discussions. The auditors should be particularly interested in learning from the interviewee:

1. The relationship and position of the interviewee in the organization.
2. The nature and purposes of his concentration of this section or division.
3. Supplanting and uses of funds and services.
4. What types of performance materials are used in his section or division.
5. Policy activities.
6. What problems and breakdowns the interviewee has observed in the operations and controls.

Likewise, internal auditors might test for compliance with organizational policies and procedures to insure that assets and activities should be examined in detail.

The auditors should also explain to each interviewee that they are interested in improving the systems and activities being examined. In particular, they should stress that they wish to maintain open

INTERVIEWS WITH STATE AUDITORS

In order to obtain a more complete perspective of SEA auditing, interviews were conducted with twenty auditors from thirteen State audit agencies in nine States. An interview guide similar to the SEA interview guide was used to structure these meetings.

TABLE 8
STATE AUDITOR INTERVIEWS

States	Number of Agencies	Number of Auditors
Alabama	2	3
California	3	4
Florida	1	1
Kentucky	2	2
Maryland	1	1
Massachusetts	1	3
Ohio	1	1
Texas	1	3
Washington	1	2
Total	13	20

FEDERAL INTERVIEWS

The project staff conducted interviews in Washington, D. C. with U. S. Office of Education personnel and auditors from the General Accounting Office and the HEW Audit Agency. Federal auditors were also interviewed in six of the nine states visited. The Washington interviews, conducted at the beginning of the Project, were more general and not as highly structured as the later State interviews.

SUPPLEMENTAL SOURCES

In addition to the interviews and questionnaires, the project staff utilized several other sources of information including:

system. . . . the actual, planned, and potential outputs or products of the function.

4. Additional Considerations

The presumption is that such an examination will provide information that the auditors can use to make recommendations for improving the activity. The auditors accomplish this through the use of logic and . . .

The personnel should be interviewed to . . . the . . . fact." . . . they should consider . . . management . . . the decision.

Review . . . Pertinent materials should be reviewed and evaluated including: accounting records, official publications, policy and procedure manuals, organization charts, job descriptions, minutes, internal memos, and other relevant materials. The keys to success in such an analysis are the auditors themselves. It has been found that as the examination proceeds certain matters will come to the auditors attention as possible problem areas. Some of the things that the auditors should look for and determine are:

Input

1. Have pre-stated plans and objectives been determined and set down in writing? Are plans and objectives stated in measurable terms?

2. What does management presently have to work with? What flows in from other organizations, groups, and/or divisions?

3. What additional funds, facilities, manpower, and information than could be made available should be made available?

4. Does management know exactly what they have to work with? Do they know what they should have to work with?

Process

How does a worksheet flow through the organization within

periodically? Could it possibly be accomplished better, cheaper, faster, easier? Could the organization structure of the division be improved?

4. Reasonable span standards should be established for optimum utilization.

5. What is each employee's job? How does it relate to other jobs and the objectives of the division or organization?

6. How are resources utilized? For example, are talents and work skills put to optimum use? Are machines and facilities employed at their maximum and best use? Are machines and facilities adequate?

7. Does each individual know what he is to do? Would new job titles accurately result in significantly better job duties?

8. Are management controls and management information systems adequate? Is information complete, prompt, factual, and meaningful? Does management know what is going on? What is going on?

9. Is there a formal system for consideration of employee suggestions?

10. Are jobs clearly defined? Are there job performance standards? Are these standards actually in use?

6. Are there any major bottlenecks or unnecessary jobs, duplications, or facilities?

7. Is there adequate protection of the organization resources (including personnel)?

8. Could employee morale, attitude, or behavior be improved? "Black Box" receives certain inputs, no satisfier to cesses and utilizes them to produce certain outputs.

2. The Inductive Systems Approach

The methodology of the systems approach to performance auditing consists of the examination of the organization and/or its subdivisions (including functions or personnel) an input-process-output point of view. Basically, the auditor should view each job, function or activity as a "Black Box" that receives certain inputs, processes and utilizes them to produce certain outputs.

Fig. 9 THE BLACK BOX CONCEPT

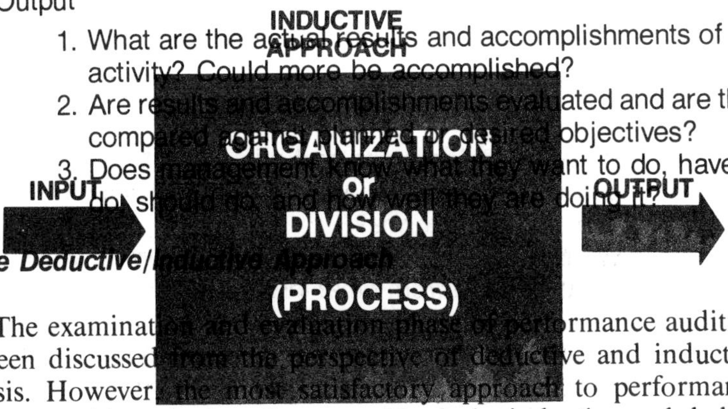

INPUT → ORGANIZATION or DIVISION (PROCESS) → OUTPUT

INDUCTIVE APPROACH

1. What are the actual results and accomplishments of the activity? Could more be accomplished?

2. Are results and accomplishments evaluated and are they compared against desired objectives?

3. Does management know what they want to do, have to do, should do, and how well they are doing it?

A detailed examination of the system(s) should be conducted to clearly determine: the actual, planned, and potential inputs or resources of the function.

3. The Deductive/Inductive Approach

The examination and evaluation phase of performance auditing has been discussed from the perspective of deductive and inductive analysis. However, the most satisfactory approach to performance auditing combines the best features of both the inductive and deductive techniques. The deductive, checklist approach will not apply perfectly to the organization being audited, since each organization is different and unique; and the auditor, using such an approach, may look problems or controls not directly suggested by an analysis of the and State program coordinators, SEA auditors, accountants and clerks. Within the nine states, a total of seventy-four persons were interviewed.

These interviews constitute the primary source of information for this chapter. In fact, we feel that the interview responses are somewhat more representative of SEA perceptions and experiences than are the questionnaire responses. In arriving at this conclusion, we were influenced by two primary factors.

1. The stratification of the interviews within each State gave consideration to all levels of SEA management.
2. It appears that SEA personnel were more likely to express their true feelings concerning "sensitive" issues in a face-to-face interview situation.

Though the interview and questionnaire responses show the same trends for a majority of questions, the questionnaire respondents did tend to give the middle or impartial answer on a few sensitive issues. For example, for the question "Does the auditor (of a particular agency) try to assist, find something wrong, or is he impartial?", the interview responses were *skewed* toward *fault-finding* while the questionnaire answers tended toward the mean (*impartial*). Therefore, a few of the findings in the following pages will rely more heavily on the interviews than upon the questionnaires.

TABLE 7
SEA INTERVIEWS

STATES	Chief State School Officer	Assistant Superintendent	Finance Officer	Program Coordinator	SEA Auditors	Accountants and Clerks	Total
Alabama	1	1	1	1	—	3	7
California	1	1	1	4	—	—	7
Flordia	—	3	2	2	—	3	10
Kentucky	1	1	2	1	—	1	6
Maryland	—	2	1	1	1	1	6
Massachusetts	—	1	1	2	1	3	8
Ohio	1	1	1	9	1	1	14
Texas	1	1	2	—	2	—	6
Washington	1	1	1	4	2	1	10
TOTAL	6	12	12	24	7	13	74

5. Whether the projects and programs are conducted in an economical and efficient manner and in compliance with the requirements of applicable laws and regulations.[2] (emphasis added)

More recently, the 1973 draft revision of the HEWAA Title I Audit Guide identifies two primary audit objectives:

(1) . . . determining if the LEA's planning, implementation, and operation of its Title I activities were in *accordance* with the intent of the program, and

(2) . . . determining the effect that any *mismanagement* of Title I resources had and/or will have on the program in meeting the special needs of educationally deprived children.[3] (emphasis added)

The introductions of both the 1966 and 1973 guides emphasize SEA/LEA responsibilities. There is no mention of *aiding* or *assisting* grantee management and no discussion concerning auditor attitudes and audit philosophy. Also, both audit guides use such negative terms as *management deficiencies, management weaknesses,.* and *mismanagement.* Thus, the focus in both the audit guides and HEW's Annual Report is primarily upon Federal perspectives and SEA/LEA accountability.

The project staff also reviewed forty audit reports provided as samples by HEW Audit Agency. These reports were issued between 1966 and 1973, covered nineteen states and involved several different education programs — including four titles of the 1965 ESEA Act, Vocational Education, and Adult Basic Education. These audit reports were found to be primarily accountability oriented. This was indicated in several ways including:

. . An examination of the scope of these reports revealed that HEWAA's findings and recommendations are primarily of a financial and compliance nature.
. One hundred fifteen findings (67%) were financial in nature (or compliance/financial).
. Fifty-four (31%) were general compliance matters (administrative or management matters covered by Federal Legislation, regulations, and/or guidelines).
. Three findings (2%) were performance in nature (management matters not covered by the program's legislation, regulations or guidelines).
. . An analysis of the *tone* of these audit reports (by subjective evaluation or syntax) indicated that 83% were im-

problems in... finding — in-
itself. Each... (I.) carefully evaluated and (II.) a
management plan... implementation... comple-
tion should... and jointly agreed upon. A series of interim
deadlines should be established and... the status of corrective action at these stages should be... reported by the principal audit recipient...
should be... and any suggestions he feels may be helpful to the
The auditee... agency should... encourage the corrective action... possible. In some instances, they may want to
(IV.) Conduct... future auditing
the same auditee should include... review of prior findings. Any findings that are still... inadequately corrected should again be
brought to... the management and, when appropriate, the
audit recipient.

In particular, the auditee representatives should be asked whether
they feel the report is accurate, fair, and fully includes the position of
the auditee organization. The audit team leader should carefully consider their comments and determine if any changes, deletions, or adjustments should...

SUMMARY AND CONCLUSIONS

V. The Final Report

An overview of the subject of auditing has been presented in this
chapter. Its purpose has been to provide the reader with a structured
conceptual framework of auditing that integrates auditing concepts
theory and practice. Hopefully, the reader will be able to put this
framework to use in his own audit environment, as he should now be
able to answer the four essential questions suggested by the conceptual
framework.

I. Why Are Audits Conducted?

Audits traditionally have been conducted for accountability purposes. As the accountability of managers has expanded so has the
scope of auditing. However, auditing has also been used in recent
years as a management control or aid technique. This, too, has forced
an expansion of the scope of auditing. Behavior theory and recent
research suggests that...

Report Structure

...whenever a significant finding or major question arises. This is for his own protection. as well as for the information of the auditee. At the meeting, the auditor should explain the problem or finding, solicit the contact official's perspective or first impressions, and, if necessary, ask the contact official to look into the matter further. It is possible that additional information may be brought to light at this time that negates or satisfactorily explains the findings. In any case, the auditee should never be "the last to know" about findings; and Management should avoid surprises during the course of the audit.

Report structure should be oriented to the needs of the audit recipient. For example, some officials prefer short, one-page reports. In general, however, the report should include:

1. Management's comments on the areas covered by the audit.
5. The significance and magnitude of the problems.
6. The causes of these problems.
7. Suggested solutions or preventive action.
8. Auditee positions regarding these recommendations, without audit rebuttal, as well as any steps that the auditee has already taken to correct the problem.
9. Overall conclusions.

It may be both possible and desirable to make an oral and audiovisual presentation of the report to the audit recipient. Such an approach often proves particularly effective in promoting action.

II. "Flash Reports" to the Audit Recipient

In some instances, it will be appropriate to notify the audit recipient of major findings before the delivery of the audit report. In fact, it may be possible to effect major savings and/or improvements before completion of the audit. It may also be that similar problems exist in other organizations or divisions not currently being audited, and that changes could also be effected promptly in these operations.

An effective tool for this purpose is a short (preferably, one page) "Flash Report," such as that used by the Army Audit Agency. This report should briefly explain the problem, its cause, and suggested solutions. The "Flash Report" should be transmitted by the audit team leader (with the concurrence of the audit agency) directly to the audit recipient and the auditee.

VI. Distribution of the Audit Report

Copies of the audit report should be made available to the auditee; the principal audit recipient, and other legally prescribed recipients. File copies should be retained by the auditor. Consideration should be given to distributing the audit report to other organizations or departments which may have similar management problems and would benefit from the audit recommendations and/or good management practices noted in the audit report. Audit reports should also be made available to other involved or interested audit agencies.

III. Draft Report

A draft report should be prepared as early as possible. This report, clearly marked "draft," should be delivered to the contact official well in advance of the audit exit conference so that the auditee agency will be able to adequately prepare a reaction. Depending upon the usual practices of the audit agency, copies of the draft may also be sent to the audit recipient.

SETTLEMENT

IV. The Audit Exit Conference

Unfortunately, the subject of audit settlement has been given little consideration in the literature of auditing. This is because many auditors feel — possibly without having really thought about it — that an audit is finished when they render their report. However, in many respects it is just beginning—since most of the work (and expense) will have been wasted if no action is taken on audit recommendations.

The audit exit conference is the counterpart of the audit entrance conference. Generally, the same individuals should be in attendance. In addition, the audit recipient may also wish to be present. The principal purpose of the exit conference is to formally explain the audit findings to the auditee. The audit team leader should conduct the exit conference. However, the auditor (or team leader) may be asked to participate in a consulting capacity (offering advice on reconciliation problems).

Settlement is not a feature of all financial audits unless financial exceptions are made or would like examined, or if the auditor could be of service in any way as a byproduct of his examination.

These responses suggest that a majority of SEA managers perceive auditing as primarily an accountability device. Also, that most auditors make no inquiry regarding SEA (auditee) needs and desires suggests that many auditors perceive the objective of auditing as accountability, e.g., inspecting, policing.

Audit objectives were also examined on an agency by agency basis.

HEW Audit Agency

The last Annual Report of the Department of Health, Education, and Welfare presents a twofold mission or objective of the HEW Audit Agency:

> . . . to insure that the Department's operations are conducted efficiently and economically; and to ascertain that Federal funds are expended properly and in *accordance* with the purposes for which they were appropriated.[1] (emphasis added)

A more specific source relating to educational audits, the 1966 "HEWAA Audit Guide for ESEA Title I Programs," identifies the objectives of HEWAA Title I reviews as determining:

1. Whether administrative and financial internal controls are adequate to provide accurate and reliable operating and financial reports essential for management evaluation and decisions.

2. Whether the expenditures made are only for the established projects and programs and in accordance with applicable Federal and State regulations and policies.

3. Whether the administrative reviews have been made by the State agency to evaluate the operations of local projects or programs.

4. Whether the State and local educational agencies have properly reported their *accountability* for grants of Federal funds for the projects or programs to which this guide is applicable.

II. What Is the Potential Scope of Auditing?

Auditing can embrace three areas: financial, compliance, and performance. As the scope of auditing has expanded into management areas, auditors and audit report users have attempted to differentiate between audits of varying scope. One result has been a confusing proliferation of adjectives modifying the word audit (e.g., performance audit, management audit, and operational audit). However, there have been several serious attempts to develop frameworks of the potential scope of auditing. Unfortunately, these frameworks, including the one used by this project, are still imperfect; and the different areas (financial, compliance, and performance) tend to overlap. Despite these limitations, these frameworks do provide a workable basis for differentiation.

III. Who Is Involved in the Audit?

The basic parties to an audit are the auditor, the auditee, and the audit recipient. Most medium to large size organizations should have an audit network consisting of both an internal audit function and an external audit activity. Of the two, the internal audit function is potentially of greater benefit to auditee management. An auditee organization may also be audited by more than one external auditor. In the governmental environment, the most common external audit network is the "Federal-State-Local Audit Network." However, this network is not yet functioning in an integrated, coordinated, and cooperative manner.

To perform an audit, the auditor must possess certain essential characteristics, namely: independence, competency, and professionalism. Also, it appears that behavioral relationships between auditors and auditees could and should be improved. This is in line with the earlier suggestion that the objective of auditing should be oriented more toward "aid to management."

IV. How Is the Audit Conducted?

A common classification of the steps of auditing is: preparation, conduct, reporting, and settlement.

Preparation should include (1) decision to make the audit, (2) selection of the audit team, (3) pre-engagement contact, (4) auditor familiarization, (5) first draft of the audit plan, (6) the audit entrance conference, (7) the walk-through, and (8) revision of the audit plan. *Conduct* should consist of (1) the preliminary survey and (2) examination and evaluation. *Reporting* should include (1) continuous reporting to the auditee, (2) flash reports, (3) the draft report, (4) the audit exit conference, (5) the final audit report, and (6) distribution of the audit report.

Settlement, the last stage of auditing, is often not considered to be part of the auditing process, per se, and is often neglected in the auditing literature. Yet, it is perhaps the most important stage. It should include (1) evaluation of audit findings and recommendations, (2) joint agreement on plan of action, (3) audit recipient review of corrective action, and (4) audit agency follow-up.

In conclusion, it appears that auditing is potentially a significant tool for the aid of auditee management. However, for any audit to be an effective management tool: its objective should be oriented as much as possible toward management aid or control, its scope should generally be performance or comprehensive in nature, the auditor should be competent and should recognize and follow modern audit standards, the relationship between the auditee and the auditor should be maximized, and progressive auditing procedures should be employed.

FOOTNOTES
Chapter III

[1]This is one of the stated objectives of the AIDE Project.

[2]E. S. L. Goodwin, "Control: A Brief Excursion on the Meaning of a Word," *The Michigan Business Review,* VIII (January, 1960), p. 14.

[3]Authur R. Pontarelli, "Accountability in Education," *Rhode Island Business Quarterly,* VII (March, 1971), p. 8.

[4]Paul O. Gaddis, *Corporate Accountability,* (New York: Harper & Row, 1964), p. viii.

[5]For example, see: Pontarelli, "Accountability in Education," p. 9.

[6]*Professional Management in General Electric, Book II: General Electric's Organization,* (New York: General Electric Company, 1955), p. 86.

[7]See: Henri Fayol, *General and Industrial Management,* trans. by Constance Storrs, (London: Sir Isaac Pitman and Sons, 1949).

[8]Goodwin, "Control," p. 28.

[9]*Ibid.,* p. 14.

[10]*Ibid.*

[11]*The American Heritage Dictionary of the English Language,* (New York: American Heritage Publishing Co., 1973), p. 290.

[12]Goodwin, "Control," p. 15.

[13]American Institute of Accountants, Special Committee on Terminology, *Accounting Terminology,* (New York: AIA, 1931), p. 17.

[14]Herman W. Bevis, "Tightening the Federal Purse Strings," *Harvard Business Review,* XXXVII (May-June, 1959), pp. 117-18.

[15]E. L. Normanton, *The Accountability and Audit of Governments,* (Manchester, England: The University Press, 1966), p. 12.

[16]United States General Accounting Office, The Comptroller General, *Standards for Audit of Governmental Organizations, Programs, Activities, and Functions,* (Washington: The GAO, 1972), p. 1.

[17]"The President's Message on Education Reform," *American Education,* VI (April, 1970), pp. 30-31.

[18]*Elementary and Secondary Education Act of 1965,* P. L. 89-10, Title I, Part D, Sec. 141(a)(6).

[19]The Institute of Internal Auditors, *Statement of Responsibilities of the Internal Auditor,* (New York: IIA, 1971).

[20]This has been demonstrated in hundreds of articles published over the years in *The Internal Auditor.*

[21]For example, the Washington State Auditor's Office and the State of California, Department of Finance.

²²For example, this has been reflected in some of the audits of the Army Audit Agency.

²³Corine T. Norgaard, "The Professional Accountant's View of Operational Auditing," *The Journal of Accountancy,* CXXVIII (December, 1969), pp. 45-48.

²⁴Corine T. Norgaard, "Extending the Boundaries of the Attest Function," *The Accounting Review,* XLVII (July, 1972), p. 441.

²⁵Robert J. Freeman, "Aspects of Performance Auditing" (Paper presented at the 3rd Annual Series of U.S. General Accounting Office Regional Workshops for State Auditors, Boston, Mass., 1972), p. 9.

²⁶Carl Heyel, ed., "McGregor's Theory X and Theory Y," *The Encyclopedia of Management,* (New York: Reinhold, 1963), p. 570.

²⁷Douglas Murray McGregor, "The Human Side of Enterprises," *The Management Review,* (November, 1957), pp. 22-28.

²⁸The Institute of Internal Auditors, *Research Committee Report 17: Behavioral Patterns in Internal Audit Relationships,* Frederic E. Mints, Project Researcher (New York: IIA, 1972).

²⁹*Ibid.,* pp. 84-85.

³⁰"Is the Term 'Audit' Too Loosely Used?" (editorial), *The Journal of Accountancy,* XCV (May, 1953), p. 552.

³¹Normanton, *Accountability.*

³²*Ibid.,* p. 415.

³³Lennis M. Knighton, *The Performance Post Audit in State Government,* (East Lansing, Michigan: Bureau of Business and Economic Research, Michigan State University, 1967).

³⁴Lennis M. Knighton, "An Integrated Framework for Conceptualizing Alternative Approaches to State Audit Programs," *The Federal Accountant,* XX (March, 1971).

³⁵*Ibid.,* pp. 10-11.

³⁶The United States General Accounting Office, *Standards.*

³⁷*Ibid.,* p. 10.

³⁸Elmer B. Staats, "Management or Operational Auditing," *The GAO Review,* (Winter, 1972), pp. 34-35.

³⁹The Institute of Internal Auditors, *Statement.*

⁴⁰American Institute of Certified Public Accountants, Committee on Terminology, *Accounting Terminology Bulletin No. 1: Review and Resume,* (New York: AICPA, 1953).

⁴¹*Ibid.,* pp. 18-19.

⁴²American Institute of Certified Public Accountants, Committee on Auditing for Federal Agencies, *Suggested Guidelines for the Structure and Content of Audit Guides Prepared by Federal Agencies for Use by CPAs,* (New York: AICPA, 1972).

⁴³*Ibid.,* pp. 2-3.

⁴⁴See: American Institute of Certified Public Accountants, Com-

mittee on Auditing Procedure, *Statements on Auditing Procedure No. 33: Auditing Standards and Procedures,* (New York: AICPA, 1963), Chapter 10.

[45]*Ibid.,* pp. 10-12.

[46]The Institute of Internal Auditors, *Statement.*

[47]The United States General Accounting Office, *Standards,* pp. 11-12.

[48]*Ibid.,* p. 2.

[49]For example, Honeywell's Operations and Analysis Department.

[50]U.S. Department of Health, Education and Welfare, *1969 Annual Report,* (Washington: Government Printing Office, 1969), p. 16.

[51]Edward W. Stepnick, "Federal-State Audit Partnership" (presentation to the "Effective Governmental Auditing Course" of the Interagency Auditor Training Center, Department of Commerce, Washington, April 20, 1971), p. 5.

[52]*Webster's New Collegiate Dictionary,* (Springfield, Mass.: G & C Merriam Co., 1961), p. 424.

[53]*The American Heritage Dictionary,* p. 359.

[54]American Institute of Certified Public Accountants, Committee on Professional Ethics, *Opinion No. 12: Independence,* (New York: AICPA, 1965).

[55]John L. Carey and William O. Doherty, *Ethical Standards of the Accounting Profession,* (New York: AICPA, 1966), p. 19.

[56]Thomas G. Higgins, "Professional Ethics: A Time For Reappraisal," *The Journal of Accountancy,* CXXI (March, 1962), p. 31.

[57]American Institute of Certified Public Accountants, *Report of the Committee on Education and Experience Requirements for CPAs,* (New York: AICPA, 1969).

[58]Robert H. Roy and James H. MacNeill, *Horizons for a Profession,* (New York: AICPA, 1967).

[59]American Institute of Certified Public Accountants, *Report of the Committee on Education,* (New York: AICPA, 1969).

[60]See: R. K. Mautz and Hussein A. Sharaf, *The Philosophy of Auditing,* (Iowa City, Iowa: American Accounting Association, 1961), p. 236.

[61]*Ibid.,* p. 237.

[62]American Institute of Certified Public Accountants, *Code of Professional Ethics,* (New York: AICPA, 1965).

[63]The Institute of Internal Auditors, *Code of Ethics,* (New York: IIA, 1968).

[64]Elmer B. Staats, "The Nation's Interest in Improving State and Local Government," (Address to Regional Conference of the American Society of Public Administrators, Topeka, Kansas, October

23, 1970), p. 10.

[65]U.S. General Accounting Office, *Standards.*

[66]These are:

(1) Neil C. Churchill, *Behavioral Effects of Audits,* (Reading, Mass: Addison-Wesley, 1966).

(2) The Institute of Internal Auditors, *Behavioral Patterns in Internal Audit Relationships,* (Cited previously).

[67]Elmer B. Staats, "The Nation's Interest," p. 9.

[68]The Institute of Internal Auditors, *Behavioral Patterns,* p. 37.

[69]Edgar H. Schein, *Process Consultation: Its Role in Organization Development.* (Reading, Massachusetts: Addison-Wesley, 1969), p. 141.

[70]O. E. Rabbensperger, "The Human Element in Auditing," *The Internal Auditor,* XXIX (January/February, 1972), p. 9.

[71]Archie McGhee, "Salesmanship for Auditors," *The Internal Auditor,* XXVII (January/February, 1971), p. 29.

[72]The Institute of Internal Auditors, *Behavioral Patterns,* pp. x-xi.

[73]R. N. Carolus, "The Who's, Why's, What's, and How's of Operational Auditing," *The Internal Auditor,* XXV (July/August, 1968), pp. 30-31.

[74]R. N. Carolus, "Some Challenges of Operational Auditing," *The Internal Auditor,* XXVI (November/December, 1969), p. 27.

[75]W. V. Bingham and B. V. Moore, *How to Interview,* (New York: Harper and Brothers, 1959).

[76]See: HEW Audit Agency, *Audit Guide for Review of Local Education Agency Programs Under Title I of the Elementary and Secondary Education Act of 1965,* (Unpublished Draft HEWAA, 1973, p.i-ii.

CHAPTER IV

THE AUDIT NETWORK

OF PUBLIC EDUCATION

INTRODUCTION

Having explained basic audit concepts and defined fundamental audit terms in Chapter III, we now have a common basis for understanding what an audit is as well as what an audit can be. This chapter will introduce those audit agencies or groups that comprise the audit network of public education. These are the agencies that have the responsibility and authority for conducting post audits of or involving Public Education Agencies. This discussion will also serve as an introduction to the next chapter, which is an in-depth examination and evaluation of the current status of Public Education auditing.

ACCOUNTABILITY AND AUDITING IN THE SEA/LEA ENVIRONMENT

The State Education Agency is part of a complex environment of accountability, management control, and auditing that includes

Fig. 10 THE AUDIT NETWORK OF PUBLIC EDUCATION

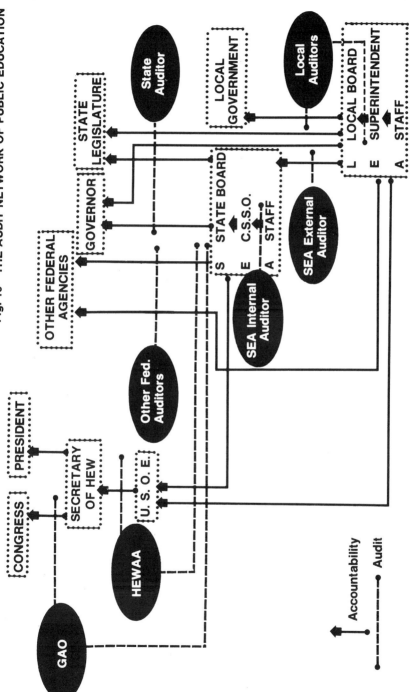

Federal, State, and Local components. At the Federal level, the U.S. Office of Education is the primary agency involved in Federal education activities. However, other Federal Agencies may fund specialized school programs, such as:

The Department of Agriculture — School Lunch Programs
The Office of Civil Defense — Civil Defense Programs
The Department of Defense — Surplus Property Programs
The Department of the Interior — Indian Education Programs

All governmental agencies are ultimately accountable to the public. But they are usually more directly and specifically accountable to those governmental bodies, agencies, and individuals that serve as higher authorities in the complex organization of government. The U.S. Office of Education, for example, is directly accountable to the Secretary of HEW, the President of the United States, and the United States Congress.

Adding assurance to the proper discharge of OE's accountability and acting as a management control device for the higher authority/audit recipients are two principal audit agencies — HEW Audit Agency and the General Accounting Office. HEW Audit Agency has the authority and responsibility to review the activities of the Office of Education (and other HEW Divisions) on behalf of the Secretary of HEW. The General Accounting Office is a legislative audit agency that has authority to review almost all executive agency activities on behalf of Congress.

The Tenth Amendment of the Constitution of the United States gives each of the fifty States the implied authority to provide for the education of its citizens. Through State Constitutions and statutes each State (and Territory) has established a State Education Agency which handles the administrative workload and provides the guidance and services inherent in the State's elementary and secondary educational efforts.[1]

State Education Agencies vary in terms of structure, organization, size, duties, and powers. To the extent that generalization is possible, the three major divisions of a State Education Agency are usually the State Board of Education, the Chief State School Officer, and his departmental staff. In this organizational structure, the departmental staff is accountable to the Chief State School Officer who is in turn accountable to the State Board of Education. Externally, the State Education Agency is accountable to the Governor of that State or his representatives, to the State Legislature, and to the citizens of the State. The SEA is also accountable to Federal Agencies, principally OE-HEW, relative to its administration of Federal programs and funds.

Cutting across these lines of accountability are a number of categories of auditing. For instance, a few State Education Agencies have internal audit groups that review the activities of the departmental staff for the Chief State School Officer (or his representative). Every State has one or more State Post Audit Agency which has the authority to review the activities of the State Education Agency. The State Audit Agency may represent the Legislature, the Executive Branch, or the State Auditor may be publically elected and directly responsible to the citizenry. The State Education Agency may also be audited with regard to Federal programs by the General Accounting Office and the HEW Audit Agency. Also, the SEA may be visited by the Department of Agriculture — Office of the Inspector General and by auditors from other Federal Agencies. These audit agencies and/or the SEA's higher authorities may also arrange for SEA audits to be conducted by independent Certified Public Accountants or for management audits to be performed by management consulting firms.

To accomplish our National and State educational goals, public elementary and secondary schools have been established in local communities in each State. The public schools are generally organized into school districts which often conform to city or county boundaries. These school districts or Local Education Agencies are usually operated by a School Superintendent and his staff who are accountable to a Local School Board, other local Governmental unit, and/or the public. The Local Education Agency, may also be directly or indirectly accountable to the State Education Agency, the Governor of the State or his representatives, and/or the State Legislature. The Local Education Agency, like the State Education Agency, can also be accountable to certain Federal Agencies relative to the administration of Federal Programs.

Serving the accountability and management control needs of these many higher authorities is a diverse and potentially large group of audit agencies. In order to satisfy the needs of the Superintendent, the School Board, the city or county government, and/or the public — the individual schools and/or the school district as a whole may be audited by management consultants, local governmental auditors, educational program auditors, or (more commonly) by CPAs or public accountants. Also, the Local Education Agency may be audited by the State Education Agency and/or one or more State Audit Agencies. The LEA is also subject to review by GAO, HEWAA, and other Federal Audit Agencies. Federal and State Agencies may also accept or require CPA or PA audits of LEAs in lieu of their own audit activities.

This complex environment of accountability and auditing is

diagrammed in Figure 10. The remainder of the chapter is devoted to a more detailed discussion of each of the major categories of auditing in the public education environment.

FEDERAL AUDIT ACTIVITIES

THE GENERAL ACCOUNTING OFFICE

The General Accounting Office was established by the Budget and Accounting Act of 1921 and functions under the direction and control of the United States Comptroller General. As an independent, nonpolitical agency in the legislative branch of government, it provides the Congress, its committees and members with information, analysis, and recommendations concerning government operations, with primary reference to the executive branch.

The GAO is concerned with how Federal departments and agencies, through their programs and activities, carry out the mandate or intent of legislation enacted by the Congress. The General Accounting Office:

. . audits or reviews department or agency financial controls and accountability, efficiency of management and use of resources, and effectiveness of program results.

. . reports its findings and recommendations to the Congress or the Federal Agencies, as appropriate.

. . renders legal opinions and furnishes legal advice.

. . suggests ways and means for financial management improvement, including prescribing principles and standards for accounting and auditing in the Federal Agencies.

. . settles claims for and against the United States.[2]

To accomplish its responsibilities, GAO has a staff of 4,600 persons located throughout the executive branch and in fifteen regional and five overseas offices.[3] With certain exceptions, GAO's audit authority and responsibility extends to all activities, financial transactions, and accounts of the Federal Government.

In recent years, GAO has reviewed four major programs administered by OE: ESEA Title I, Teacher Corps, Follow Through, and Teacher Training. GAO's primary effort, however, has been with regard to ESEA Title I.

This Title authorizes financial assistance to Local Education Agencies to meet the special educational needs of educationally deprived children living in areas having high concentrations of children from low income families. This program is the largest single commitment of the Federal Government to strengthen and improve the educational opportunities in elementary and secondary schools across the nation, and has been funded at about $1.5 billion in each of the fiscal years 1971-73.

GAO has made four audits of this program since its inception. Three of these were concerned principally with the efficiency of Federal, State, and Local administration of the program in three selected States (West Virginia, Ohio, and New Jersey). The fourth review, conducted at three Local Education Agencies in one State (Illinois), was concerned primarily with the effectiveness of selected projects in meeting the needs of that State's educationally deprived children.[4]

In addition to their regular audit program, approximately 10% of GAO's audits are initiated as a result of special requests from Congress. These special audits are available to the public only if released by the Congressman that requested them. On occasion, these special request audits might concern a SEA, LEA, or specific school.

GAO recommendations are frequently adopted by the agencies without the intervention of Congress or its committees. In cases where GAO audits of Federal programs involve SEAs or LEAs, the audit settlement procedure is conducted by the Office of Education. Then, approximately six months after audit settlement, GAO will usually conduct an audit follow-up to determine the extent to which their recommendations have been initiated.

HEW AUDIT AGENCY

The HEW Audit Agency (HEWAA) was established in 1965 as a result of the recommendations of an advisory panel appointed by the Secretary of HEW. Prior to this time, audits of HEW activities were conducted by fifteen separate audit organizations within the Department.

The Washington headquarters of the HEW Audit Agency is organized into five operating divisions, each headed by an assistant director; these divisions are: State and Local Audits, University and Nonprofit Audits, Social Security Audits, Installation and Management Audits, and Audit Coordination. The field staff is organized into ten regions, each of which operates under a regional director. In addition to regional office staffs, there are more than forty-five branch offices and residencies. The HEWAA staff of 700 professional employees, issues over 4,000 audit reports annually. This represents a sampling of more than 1,000 department installations, 545 state agencies, 20,000 local government units, 4,000 universities and other private organizations, 11,500 hospitals and extended care facilities, and 1,600 home health agencies.[5]

HEW Audit Agency represents and reports to the Secretary of HEW through the Office of the Assistant Secretary Comptroller. HEWAA performs an internal audit function with regard to its reviews of departmental activities, but from the perspective of grantee agencies, such as SEAs and LEAs, it is an external audit agency. In general, HEWAA's objectives are to:

> Determine whether the Department's operations are being conducted economically, and efficiently.

> Provide a reasonable degree of assurance that Federal funds are being expended properly and for the purpose for which they were appropriated.[6]

Because of recent trends in program requirements, increased accountability, and legislative mandates, HEWAA audit emphasis is increasingly being placed on current or potential problems of grantee or Departmental management. These expanded audits may contain a professional judgement, statement, or opinion by the auditor on the conditions of program performance and the report may contain specific suggestions to management for improving the program operations.

OTHER FEDERAL AUDIT ACTIVITIES

Whenever an SEA and/or LEA participates in a program supported in whole or part by Federal funds, they become subject to audit by the administering Federal agency. Almost all Federal programs dealing with Education and affecting SEAs and LEAs are administered by HEW. However, there are a few Federal programs outside the domain of HEW that may involve State and Local Education Agencies. Some of the Federal Agencies administering such programs include:

> The Department of Agriculture
> The Office of Economic Opportunity
> The Office of Civil Defense
> The Veterans Administration
> The Department of the Interior
> The Department of Defense

The Federal School Lunch Program illustrates a situation in which an SEA or LEA may be involved with a Federal Agency other than HEW. The Department of Agriculture, Office of the Inspector General (OIG) audits the administration of this program at the State and Local level. Their audit program stresses four areas of financial and compliance accountability by instructing the auditor to determine if:

> . . controls are adequate to account for the receipt and disbursement of program funds.
> . . accounting records and reports accurately reflect the financial condition of the program.
> . . funds accruing to the program are expended in accordance with program regulations and instructions.
> . . claims for reimbursement are accurate.[7]

The auditor is also directed to determine whether Government commodities are used effectively and only for the purpose intended. Other program operations reviewed by the OIG auditor include the adequacy of the free meal plan and whether there is discrimination between children receiving free meals and those who pay the full price.

In many cases, HEW Audit Agency may conduct SEA or LEA Audits for other Federal agencies in conjunction with their own audit activities. With regard to this policy, *Federal Management Circular 73-2* directs:

> To conserve manpower, promote efficiency, and minimize the impact of audits on the operations of the organizations subject to audit, each Federal agency will give full consideration to establishing cross-servicing arrangements under which one Federal agency will conduct audits for another — whenever such arrangements are in the best interest of the Federal Government and the organization being audited. This is particularly applicable in the Federal grant-in-aid and contract programs where two or more Federal agencies are frequently responsible for programs in the same organization or in offices located within the same geographical area.[8]

Federal agencies may also accept audits of SEAs and LEAs performed by State Auditors, internal auditors, or CPAs.

> Reports prepared by non-Federal auditors will be used in lieu of Federal audits if the reports and supporting workpapers are available for review by the Federal agencies, if testing by Federal agencies indicates the audits are per-

formed in accordance with generally accepted auditing standards (including the audit standards issued by the Comptroller General), and if the audits otherwise meet the requirements of the Federal agencies.[9]

STATE AUDIT ACTIVITIES

STATE AUDIT AGENCIES

The Project identified 68 State Agencies in the 50 States with authority to post audit other State and/or Local Agencies. Thirty-four States have one State Agency, fourteen have two, and two States have three. Of these, fifty (in 46 States) audit their State Education Agency and forty-four (in 40 States) audit their Local Education Agencies.

The Director of a State Post Audit Agency is most commonly called State Auditor. However, in seven States the official in charge of the State pre-audit function if referred to as the State Auditor. In addition, some State Audit Agencies and Auditors do not have the word "audit" in their official titles. In some States, for example, a State Auditor is called Public Examiner, Tax Commissioner, Legislative Analyst, State Comptroller, or Budget Assistant.

A State Auditor may be selected by (1) popular election, (2) appointment by the State Legislature or Legislative Committee, (3) appointment by the Governor or by other executive appointment such as civil service examination, or (4) some combination of (2) and (3). In all, 19 State Auditors are popularly elected, 35 are legislative auditors, and 14 have some type of executive appointment.

In recent years, the number of legislative audit agencies has been increasing. This trend is in line with the consensus of authoritative opinion which is that every State should have at least one strong Audit Agency responsible to the State Legislature (as GAO is responsible to Congress).

The size of the State Audit Agency's professional staff can vary from less than ten in a few instances to more than 100 (in at least seven States). Sixteen States require that the State Auditor must be a Certified Public Accountant.

At the present time, most State Audit Agencies conduct financial/compliance audits. But there is a clear and growing trend to expand the scope of State Auditing into operational or performance areas. The Constitution or statutes of at least ten states — Montana, New Hampshire, Wisconsin, Idaho, Florida, Colorado, New Jersey, California, Michigan, and Maryland — require performance post audits. Performance audits of varying degrees of sophistication have also been conducted in at least three other States (Washington, New York, and Hawaii).

STATE EDUCATION AGENCY AUDITS

Thirty-two State Education Agencies conduct some type of audit of their Local Education Agencies. Thirteen of these are major activities with a staff of three or more auditors and regularly scheduled visits to each LEA. Eleven are limited to certain Federal programs such as ESEA Title I projects. For the most part, these audits are fiscal and compliance in nature. However, at least five State Education Agencies are presently conducting performance audits of their Local School Systems.

In response to our inquiries, seventeen SEAs reported that they have an internal audit staff. However, supplemental information indicated that:

. . One is actually part of the State Audit Staff.
. . Seven conduct LEA Audits exclusively.
. . Five conduct only a pre-audit function.

Of the remaining four, only two conduct performance post audits of the SEA on a regular basis.

Thus, the vast majority of State Education Agencies do not at the present time have a satisfactory internal audit activity. This is a serious weakness of the SEA audit network which is discussed more fully in the next chapter.

OTHER STATE AUDIT ACTIVITIES

Independent auditing firms, management consultants, and special study commissions may in certain situations conduct State Audits of SEAs and/or LEAs.

Twelve State Education Agencies report that they are audited by Certified Public Accountants. In seven cases, this audit is conducted on a regular basis (usually annually). In five of these States, the CPA audit substitutes for the audit of the State Audit Agency.

In general, CPA audits of LEAs are more properly classified as local audits (next section). However, the distinction is rather fine. CPAs are usually hired by the District's Board of Education while the authority for such audits is often State law.

A majority of State Education Agencies have on occasion utilized the services of management consultants and/or been examined by special study commissions. In a number of instances, such reviews are in fact performance audits. This would prove to be the case if the primary recipient of the recommendations was the SEA's higher authority (such as the State Board of Education, the Governor's Office, or the State Legislature) and if the SEA was expected to abide by the recommendations or show cause.

LOCAL AUDIT ACTIVITIES

CERTIFIED PUBLIC ACCOUNTANTS

The largest category of local audits of LEAs is that performed by Certified Public Accountants. Local Education Agencies in thirty-eight States are audited on a regular basis by CPAs (five other States report occasional CPA audits). In at least four States, however, only certain categories of LEAs—such as city districts—have CPA audits.

CPA audits may either supplement or supplant State Audit Agency audits. In all, fifteen States have both State audits and CPA audits of LEAs, thirteen States give the option of either State or CPA audits, twelve States have principally State Audits, and ten States have primarily CPA audits. In thirty-one States, public accountants (PAs) may on occasion be used instead of Certified Public Accountants (CPAs).

The CPA is usually hired by and is primarily responsible to the LEAs next higher authority which is the School Board or local governmental unit. In a majority of cases, their audit reports are also transmitted to the State Education Agency and in a few cases (13 States) to a State Audit Agency.

In most instances, the CPA audit is strictly financial in scope. A small percentage may also consider compliance matters. There is, however, a discernable trend toward increased compliance evaluations particularly with regard to Federal programs (such audits are now required by Federal regulations). On the other hand, performance audits by CPAs are quite rare. As mentioned earlier, CPAs are slowly moving into performance auditing but are hampered by many things including (1) lack of firm or absolute performance standards, (2) possible conflicts of interest (independence), and (3) fear of possible legal liabilities. CPAs may in some cases submit an internal management letter that comments on observed weaknesses in internal controls and many CPA firms offer management "reviews" as a separate service.

OTHER LOCAL AUDIT ACTIVITIES

Local Education Agencies may also be audited by local governmental auditors, municipal accountants, management consulting firms, and educational program auditors.

Five States report that certain of their LEAs are audited by local governmental auditors. This occurs almost exclusively in Districts located in large metropolitan areas. Local governmental audits are principally financial in scope with some compliance coverage. However, performance auditing is beginning to reach even the local levels of governmental auditing. For instance, the County Auditor of King County, Washington (Seattle) is directed to:

> . . . report matters concerning the effectiveness and efficiency of the programs and operation of the County.
>
> ·
>
> This step involves not only an examination of the financial statements and of the legality of expenditures but also of the prudence of expenditures and the efficiency of the use of all resources including the elimination of wasteful practices.[10]

LEAs in at least two States, Kansas and New Jersey, may be audited by a special category of auditor called a Licensed or Registered Municipal Accountant. This is an accountant licensed by the State as competent to conduct municipal audits and perform other municipal accounting services.

Sometimes a management consulting firm may be engaged to make a special examination of a Local Education Agency. Such evaluations are often quasi-audits particularly when the consulting firm is hired by the School Board or local governmental unit. Although the actual incidence of such examinations is relatively low, several have been worthy of write-ups in professional publications.[11]

Since 1969, the U.S. Office of Education has promoted the concept of educational program auditing (also called independent accomplishment auditing). In particular, educational program auditing has been tried experimentally in certain ESEA Titles III, VII, and VIII Projects.

Basically, these projects, which are administered by Local Education Agencies, must have as a minimum staff: a Director and an Evaluator. The Evaluator develops testing and evaluation procedures to measure the accomplishments of the project. An outside Educational Program Auditor (EPA), also an educator, reviews the Evaluator's reports and procedures and attests to their adequacy.

The objective of educational program auditing is to assist school administrators in verifying the quality of their educational programs. Throughout the audit process, the EPA searches for discrepancies between proposed evaluation design, reported accomplishments, and on-going evaluation techniques. The EPA provides feedback designed to help the Project Director adjust his operations to meet the demands of complex and/or changing situations.

SUMMARY

State and Local Education Agencies are members of a complex environment of accountability and management control. Adding assurance to the proper discharge of accountability and acting as a management control device for the many higher authority/audit recipients is an integrated and overlapping network of auditing that includes Federal, State, and Local components. The purpose of this chapter has been to introduce and briefly describe the audit agencies that comprise this audit network. In the next chapter, the current status of the SEA/LEA audit activities of these agencies will be examined in much greater detail.

FOOTNOTES

Chapter IV

[1]For a detailed discussion of the administration and organization of State Education Agencies see: Sam P. Harris, *State Department of Education, State Boards of Education, and Chief State School Officers,* Department of Health, Education, and Welfare Publication No. (OE) 73-07400, (Washington: U.S. Government Printing Office, 1973).

[2]United States General Accounting Office, *GAO,* (Washington: GAO, 1970), p. 3.

[3]Elmer B. Staats, "The Role of the General Accounting Office in Reviewing the Results of Federal Programs," *The GAO Review,* (Summer, 1971), p. 81.

[4]Elmer Staats, "Evaluation of Federally Funded Education Programs," *Government Executive,* V (February, 1973), p. 49.

[5]U.S. Department of Health, Education, and Welfare, *1969 Annual Report,* (Washington: U.S. Government Printing Office, 1970), p. 16.

[6]*Ibid.,* p. 15.

[7]U.S. Department of Agriculture, *Inspector General Audit Guide 7027.3,* March, 1973 (Internal Document), pp. 16,20.

[8]General Services Administration — Office of Federal Management Policy, *Federal Management Circular 72-3: Audit of Federal Operations and Programs by Executive Branch Agencies,* (Washington: GSA, 1973), p. 4.

[9]*Ibid.*

[10]"Responsibilities of Auditor — King County, Washington," *The GAO Review,* (Summer, 1972), p. 74.

[11]See for example: "How to get Ready for a Management Audit," *Nation's Schools,* LXXVIII (September, 1966), pp. 66-68. (and) William M. Staerkel, "How a School Management Audit Works," *Nation's Schools,* LXVVI (December, 1965), pp. 33-36.

SUMMARY AND ANALYSIS OF CONTEMPORARY SEA/LEA AUDIT PRACTICES AND PERCEPTIONS

INTRODUCTION

The previous chapter identified the audit agencies that are members of the SEA/LEA audit network. In this chapter the educational audit activities of these agencies are analyzed. The conceptual framework of auditing, developed in Chapter III, is used to structure this discussion and to identify significant concepts and relationships.

This chapter provides factual information for educational managers and auditors so they may compare and evaluate their own audit activities and experiences. It also provides a basis for recommendations directed toward strengthening the SEA/LEA audit process and, in particular, enhancing the potential of auditing as a significant aid to SEA/LEA management. The information contained in this chapter is based upon:

1. SEA questionnaires
2. Interviews with SEA managers
3. Interviews with State auditors
4. Interviews with Federal auditors and U. S. Office of Education personnel
5. Supplemental sources

SEA QUESTIONNAIRES

The Chief State School Officer in each of the states and territories in which interviews were not conducted was asked by Alabama's Superintendent of Education to participate in the Project. All State Officers and one Territorial Officer responded favorably to this request and each designated a contact official for his respective state or territory.

A detailed questionnaire and cover letter were forwarded to each contact official (see Appendix A), a follow-up letter was mailed to nonrespondents four weeks after the initial contact, and those states that had not responded to the questionnaires after eight weeks were contacted by telephone. As a result, thirty-six out of forty-one states answered and returned usable questionnaires (see Table 6), giving an 88% state response — or a total for both interviews and questionnaires of 90% (forty-five out of fifty states).

SEA INTERVIEWS

Interviews with SEA personnel were conducted in nine states: Alabama, California, Florida, Kentucky, Maryland, Massachusetts, Ohio, Texas and Washington. These states were chosen in order to obtain a representative sample (a) geographically and (b) by size and organization structure of the State Education Agencies.

A detailed interview guide was prepared. Generally, the same questions were asked in the interview guide that were asked in the questionnaire. Each interviewee was asked to respond only to those questions that pertained to his background and experience with auditing. However, every question was answered by at least one person in each state.

In order to obtain a complete perspective, a variety of SEA personnel were interviewed. For example, a typical series of interviews within a given state could include: the Superintendent of Education, several Assistant Superintendents, the chief financial officer, Federal

TABLE 6
QUESTIONNAIRE RESPONSE

States and Territories Responding	States and Territories Not Responding
Alaska	Colorado
Arkansas	Idaho
Arizona	Illinois
Connecticut	New Hampshire
Delaware	New Jersey
Georgia	American Samoa
Hawaii	Guam
Indiana	Puerto Rico
Iowa	Trust Territory of the
Kansas	Pacific Islands
Louisiana	Virgin Islands
Maine	
Michigan	
Minnesota	
Mississippi	
Missouri	
Montana	
Nebraska	
Nevada	
New Mexico	
New York	
North Carolina	
North Dakota	
Oklahoma	
Oregon	
Pennsylvania	
Rhode Island	
South Carolina	
South Dakota	
Tennessee	
Utah	
Vermont	
Virginia	
West Virginia	
Wisconsin	
Wyoming	

TOTAL QUESTIONNAIRE RESPONSE — 36 States

and State program coordinators, SEA auditors, accountants and clerks. Within the nine states, a total of seventy-four persons were interviewed.

These interviews constitute the primary source of information for this chapter. In fact, we feel that the interview responses are somewhat more representative of SEA perceptions and experiences than are the questionnaire responses. In arriving at this conclusion, we were influenced by two primary factors.

1. The stratification of the interviews within each State gave consideration to all levels of SEA management.
2. It appears that SEA personnel were more likely to express their true feelings concerning "sensitive" issues in a face-to-face interview situation.

Though the interview and questionnaire responses show the same trends for a majority of questions, the questionnaire respondents did tend to give the middle or impartial answer on a few sensitive issues. For example, for the question "Does the auditor (of a particular agency) try to assist, find something wrong, or is he impartial?", the interview responses were *skewed* toward *fault-finding* while the questionnaire answers tended toward the mean (*impartial*). Therefore, a few of the findings in the following pages will rely more heavily on the interviews than upon the questionnaires.

TABLE 7
SEA INTERVIEWS

STATES	Chief State School Officer	Assistant Superintendent	Finance Officer	Program Coordinator	SEA Auditors	Accountants and Clerks	Total
Alabama	1	1	1	1	—	3	7
California	1	1	1	4	—	—	7
Flordia	—	3	2	2	—	3	10
Kentucky	1	1	2	1	—	1	6
Maryland	—	2	1	1	1	1	6
Massachusetts	—	1	1	2	1	3	8
Ohio	1	1	1	9	1	1	14
Texas	1	1	2	—	2	—	6
Washington	1	1	1	4	2	1	10
TOTAL	6	12	12	24	7	13	74

INTERVIEWS WITH STATE AUDITORS

In order to obtain a more complete perspective of SEA auditing, interviews were conducted with twenty auditors from thirteen State audit agencies in nine States. An interview guide similar to the SEA interview guide was used to structure these meetings.

TABLE 8
STATE AUDITOR INTERVIEWS

States	Number of Agencies	Number of Auditors
Alabama	2	3
California	3	4
Florida	1	1
Kentucky	2	2
Maryland	1	1
Massachusetts	1	3
Ohio	1	1
Texas	1	3
Washington	1	2
Total	13	20

FEDERAL INTERVIEWS

The project staff conducted interviews in Washington, D. C. with U. S. Office of Education personnel and auditors from the General Accounting Office and the HEW Audit Agency. Federal auditors were also interviewed in six of the nine states visited. The Washington interviews, conducted at the beginning of the Project, were more general and not as highly structured as the later State interviews.

SUPPLEMENTAL SOURCES

In addition to the interviews and questionnaires, the project staff utilized several other sources of information including:

. . Federal Audit Reports. The Project staff reviewed forty HEW audit reports, four GAO Title I audits, and several miscellaneous Federal audits.

. . State Audit Reports. Audit reports were obtained from thirteen states. These included State Audits of SEAs and LEAs, independent CPA audits of LEAs, SEA audits of LEAs, and SEA internal audits.

. . Audit Guides and Memorandums. Audit guides and memorandums were submitted by HEW Audit Agency and by several State Audit Agencies and CPA firms.

. . Audit Conferences. The staff attended and participated in a number of conferences and meetings dealing directly or indirectly with SEA auditing.

. . Other Sources. Official audit agency publications, articles by leading authorities, reports from other auditing and education research projects, and miscellaneous memos, reports, letters and other documents were also consulted.

The following report on the condition and status of SEA/LEA auditing is based upon these sources. The discussion is organized into four major sections corresponding to the four divisions of the conceptual framework of auditing, namely: *objective, scope, parties,* and *process.* Each section is further divided into three parts (1) a brief *background review* of the topic as it was discussed in Chapter III, (2) the *findings* of the project concerning this aspect of SEA Auditing, and (3) *conclusions* of the project staff.

THE OBJECTIVES OF SEA/LEA AUDITING

BACKGROUND REVIEW

Historically, auditing has been primarily an accountability device. In this frame, the auditor acts as an inspector, examiner, or policeman — his chief function being to assure a higher authority that an auditee has properly discharged his responsibilities or obligations. However, the scope of auditing in all fields has been expanding in recent years to encompass management or performance matters. Hence, contemporary auditing, particularly in the governmental environment, often has as a major purpose the upgrading or strengthening of management.

But there is a dichotomy in attempting to *improve management* through *policing.* Both behavior theory in the area of human motivation and recent research suggests that this approach is not the most effective method in which to promote change.

Yet, auditing is irrevocably an accountability technique since the primary audit recipient is, at least theoretically, the auditee's higher authority. However, it has been demonstrated by many auditors that the accountability aspect of auditing can be de-emphasized, and management control or aid emphasized. Hence, even when there is an environment of accountability, the emphasis and philosophy of an audit can be focused upon assisting management, rather than evaluating or inspecting. Thus, it would appear that the cooperative, participative type audit — with accountability neither emphasized, nor completely ignored — could result in increased acceptance and implementation of auditor recommendations.

FINDINGS

SEA managers were asked a series of question designed to determine their attitudes regarding current SEA audit objectives.

. . When asked, "In general, how does your SEA management view the current audit process?", 59% of those interviewed (22 total responses) answered negatively (23%) or indifferently (36%).

. . Slightly more than half (60%) of 55 total responses to the interviews and questionnaires indicated that manager attitude toward auditors and auditor attitude regarding management is *not* of a positive nature.

. . As reflected by both interviews and questionnaires (65 responses) a majority of SEA managers (78%) believe that auditors in general feel that they must make a finding of some kind.

. . A significant minority, 23 out of 53 respondents (43%) to both the questionnaires and interviews, felt that *none* of the audits of their SEA had ever identified an important management problem.

. . Only 19% of the SEA managers interviewed (5 out of 27 total responses) view the objective of Federal auditing as assistance to SEA Management.

. . A large majority (85%) of SEA managers interviewed (33 total responses) report that auditors, in general, never ask if there are any specific areas that the SEA would like examined, or if the auditor could be of service in any way as a byproduct of his examination.

These responses suggest that a majority of SEA managers perceive auditing as primarily an accountability device. Also, that most auditors make no inquiry regarding SEA (auditee) needs and desires suggests that many auditors perceive the objective of auditing as accountability, e.g., inspecting, policing.

Audit objectives were also examined on an agency by agency basis.

HEW Audit Agency

The last Annual Report of the Department of Health, Education, and Welfare presents a twofold mission or objective of the HEW Audit Agency:

> . . . to insure that the Department's operations are conducted efficiently and economically; and to ascertain that Federal funds are expended properly and in *accordance* with the purposes for which they were appropriated.[1] (emphasis added)

A more specific source relating to educational audits, the 1966 "HEWAA Audit Guide for ESEA Title I Programs," identifies the objectives of HEWAA Title I reviews as determining:

1. Whether administrative and financial internal controls are adequate to provide accurate and reliable operating and financial reports essential for management evaluation and decisions.

2. Whether the expenditures made are only for the established projects and programs and in accordance with applicable Federal and State regulations and policies.

3. Whether the administrative reviews have been made by the State agency to evaluate the operations of local projects or programs.

4. Whether the State and local educational agencies have properly reported their *accountability* for grants of Federal funds for the projects or programs to which this guide is applicable.

5. Whether the projects and programs are conducted in an economical and efficient manner and in compliance with the requirements of applicable laws and regulations.[2] (emphasis added)

More recently, the 1973 draft revision of the HEWAA Title I Audit Guide identifies two primary audit objectives:

(1) . . . determining if the LEA's planning, implementation, and operation of its Title I activities were in *accordance* with the intent of the program, and

(2) . . . determining the effect that any *mismanagement* of Title I resources had and/or will have on the program in meeting the special needs of educationally deprived children.[3] (emphasis added)

The introductions of both the 1966 and 1973 guides emphasize SEA/LEA responsibilities. There is no mention of *aiding* or *assisting* grantee management and no discussion concerning auditor attitudes and audit philosophy. Also, both audit guides use such negative terms as *management deficiencies, management weaknesses,* and *mismanagement.* Thus, the focus in both the audit guides and HEW's Annual Report is primarily upon Federal perspectives and SEA/LEA accountability.

The project staff also reviewed forty audit reports provided as samples by HEW Audit Agency. These reports were issued between 1966 and 1973, covered nineteen states and involved several different education programs — including four titles of the 1965 ESEA Act, Vocational Education, and Adult Basic Education. These audit reports were found to be primarily accountability oriented. This was indicated in several ways including:

. . An examination of the scope of these reports revealed that HEWAA's findings and recommendations are primarily of a financial and compliance nature.

. One hundred fifteen findings (67%) were financial in nature (or compliance/financial).

. Fifty-four (31%) were general compliance matters (administrative or management matters covered by Federal Legislation, regulations, and/or guidelines).

. Three findings (2%) were performance in nature (management matters not covered by the program's legislation, regulations or guidelines).

. . An analysis of the *tone* of these audit reports (by subjective evaluation or syntax) indicated that 83% were impartial or slightly negative. None were deemed either wholly positive or negative in tone.

Positive	0	(0%)
Fairly Positive	7	(17%)
Impartial	21	(53%)
Slightly negative	12	(30%)
Negative	0	(0%)

Also, 14 audit reports (35%) included particularly negative words and phrases such as: "significant deficiencies," "inadequate," "failure," "weaknesses."

. . Only one audit report (3%) noted any positive achievement by the SEA.

On the other hand, an HEWAA audit report that was very positive in tone came to our attention during the course of our research. (It was not included in the sample of forty provided by HEWAA.) This report concerned a follow-up review of ESEA Title V activities in the State of Connecticut.

Relating to our current review, we noted definite progress on the part of the SEA to accommodate our recommendations.

. . . .

. . . . we believe that the SEA has made definite strides forward toward developing meaningful project applications and reports of accomplishments.

. . . .

Our current review of the procedures established and used by the ESEA Title V program funds showed that they were quite effective.[4]

We were informed that this audit was conducted experimentally and hope that it proved of sufficient success to warrant similar approaches in the future.

The General Accounting Office

The 1969 edition of *GAO*, an official publication describing the purpose, function, organization and services of the U. S. General Accounting Office, contains the following statement:

GAO often is called Congress' 'watch dog' over Government spending. Its constructive role in appraising and reporting on a wide range of Government activities and operations more accurately reflects its services to the Congress and the Nation.[5]

The 1970 edition of that publication contains the following new paragraph:

Briefly, GAO is concerned with how the Federal departments and agencies, through their programs and activities, carry out the mandate or intent of legislation enacted by the Congress. Therefore, it plays an important part in the legislative oversight role of the Congress.[6]

Both editions convey the idea that GAO performs an "oversight," or "policing" function — and, in fact, its staff newsletter is titled "The Watchdog." This view is also shared by some members of Congress. For example, the following statement was made recently by the Chairman of the Subcommittee on Legislative Branch Appropriation:

I do not think there is any question but that the General Accounting Office is doing a good job. As the gentleman well knows Government expenditures are increasing year by year by year and I continually hope that we can see the end in sight. But so far we have not. And the more money the Government Agencies spend the more need there is to have, figuratively speaking, *that policeman* on the beat. And the General Accounting Office will make them do right, in many instances *catch them* and if they do wrong, *see they are punished,* and then collect the money that the Government otherwise would not get.[7] (emphasis added)

However, the recent *Standards for Audit of Governmental Organizations, Programs, Activities and Functions* published by the GAO provides for a governmental auditing function that is cooperative in tone and perspective. For example, it is stated therein that each audit report shall:

. . Place primary emphasis on improvement rather than on criticism of the past; critical comments should be presented in balanced perspective, recognizing any unusual difficulties or circumstances faced by the operating officials concerned.

. . Include recognition of noteworthy accomplishments, particularly when management improvements in one program or activity may be applicable elsewhere.

. . Include recognition of the views of responsible officials of the organization, program, function, or activity audited on the auditor's findings, conclusions, and recommendations. . . .[8]

With the publications of these new audit standards, it is reasonable to expect future GAO audits to be more aid-to-management oriented. In this regard, our interviews with GAO officials revealed that an intentional effort is underway to de-emphasize the heavy policing or "watch dog" philosophy of the past and to move toward a more "constructive" approach.

The Project staff analyzed the four audit reports that represent GAO's major review effort in recent years in the area of Federal Aid to Elementary and Secondary Education. These were reviews of the ESEA Title I Programs in West Virginia, Ohio, New Jersey, and Illinois. In our opinion, these reports reflect a more positive and cooperative attitude than do those of many other Federal and State audit agencies. This was indicated in several ways, including:

. . An examination of the scope of these audit reports revealed that GAO's findings and recommendations were primarily compliance in nature.
  . Five findings (13%) were financial in nature (or financial/compliance).
  . Thirty (77%) were general compliance matters (administrative or management matters covered by Federal legislation, regulations, and/or guidelines).
  . Four findings (10%) were performance in nature (management matters not covered by the program's legislation, regulations, or guidelines).
. . An analysis of the *tone* of these GAO audit reports indicates that they are fairly positive.

Positive	0	(0%)
Fairly positive	4	(100%)
Impartial	0	(0%)
Slightly negative	0	(0%)
Negative	0	(0%)

There was an obvious *avoidance* of the use of negative words and phrases, such as: Inadequate, failure, deficiency, and weaknesses. Findings were generally "areas needing improvement."
. . Positive accomplishments of the SEA were noted in all

four audit reports. All included HEW, SEA, and LEA comments and attitudes, without rebuttal, and some findings were made indirectly by giving HEW's or the SEA's *own* observation concerning problem areas.

State Auditing

Although we obtained a number of exceptional State audit reports, we did not obtain a representative sample of State audit reports of SEAs and LEAs. However, SEA managers were asked several questions relating to State audits of their SEA.

. . When asked, "Does the State auditor note positive as well as negative aspects?" — 14% said "seldom" and 86% said "never" (14 total interview responses — 9 states).

. . In response to, "Does the State auditor ask if you have any specific areas you would like examined or if he could be of service to you as a byproduct of his investigation?" — 57% said "seldom" or "never."

	Number	Percentage
Always	4	7%
Usually	12	22%
Occasionally	7	13%
Seldom	7	13%
Never	24	44%
TOTAL	54	99%

(both questionnaire and interview responses)

State auditors from 13 state audit agencies in nine states were also asked a number of questions about state auditing. In response to "Can an auditor be both a watchdog and an aid to management?", they indicated:

	Number	Percentage
Yes	3	15%
No	5	25%
Possibly	12	60%
TOTAL	20	100%

It would appear from these responses, a review of the literature, and conversations with various authorities, that State auditing generally serves primarily as an accountability function. There are some exceptions, however. As the scope of auditing in many states is expanding to concern performance matters, there is a simultaneous movement to make State auditing more management control oriented.

SEA Internal Auditing

Our research revealed that most State Education Agencies (90%) do *not* have an internal audit function. (See SEA Internal Auditing, page 148.) Therefore, a general statement concerning the current objectives of SEA internal auditing cannot be made. However, past experiences in other areas reveal that internal auditing is generally *more* oriented toward management needs and uses than is external auditing.

Local Auditing

All of the 16,000 or so Local Education Agencies (public school districts) in the United States are audited by some combination of Federal, State, and Local auditors. Our statistics indicate that approximately 88% are audited by State auditors, 76% are audited by CPA's, and 64% are audited by their State Education Agency.

We received responses from 42 states (both questionnaires and interviews) concerning the objective of LEA auditing as indicated by its "use." Thirty-five SEAs (83%) indicated that the objective of LEA auditing in their state was accountability and seven SEAs indicated management aid (17%). A related statistic is that most LEA audits are financial and compliance in scope. Our responses indicate: 99% financial, 55% compliance, and 12% performance or program.

CONCLUSIONS

It appears that the current objective of SEA and LEA auditing is more "accountability" than "aid to management." However, there is a discernible trend toward more positive and cooperative audits — a trend which should be encouraged.

The AIDE staff recognizes the continued need for accountability in governmental activities and the important role of auditing in the accountability process. But, we also feel that there is a "happy medium" somewhere between outright policing and absolute cooperation. As it now stands, many SEA auditors view themselves as examiners and/or inspectors; and this view is shared by the SEA auditees. As a result, relationships can be strained and implementation of auditor recommendations may be resisted. We would hope to see auditors adopt a more cooperative, participative approach and to see *clear* statements of audit philosophy from each audit agency.

In this regard, it is significant that SEA respondents reacted favorably to the *potential* of auditing as an aid to management.

> An overwhelming 88% of the SEA managers queried (59 interview and questionnaire responses) felt that the auditor could be *both* a watchdog and an aid to management.
>
> A majority (79%) of the SEA managers from both the questionnaire and interviews (61 responses), felt that the *usefulness* and *practicality* of performance auditing was "excellent" or "very helpful."

It would appear, that although the current objective of most SEA auditing is perceived as accountability, SEA managers would be receptive to — and are optimistic about — the potential usefulness of management-oriented auditing.

THE SCOPE OF SEA/LEA AUDITING

BACKGROUND REVIEW

Most people perceive auditing as a financial review conducted by an accountant-auditor. This has been the traditional role of auditing and in many instances it is the current role. However, there has been a definite expansion of the scope of many audits in recent years to encompass matters of a management or performance nature. This has been caused by several factors: (1) the accountability of managers, particularly governmental managers, has been expanding; (2) auditing is increasingly recognized by managers themselves as potentially a useful, management tool; and (3) there is a growing awareness within the auditing profession of the potential contribution of broad scope auditing toward enhancing the economy, efficiency, and effectiveness of operations.

These "modern," comprehensive audits are labeled with various names, including: operational audits, management audits, program audits, and performance audits. The framework used by the AIDE

Project to describe the potential scope of auditing is:

1. Financial auditing — which concerns accounting error, fraud, financial controls, and fairness of financial statements.
2. Compliance auditing — which concerns faithful adherence to administrative and legal requirements, policies, and regulations.
3. Performance auditing — which goes beyond the "traditional" encompassing such matters as the economy, efficiency, and/or effectiveness of operational controls, management information systems, and programs.

However, compliance is a somewhat ambiguous category in that matters of a financial, administrative, and performance nature may be required by law.

For instance, Federal legislation, regulations, and guidelines may be so explicit with regard to grant-in-aid programs as to encompass many aspects of the management process.

This framework reflects the *potential* scope of auditing. The scope of any particular audit depends upon the needs and desires of the audit recipient, the ability (time, competency, cost, etc.) of the auditor, and the nature, size, and willingness of the auditee.

Comprehensive, broad-scope auditing is now considered by most experts to generally be the best approach to governmental auditing. In particular, such auditing has great potential as a significant aid in the management of State *and Local* Education Agencies.

FINDINGS

The audit scope framework was explained to both the SEA interviewees and the respondents to the SEA audit questionnaire. They were then asked to describe the scope of audits of their own SEA as they perceived them. The results were as follows:

TABLE 9
SCOPE OF SEA AUDITS AS PERCEIVED
BY SEA MANAGERS

Scope	HEW Audit Agency	GAO	State Audit Agency	CPA	SEA Internal Audit
Financial	85%	86%	96%	100%	69%
Federal Compliance	87%	100%	30%	33%	56%
State Compliance	15%	0%	80%	50%	56%
Performance	49%	29%	26%	0%	13%

Some important observations can be drawn from this data. For example, SEA managers feel that:

. . . Federal audit agencies are ahead of State audit agencies in extension of audit scope.

. . . Federal auditors generally do not conduct "State compliance audits."

. . . CPAs and SEA Internal Auditors seldom conduct performance audits.

The following discussion examines these statistics more closely on an Agency by Agency basis.

HEW Audit Agency

Sixty-one SEA managers perceived HEWAA audits as being:

Financial	85%
Federal Compliance	87%
State Compliance	15%
Performance	49%

To gain a greater insight into the scope of HEW audits the Project Staff also analyzed the forty audit reports provided as samples by HEW Audit Agency. The scope of these audits as reflected by types of findings and recommendations was:

TABLE 10
SCOPE OF HEWAA AUDIT REPORTS

Scope	By Number of Findings (172)	%	By Number of Audit Reports (40)	%
Financial	74	43%	29	73%
Compliance (Financial)	41	24%	22	55%
Compliance (Administrative)	3	2%	1	3%
Compliance (Performance)	51	30%	28	70%
Performance	3	2%	1	3%

The percentages in the last column do not add to 100% because an audit report usually contains more than one finding: thus, one audit could be financial, compliance, and performance in scope. Below is a more detailed breakdown of the number and types of findings that are categorized under each of the above headings.

FINANCIAL (74; 43%)
Inadequate Records (3)
Accounting Error (5)
Improper Voucher and Documentation (17)
Unsubstantiated Allocation or Proration of Overhead (10)
Charges Based on Budgeted — Not Actual (5)
Improper Adjusting Entries (9)
Accounting Reports Inadequate or Not Timely (9)
Federal Income Not Recorded (2)
LEA Financial Reports Not Adequately Reviewed (1)
Inadequate Budget (1)
Lack of Internal Controls (1)
Miscellaneous (11)

COMPLIANCE — FINANCIAL (41; 24%)
Exceeded Budget (2)
Expenditures Made Before or After Grant Period (6)
Failed in Matching, Supplanting, and/or
    Maintenance of Effort (8)
Improper Purchase Order Procedures (2)
No Letter of Credit Procedures (6)
Improper Charges (8)
Excess Cash on Hand (5)
Delays in Advancements of Funds to LEAs (3)
Obligations Not Liquidated Promptly (1)

COMPLIANCE — ADMINISTRATIVE (3; 2%)
Written Contracts Not Issued (1)

Contracts Not Submitted to OE (1)
Consultants Receiving Dual Compensation (1)

COMPLIANCE — PERFORMANCE (51; 30%)
Inadequate LEA Audits (16)
Property Not Properly Controlled or Inventoried (10)
Equipment Not Justified, Used Elsewhere (7)
Project Not in Line With Objectives of the Act (2)
Inadequate Assessment of Needs, Targets, Objectives (7)
Inadequate Reviews of Proposals (2)
Projects Inadequately Monitored (2)
Evaluation of Project Accomplishments Inadequate (5)

PERFORMANCE (3; 2%)
Data Processing Department Needs Additional Staff and
   Improvement in Workloads (1)
Manager Job Descriptions Need Clarification (1)
Project Did Not Accomplish Objectives (1)
(Interestingly all three performance findings were made in the
   same audit report.)[9]

As can be seen from the above, HEW audit agency has definitely extended the scope of their SEA/LEA audits to frequently include matters of a performance nature. For the most part, however, the HEW auditor has to date limited his management comments to those matters that are clearly covered by appropriate legislation, regulations, and guidelines. In other words, he has refrained from commenting upon issues of a *general management* nature. This is probably due in part to some of the following factors.

Authority — HEWAA has *clear* authority to audit only financial and Federal compliance matters: matters in the tradition of auditing and/or specifically required by Federal laws, regulations and guidelines. HEW's primary authority to audit SEAs is Public Law 90-577. This is the Intergovernmental Cooperation Act of 1968, which states in Section 202:

> The Head of the Federal Agency and the Comptroller
> General of the United States or any of their duly authorized
> representatives shall have access for the purpose of audit
> and examination to any books, documents, papers, and
> records that are pertinent to the grant-in-aid received by the
> States.

The question here seems to be in the definition of the word "audit." Although the modern definition of the term extends into performance areas, as indicated in the new Governmental Audit Standards, the legislation itself is unclear as to the specific scope of the word.

Cooperation — HEWAA auditors are not encouraged by the SEA to extend the scope of their audit because of the traditional accountability objective of auditing.

Time — HEWAA auditors have a heavy workload and limited time to conduct an audit. To do a comprehensive job of evaluating performance may be impossible in the time available for a particular engagement.

Competency — Performance auditing is a relatively new concept, and specific approaches are still in the formulative stages. SEAs are basically administrative units, and administrative activities are the most difficult to completely, and comprehensively evaluate.

However, there is a clear trend toward extension of the scope of HEW audits and HEW's top management is clearly committed to this broad approach. For instance a recent draft of HEW's ESEA Title I audit guide states:

> The management audit approach is to be used in making this review. This approach requires that primary emphasis be placed on evaluating the efficiency and effectiveness of policies and procedures used by the LEA in managing projects meeting the intent of the Title I Program. In line with this approach, the auditor should keep in mind that good management practices include more than compliance with rules and regulations. Attention should be focused on the appropriateness of management decisions and actions in view of available information, resources, and alternative approaches. It is the LEA's performance that determines the quality and success of its Title I projects.[10]

The General Accounting Office

SEA managers perceived GAO audits as being:

Financial	86%
Federal Compliance	100%
State Compliance	0%
Performance	29%

Analysis of the four ESEA Title I audit reports that represent GAO's major efforts in recent years in the areas of elementary and secondary education disclosed the following audit scope.

TABLE 11
SCOPE OF GAO AUDIT REPORTS

Scope	By Number of Findings (39)	%	By Number of Audit Reports (4)	%
Financial	3	8%	2	50%
Compliance (Financial)	2	5%	2	50%
Compliance (Administrative)	3	8%	3	75%
Compliance (Performance)	27	69%	4	100%
Performance	4	10%	3	75%

Below is a more detailed breakdown of the number and types of findings that are categorized under each of the above headings.

FINANCIAL (3; 8%)
Improper Proration of Salaries (1)
Sick Leave Charged That Was Not Used (1)
Federal "Income" Not Credited (1)

COMPLIANCE — FINANCIAL (2; 5%)
Purchases or Transactions in Closing Day of the Project (1)
Obligation Incurred Prior to Effective Date of SEA Approval (1)

COMPLIANCE — ADMINISTRATIVE (3; 8%)
Equipment and Supplies Purchased Without SEA Approval (1)
Documentation of "Attendance Area Selection" Not Maintained
    or Retained (2)

COMPLIANCE — PERFORMANCE (27; 69%)
Inadequate LEA Audits (4)
Project Application Form Inadequate (1)
Equipment Not Needed; Not Utilized (2)
Equipment Purchases — Not Used Just for Title I Purposes (3)
SEA Failed to Review Inventories (1)
Facilities Purchased/Constructed — Not Just for Title I Use (2)
Improper Selection of Attendance Areas or Target Schools (3)
Services — Not Just Furnished to Deprived Children (1)
Selection of Participating Children — Not Adequate (1)
Project Not Designed for Special Needs of Educationally
    Deprived (2)
Did Not Involve Parents or Representatives of Community
    Organizations (1)
Private Schools Not Adequately Participating (2)
Need for Periodic Review and Monitoring of Projects (2)
Inadequate Evaluation of Project Accomplishments (2)

PERFORMANCE (4; 10%)

SEA Failed to Determine if Additional Funding (for Multi-agency Project) Actually Was Available When the Project Was Approved (1)

OE Should, in Their Field Visits, Determine if Attendance Criteria Is Being Properly Applied (1)

OE Is Not Resolving Audits on a Timely Basis (1)

OE Needs to Consolidate Title I Guidelines (1)

As can be seen from the above, GAO has definitiely extended the scope of their SEA audits to frequently include matters of a performance nature. In fact, GAO's audits of SEAs have, in general, been somewhat broader in scope than HEWAA's. But in recent years this difference has become less apparent. However, GAO — like HEW — has also limited the scope of their SEA audits to principally those management matters covered by appropriate legislation, regulations, and guidelines.

There are indications, however, that both HEWAA and GAO hope to extend the scope of their SEA audits to encompass "Program Effectiveness." As noted earlier, such a broad-scope audit concept is reflected in GAO's new *Governmental Audit Standards*.

State Auditing

The Project staff identified sixty-eight State audit agencies in the fifty states that audit State Education Programs at the SEA and/or LEA level. We received replies from forty-five SEA respondents concerning fifty-four of these agencies. In general, the scope of State audits of educational activities as perceived by SEA managers is:

TABLE 12
SCOPE OF STATE AUDITS AS PERCEIVED BY
SEA MANAGERS

Scope	SEA AUDITS	LEA AUDITS
Financial	96%	100%
Federal Compliance	30%	41%
State Compliance	80%	85%
Performance	26%	6%

At the present time, most State Audit Agencies conduct financial/compliance audits. But there is a clear and growing trend to expand the scope of State Auditing into operational or performance areas. However, not all State auditors are in favor of this movement. Some feel that it is not the place of the State audit agency to make such recommendations and/or they do not have the staff or present ability to conduct a performance audit. The Project staff interviewed twenty representatives of thirteen State audit agencies in nine States. All were aware of the national movement toward performance State audits. Seven audit agencies were strongly in favor of this movement, five were neutral, and one was opposed to the movement.

Ten SEAs reported that they had been "performance audited" by a State Audit Agency. However, supplemental information indicated that not all of these were performance auditing as the term is generally used. It appears that to date, few performance audits of SEAs have been conducted by State auditors.

The staff was able to locate and review only four SEA State audits that were performance in scope. One of these was conducted in 1968 by the Office of the Washington State Auditor, Robert V. Graham.[11] An excellent performance audit of Washington's State Education Agency, it included such recommendations as:

. . A major division "Staff Services" should be created to be headed by an Assistant Superintendent.
. . Within the scope of Electronic Data Processing operations, the agency should develop written plans and objectives and coordinate such plans and objectives with statewide EDP developments.
. . The agency should locate and store "backup" tapes in some area other than that occupied by the computer.
. . Priority attention should be given to more efficient management of office space throughout the agency to promote a more coordinated and more orderly document flow.
. . The Superintendent should institute a program of form design and control with emphasis on consolidation of information and elimination of extraneous efforts in reporting and procurement procedures.
. . The agency should install an internal audit unit which will report directly to top administrative officials.

Another example of an SEA Management Audit by a State Audit Agency was released in 1973 by the Legislative Auditor of Hawaii.[12] Some of the many management recommendations made, include:

. . The need to redefine organizational patterns to insure a more effective and efficient attainment of educational objectives.

. . The SEA should clarify through job descriptions, the roles and responsibilities of staff personnel.

. . The SEA should develop personnel staffing policies at both the State Department of Education and in the district agencies.

. . The development of a comprehensive training program should be implemented for Department of Education personnel.

. . There is a need for closer communication between the State Department of Education and the District Agencies.

. . The State board should develop policies which clearly delineate the responsibility for curriculum development.

. . All new education programs should be pilot-tested before being implemented on a statewide basis.

. . All new programs should be the products of analysis.

. . The Department of Education should consider developing a reporting system that would provide for closer supervision of educational programs.

Performance auditing is a relatively new development in State auditing. It began in Michigan in 1964 and is now spreading rapidly. There is little doubt but that increasing numbers of SEAs will be performance audited by State auditors in the near future.

SEA Internal Auditing

As mentioned earlier, most State Education Agencies do not have an internal audit activity (see SEA Internal Auditing, page 148). Therefore, a meaningful assessment of the scope of SEA internal auditing cannot be made. However, it is generally recognized that the scope of modern internal auditing should encompass operational or performance matters.

Local Auditing

Our SEA respondents reported the following scope of LEA auditing:

TABLE 13
SCOPE OF LEA AUDITS
AS PERCEIVED BY SEA MANAGERS

Scope	State Audit Agency	SEA External Audit	CPA/PA	Local Government Audit
Financial	100%	100%	97%	100%
Federal Compliance	41%	90%	37%	25%
State Compliance	85%	65%	34%	25%
Performance	6%	25%	12%	0%

In general, local school audits are principally financial in scope, with some compliance coverage, and little performance emphasis.

CPA Audits

As discussed in the previous chapter, the largest category of LEA audits is that performed by CPAs or PAs. Most CPA audits result in a short, two paragraph opinion on the fairness of an entity's financial statements. In recent years, however, a few CPAs have begun to issue narrative financial/compliance reports for certain governmental audits — particularly audits of federal programs. However, at the present time, performance audits by CPAs are quite uncommon.

Recently, HEW Audit Agency has cooperated with the American Institute of Certified Public Accountants in the development of three audit guides for those CPAs who audit the following programs:

(1) National Direct Student Loan Program, College Work-Study Program, and Supplemental Educational Opportunity Grants Program. (These are University level programs.)
(2) Upward Bound Program. (This is a LEA program.)
(3) Head Start Program and other Office of Child Development Programs. (These are LEA programs.)
(4) A joint ESEA Title I audit guide is now in the process of being developed.

These audit guides suggest that the CPA give both (1) "an opinion on financial statements" and (2) "conclusions on internal accounting and administrative controls and compliance information." There is also a recommended common format for the audit report.

Part I   — Introduction
Part II   — Financial
            Auditor's Opinion on Financial Statements
            Exhibits and Schedules
            Findings and Recommendations — Financial
Part III — Auditor's Conclusions on Internal Accounting and
            Administrative Controls and Compliance Infor-
            mation
            Findings and Recommendations — Compliance,
            and Internal Accounting and Administrative
            Controls
Part IV   — Prior Audit Reports
Part V   — Exhibits and Schedules

SEA Audits

Most performance audits of Local Education Agencies have been conducted or sponsored by the SEAs. All SEAs review LEA activities in some way. A majority (64%) conduct a fiscal audit, and many conduct program or school district reviews on a periodic or unscheduled basis.

An excellent example of a "performance audit" conducted by an SEA is the Administrative Survey conducted periodically by the Kentucky Department of Education.[13] A recent audit of a large Kentucky school district covered a number of significant areas, including the need for:

. . . Job specifications.
. . . A position of Assistant Superintendent.
. . . An organization chart clearly showing lines of au-
      thority and responsibility.
. . . Revised personnel application forms.
. . . A more desirable relationship with the local news
      media.
. . . A more effective districtwide communications system.
. . . An effective teacher orientation program for newly
      employed professionals.

CONCLUSIONS

In summary, the scope of SEA and LEA auditing in all areas and levels is slowly expanding to encompass matters of a management or performance nature. The AIDE Project believes that this expansion should be encouraged and that performance auditing *can* make a significant contribution to SEA management — particularly if the objectives of the audit are oriented more toward helping management than policing.

Some authorities have implied that SEAs may be hostile to the concept of performance auditing. Burton D. Friedman and Laird J. Dunbar state that:

> Federal audit agencies are aware that substantive auditing is constructive and necessary. It is not clear, however: To what extent is it appropriate for federal auditors to perform substantive audits with respect to agencies of state and local governments? Is it a proper task of a federal auditor to sit in judgement on the performance of a state government? To what extent and under what conditions is it appropriate?
>
> As long as such matters remain unresolved, it seems clear that any effort by federal auditors to make substantive audits of State Education Agencies will be resented and may be resisted by state officials.[14]

There is no doubt some truth in these remarks, particularly with regard to accountability audits. However, our investigations reveal that SEA officials are not so much opposed to the idea of performance audits as they are concerned about the auditor's competency to conduct such reviews.

- . . A majority (79%) of the SEA managers — from both the questionnaire and interviews (61 total responses) — felt that the (potential) usefulness and practicality of performance auditing was excellent or very helpful.
- . . Seventy-eight respondents for both the questionnaires and interviews answered, "In your opinion in which areas are auditors (in general) presently qualified to conduct audits?" On a scale from 1 (highly qualified) to 4 (not qualified):

Fiscal ranked 1.6
Compliance ranked 2.2
Performance ranked 3.5

Competency and other matters relating to "The Parties to SEA Auditing" are discussed in the following section.

THE PARTIES TO SEA/LEA AUDITING

The most basic of audits involves a minimum of three parties: auditor, auditee, and audit recipient. In this section, the interrelationships and characteristics of these parties will be examined under the following topics.

1. SEA Internal Auditing
2. The SEA External Audit Network
3. Characteristics of SEA Auditors
4. Behavioral Considerations

SEA INTERNAL AUDITING

BACKGROUND REVIEW

Modern internal auditing is considered by management experts to be an essential and highly effective management control device. In many instances, a competent internal audit staff can perform studies and evaluations for which the organization would otherwise have to hire management consultants or accounting firms. These might include, for instance: organizational reviews, functional reviews, job studies, analyses of work flow, form studies, EDP plans and programs, development and evaluation of management information systems, formula plans for funding education, and LEA program reviews.

Because the internal audit staff can devote their full attention to the organization, and because their recommendations are for internal use, internal auditing has the potential to make a greater contribution to an organization's management than does external auditing. Also, an Internal Audit Division can plan, assist, direct, and in some cases implement and evaluate lower level external audits (such as audits of LEAs); and can work closely and cooperatively with the organization's higher level external auditors (such as working with HEWAA and GAO auditors).

FINDINGS

As reported in Chapter IV, seventeen SEAs indicated that they had an internal audit division or group. Supplemental information indicated, however, that only four of the seventeen have an internal audit activity in the true sense of the term; and only two SEAs, (Hawaii and Illinois) have internal audit groups that conduct *perfor-*

mance audits of SEA activities.

As an example of the kind of performance recommendations that an internal SEA audit staff can actually make, consider the Organizational Review conducted by Hawaii's Management Audit and Review Branch in 1969.[15]

Their report determined and clarified the *de facto* organization structure of the SEA, identified and documented major organizational issues and problems, and presented a few "urgent" recommendations. Just a few of the many issues and questions noted were:

- . . We must begin to reexamine the emerging role of the Board.
- . . Some thought might be given to placing the Office of Federal Programs in the Office of Business Services.
- . . Should maintenance services have branch level status?
- . . Should the payroll function be assumed by the Office of Personnel Services?
- . . Should the Statistical Branch be in the Planning Office?
- . . Is it important to set up a central information office to answer inquiries about the public schools?

The three "urgent" recommendations were:

1. The Management Audit and Review staff should be called upon to develop procedures and necessary guidelines and instructions for the development, review and adoption of organizational proposals.
2. The Office of Personnel Services should take immediate steps to develop an effective system of position control and inventory. The responsibility for maintaining position control should clearly be assigned to that office.
3. The Board of Education should authorize a comprehensive and intensive study of organization over the next several months with the aim of developing a program-oriented organization and management structure. This study should be considered a major undertaking with high priority in the application of manpower and supplemental support.

CONCLUSIONS

The obvious conclusion is that modern internal auditing, as it now exists in many industries and governmental agencies, is practically nonexistent in the SEA environment. This represents a serious weakness of SEA management control on a nationwide basis.

Internal auditing has proven itself in industry and the Federal government. The General Accounting Office considers internal auditing ". . . one of the essential tools of management complimenting all other elements of management control."[16]

The virtual nonexistence of modern internal auditing in the nation's State Education Agencies when it is so widely recognized and endorsed as an essential element of management control is an untenable situation in need of immediate correction. We urge all SEAs to develop and implement a *vigorous, broad-scope, management oriented, internal audit function.*

THE SEA/LEA EXTERNAL AUDIT NETWORK

BACKGROUND REVIEW

Any medium to large size organization, public or private, should have as a minimum both an internal and an external audit function. Together, these form the most basic type of audit network: one external audit activity coupled with one internal audit activity. For those organizations operating in a complex accountability environment (such as SEAs), it is necessary that this simple dual system be expanded into a more complex, integrated audit network (such as was discussed in Chapter IV) that satisfies the needs of all "higher authorities." In the governmental environment, this network is often called the "Federal-State-Local Audit Network." Ideally, this audit network should be integrated, coordinated, and cooperative in order to minimize audit duplication and maximize audit effectiveness.

FINDINGS

The U. S. Bureau of the Budget, now called the Office of Management and Budget (OMB), established the Federal Government's basic policy with regard to grantee audits in circular number A-73, August 4, 1965, *Audit of Federal Grants-in-Aid to State and Local Governments.*

> *Coordination of Federal, State, and Local Audits.* Federal agencies responsible for conducting audits of grant operations will foster close cooperation and coordination among the auditors of the respective jurisdictions. Continuous liaison, including the exchange of audit standards and objectives, should be maintained among the Federal, State,

and Local audit groups involved. As a minimum, these groups will collaborate in the development of audit schedules to minimize the amount of effort required, as well as the impact on operations of the grantee offices. While the Federal Government cannot automatically accept audits performed by a representative of the grantee, maximum use should be made of audits performed by grantee's internal or independent auditors, so as to avoid unnecessary duplication by Federal auditors.[17]

Both HEWAA and GAO have attempted to develop an effective Federal-State-Local Audit Network, but the task has proven formidable. To quote, Comptroller General Staats:

As the Joint Financial Management Improvement Project report of September, 1969 pointed out, Federal Agencies have made some gains in working with State and local governments to achieve greater reliance on and use of non-Federal audits, but far less than the maximum potential has been realized.[18]

GAO has sponsored several intergovernmental audit workshops, and their officials have discussed audit network problems and potentials on numerous occasions, including several Congressional appearances. GAO's greatest contribution to date, however, may well be their recently issued *Statement of Governmental Audit Standards.*[19] The lack of uniform standards, benchmarks from which to base acceptable intergovernmental audit programs, has seriously hampered the development of a viable audit network. With the recent issuance of the Standards, governmental auditors now have a basis from which to establish dialogue.

HEW Audit Agency has also actively encouraged, and promoted the cooperative intergovernmental audit network concept. For example, HEWAA has (1) established a permanent Directorship for this purpose called the Special Assistant for Intergovernmental Audit Relations; (2) sponsored a number of intergovernmental audit demonstration projects; and (3) instigated a policy of sharing audits, audit guides, and programs with interested State and Local Audit Agencies. With regard to these activities, Robert B. Brown, HEWAA Assistant Director and Edward W. Stepnick, HEWAA Director, have stated:

. . . one of our long range goals is to develop a national audit network that maximizes the use of outside audit capability. Accomplishment of this goal will provide the Department with reliable assurances that Federal funds are being expended for the purposes for which they were made available with only limited test checking by the Department's auditors. The audit coverage thus provided will release additional Audit Agency manpower for broader review work, such as the evaluation of program performance against established standards, policies, and procedures.

. . . .

We have found that no one set of mutual audit arrangements can serve effectively in all States. The wide variety of organizational responsibility, management attitudes and capabilities, and audit philosophies in the States make a pragmatic and flexible approach to cooperative auditing a necessity.

. . . .

A major point . . . is the importance of regular two-way communication between the parties involved. We have found that merely transmitting audit guides and programs for the States to follow has proved insufficient to insure quality audit reports from State and local governments.[20]

We asked fifty-one SEA managers what they envisioned as the major problems in implementing a program that would allow Federal reliance on audits conducted by the State Audit Agency. The most common responses were, in order of frequency:

. . lack of State auditor competency and ability (13).
. . lack of State manpower, time, money (13).
. . lack of uniform audit standards (10).
. . Federal "over hesitancy" to accept satisfactory State audits (6).
. . different needs, pressures, and goals (4).

We also discussed intergovernmental auditing with the twenty State auditors we interviewed. All felt that "We were far from achieving a viable audit network." The major problems, as they perceive them, were:

. . lack of money which in turn contributes to lack of manpower and competency (14).
. . lack of uniform audit standards and different needs and goals (12).
. . the audit network concept is, to paraphrase, a one way street for the Federal Government — what we can do for them, not what we can do together (9).

CONCLUSIONS

HEW Audit Agency and General Accounting Office efforts to promote intergovernmental audit cooperation are commendable. Realistically, the development of an effective audit network is an awesome and complex task that may never be adequately accomplished. It appears that in the short run, at least, the Federal Audit Agencies will likely continue efforts already initiated. However, achieving the long-run goal of a viable, integrated, cooperative, and effective audit network may ultimately prove to require more extreme measures than those taken to date. In this regard, we feel that the most pressing need is legislation specifically authorizing Federal assistance to State and local audit agencies.

We now have a Federal program that can be used to some extent in this regard — The Intergovernmental Personnel Act of 1970, which:

> Authorizes the Civil Service Commission to furnish technical assistance on personnel administration to State and local governments, and to make grants, on a matching fund basis, for personnel administration improvement.

> Authorizes Federal assistance in training State and local employees and provides for grants by the Civil service Commission on a matching fund basis to State and local governments to train their employees.

> Authorizes grants to certain other organizations to cover in part the costs of training State and local employees.

> Provides authority for the Civil Service Commission to make grants to support programs for 'Government Service Fellowships' for State and local personnel.

> Authorizes the temporary assignment of personnel between the Federal Government and State and local governments and institutions of higher education.

> Transfers to the Civil Service Commission responsibility for administering laws requiring merit personnel administration in certain Federal grant programs.

> Provides for the establishment of an advisory council to the President on intergovernmental personnel policy.[21]

Under this Act, the Governor of each State submits a comprehensive plan and program for his State as a whole. Eighty per cent of each year's appropriated funds is apportioned to the States on the basis of a weighted formula — twenty per cent is discretionary.

The Intergovernmental Personnel Act is a comparatively new piece of legislation. It has not, as of yet, had a significant impact on State auditing. And because it is general aid for all State and local programs, it may never have a major impact. Thus, legislation specifically authorizing assistance for State and local auditing should be actively sought.

Federal "Revenue Sharing" significantly increases the need for immediate action in this regard. Although called "no-strings-attached money" by the press, accountability is required and the Secretary of the Treasury has wide latitude in specifying the degree and nature of necessary audit coverage. Because of the extent of Revenue Sharing, the Federal Government will have to increasingly rely upon State and local audits. Thus, an effective Federal-State-Local Audit Partnership is more essential than ever before and is apt to receive increased Federal attention and support.

CHARACTERISTICS OF SEA/LEA AUDITORS

BACKGROUND REVIEW

To conduct a good audit requires special skills and attributes. The most important of these are *independence, professionalism,* and *competency.*

Independence is one of the essential characteristics of auditing. This is not to say that useful investigations cannot be conducted by individuals closely associated with the auditee. But to be an audit, by definition and custom, it must be the work of a person who is independent in mind, in fact, and in appearance.

Professionalism has two basic components: *ethics* and *standards.* The nature of auditing and the need for continuing public respect evidence the special obligations and responsibilities that auditors in all fields have as members of the profession of auditing. Thus, both the AICPA and the IIA have developed Rules of Professional Conduct (ethics) for Auditors.

Auditing standards are criterions of both audit acceptability and excellence. Though the most widely accepted auditing standards are those of the AICPA, the General Accounting Office recently (June, 1972) issued a set of standards which are much more appropriate for governmental auditing.

The auditor's knowledge of auditing, coupled with his care in conducting an audit, are referred to as auditor *competency.* The auditor must possess satisfactory knowledge to conduct an adequate review. Background or experience in accounting is required for a financial audit. For a compliance audit, familiarity with programs, legislation, regulations, guidelines, rules, and policies is needed. A performance audit *may* require additional auditor skills. For example, recommendations in a technical field require that the auditor either possess technical knowledge or have technical assistance available.

However, the auditor — through his college training, special training, and experience — is an expert in the area of internal controls, both financial and management. These are basic controls which are necessary for any organization to operate economically, efficiently, and effectively — as good business practices apply to almost any activity. Through their familiarity with analytical procedures, coupled with intelligence, auditors can often make meaningful recommendations in technical areas. Too, they can measure against objectives and standards prepared by experts, or note that objectives and standards have not been established.

Though it is difficult for one individual to be qualified in all areas, the audit staff — either as a whole or through the use of experts in special situations — should be qualified in all areas that they are called upon to evaluate. The best competencies for the individual auditor are: rigorous college training in accounting and management, continuing professional development and special training, plus that innate ability often referred to as "good common sense."

Thus, an auditor should possess the following characteristics: (1) he should be *independent* of the auditee and the auditee's activities; (2) he should be *professional,* that is — he should practice *ethical* conduct and recognize and abide by modern audit *standards;* and (3) he should be *competent* to conduct the audits he is called upon to perform.

FINDINGS

Our study of the audit environment of public education revealed no general weaknesses with regard to either auditor *independence* or *ethics.* However, we did note that there is presently no "Code of Ethics" especially tailored for, and adopted by, governmental auditors.

With regard to audit *standards,* it has been noted previously that there is a need for widespread adoption and implementation of uniform audit standards that conform to the modern concept of governmental auditing. The General Accounting Office has provided such standards in their publication, *Standards for Audit of Governmental Organizations, Programs, Activities, and Functions.*[22]

SEA managers were asked a number of questions that ranked

auditor competency by category or agency.

   . . 44 SEA managers answered, "What is your general
   opinion of the quality of LEA audits?" On a scale from
   1 (excellent) to 4 (poor):
   >   Federal auditors ranked 1.8
   >   SEA auditors ranked 2.2
   >   State auditors ranked 2.4
   >   CPA auditors ranked 3.2

   . . 35 SEA managers answered, "Which audits are most
   beneficial to your SEA management?" On a scale from
   1 (most) to 4 (least):
   >   State audits ranked 1.6
   >   Federal audits ranked 2.9
   >   CPA audits ranked 3.4

   . . 34 SEA managers answered, "Which auditors seem to be
   the best qualified and most competent?" On a scale from
   1 (best) to 4 (least):

   >   For *Fiscal* Audits
   >   State auditors ranked 1.8
   >   Federal auditors ranked 1.9
   >   CPA auditors ranked 3.2

   >   For *Educational Program* Audits
   >   Federal auditors ranked 1.9
   >   State auditors ranked 2.6
   >   CPA auditors ranked 3.6

The most critical matter with regard to SEA auditor competencies was a general feeling reflected in both the interviews and questionnaires that auditors are *not* presently qualified to conduct performance audits. Seventy-eight SEA managers answered, "In your opinion in which areas are auditors (in general) presently qualified to conduct audits?" On a scale from 1 (highly qualified) to 4 (not qualified):

>   Fiscal ranked 1.6
>   Compliance ranked 2.2
>   Performance ranked 3.5

This does not necessarily mean that auditors are *actually* unqualified to conduct performance audits. What it does indicate is a lack of confidence in auditor ability on the part of SEA managers. It should be remembered that these same managers were receptive to the potential usefulness and practicality of performance auditing (79% responded with "excellent" or "very helpful"). Hence, it appears that lack of confidence in current auditor competency is a major, if not *the* major, objection that SEA managers would have to performance audits of their State Education Agencies.

In order to gain a clearer perspective of current auditor competencies, we examined the background and training of the auditors of HEW Audit Agency, GAO, the State Audit Agencies, and the CPA profession.

HEW Audit Agency

The majority of personnel vacancies in the HEW Audit Agency are filled by auditor interns recruited from colleges and universities. Approximately 125 interns were recruited from 1965-1969, all of which had, as a minimum, a general background in accounting and auditing as part of their college training.

New trainees receive three weeks of formal training during their first six months of employment. The first week is given by the appropriate regional office and the second and third weeks are conducted by the central office. Basically, this initial instruction covers orientation and indoctrination in the Audit Agency's programs, policies, and audit techniques.

Throughout his career with HEWAA, the auditor receives continual training, averaging approximately three weeks per year. The agency offers over twenty different courses in the general areas of Audit Techniques, Management, Behavioral Sciences, and Communication. To encourage off-duty training HEWAA reimburses the full cost of work-related courses in graduate schools, CPA coaching courses, and programs sponsored by professional societies.[23]

The General Accounting Office

GAO recruits new employees from universities, other governmental agencies, accounting firms, and industry. Most are hired without pre-employment testing on the basis of their backgrounds and promotions are based upon ability and performance. A special GAO division, the Office of Personnel Management, is devoted to auditor recruitment and training. Direct training costs of the General Accounting Office amount to nearly two million dollars annually.

In the early stages of the auditor's preparation, training emphasis is placed upon conceptual understanding. Procedural instruction comes primarily from on-the-job training. The new auditor quickly gets exposure—two or three audits in the first few months, interspersed with in-house training seminars.

Sometime during his first few months of the job, the new auditor attends a General Orientation Program. During this five-day orientation, instructors give new employees a concrete idea of the work they will be doing through discussion of audit techniques, the use and analysis of evidence, and relations with the Congress and Executive Agencies.

Within their first six months in GAO, new auditors attend a one week Central Orientation Program in Washington. This comprehensive orientation on how GAO operates, includes presentations by Division Directors and the Comptroller General. First year auditors also attend six short technical seminars covering specific audit and management techniques used by GAO. In the second and third years, the auditor attends a two week intermediate training seminar concerning (1) communication skills, (2) evidence, (3) system analysis, (4) statistical sampling, and (5) audit approaches.

State Audit Agencies

As would be expected, the background, training, and qualifications of the state audit agency staffs varies greatly from state to state. A few states have little or no requirements, while others require an accounting degree and high class ranking. SEA managers were asked to report the qualifications of their state audit staff(s). Concerning 53 state audit agencies, they report:

> CPA certificate - 9 (17%)
> Accounting degree - 37 (70%)
> State examination - 21 (40%)
> Experience - 18 (34%)
> No requirements - 3 (6%)
> (Does not add to 53 because some State Audit Agencies require a combination of qualifications.)

Certified Public Accountants

A majority of states require or will soon require a college degree with a major in accounting as the minimum education requirement for the CPA certificate. In addition, most states require a certain amount of prior accounting experience. Two years is the most common experience requirement with some states allowing graduate education as a substitute for at least one year's experience.

The "uniform" part of CPA certification is the examination. All states have adopted the uniform CPA Exam prepared and graded by the Board of Examiners of the AICPA. This is a rigorous two-and-a-half day examination in accounting practice, accounting theory, auditing, and business law. It is offered twice a year and the percentage of passing grades is rather low.

Many practicing CPAs participate actively in a State Society of CPAs. They may also belong to one or more of the national accounting societies. These associations provide a variety of services and programs, many of which contribute directly to the CPA's continuing education; also many CPA firms sponsor or support training and continuing education programs for their staff. Currently, the CPA profession is considering the feasibility of amending statutes and regulations to require all public accountants to give evidence of a certain number of hours every three years in professional development courses as a basis for continuing registration.

Educational Program Competency

What the foregoing information concerning HEWAA, GAO, State, and CPA auditors does not show is individual differences in auditor competency. As in any field, similar exposure to training and instruction can have varying impacts on different individuals. Thus, there exists today a wide range of actual auditor competencies. But to the extent that generalization is possible, it appears that auditor background and training is, for the most part, adequate.

Auditors of SEAs are generally well-qualified with regard to accounting practices and auditing techniques. Also, college accounting curriculums usually include courses in management theory and controls. Continuing education programs and training courses for auditors may also be management oriented and on-the-job audit experiences in a variety of organizations gives the auditor further exposure to management systems and techniques. This background in management coupled with the auditor's analytical ability (as demonstrated by his training in accounting) makes him generally well-qualified to review, analyze, and evaluate management control systems. He can also evaluate technical activities by comparing against standards prepared by experts.

Further questioning revealed a more specific concern on the part of SEA managers relative to auditor competencies.

. . Sixty-three SEA managers answered, "Which term best

describes the auditor's competency (by governmental agency)?" On a scale from 1 (excellent) to 5 (poor):

For *Fiscal* Audits

a. GAO auditors ranked 1.5
b. State auditors ranked 2.1
c. HEW auditors ranked 2.2

In *Educational Program* matters

a. GAO auditors ranked 3.2
b. State auditors ranked 3.6
c. HEW auditors ranked 4.1

The Project staff would not necessarily agree with the agency rankings, but the difference between the SEA managers' opinion of Fiscal Audit competency and Educational Program Audit competency is strikingly clear. Apparently, SEA managers question the auditor's competency to conduct performance audits of SEAs because they believe that a knowledge and background in Education is a necessary requisite for such auditing. Ideally, this would include a knowledge of compliance matters that affect State Education Agencies, familiarity with major Educational programs and the environment of Education, and a background in Educational theory and technique.

SEA managers did seem to feel, however, that this weakness could be overcome through the use of audit teams and/or auditor specialization.

. . Thirty-two SEA managers answered, "What would be your reaction to a team approach to auditing (e.g., OE program people working with the HEW auditors, for example)?"

87% were receptive, positive, or hopeful.

13% were cautious or negative.

. . Thirty-three SEA managers answered, "What would be your reaction to Federal Auditors specializing in Educational Audits?"

85% were receptive, positive, or hopeful.

15% were cautious or negative.

CONCLUSIONS

With regard to auditor *ethics*, we feel that there is a need for a code of ethics especially tailored for governmental auditors. For State auditors, such a code could possibly be developed through the auspices of either the National Legislative Conference or the National

Association of State Auditors, Comptrollers, and Treasurers.

Relative to audit *standards,* the AIDE Project strongly endorses the recently issued *Standards for Audit of Governmental Organizations, Programs, Activities and Functions.*[24] We urge the formal adoption and promulgation of these standards by all governmental audit agencies.

In general, the ranking of auditor *competencies,* as perceived by SEA managers was: (1) Federal Agencies, (2) State Agencies, and (3) CPAs. This may come as a surprise to many members of the CPA profession. Though we have no direct evidence, we feel that there is a link between the SEA's opinion of CPA's competencies and CPA reluctance to conduct compliance and performance audits. Thus, we believe that CPAs should seriously consider improving their contribution to State Education through changed audit approaches.

To the extent that generalization is possible, auditors of SEAs appear to be competent in the areas of accounting and management controls. However, a majority of SEA managers feel that auditors are not presently qualified to conduct performance audits of SEAs. This *does not* necessarily mean that auditors are unqualified to conduct such audits. It does mean that SEA managers lack confidence in the auditor's ability.

More specifically, SEA managers are particularly concerned about the auditor's knowledge of *Educational* matters. Theoretically, a meaningful performance audit of controls can be conducted without such technical knowledge. However, we feel that auditors of SEAs and LEAs should seriously consider (1) including an educator on the audit team, and/or (2) developing audit teams that specialize in educational audits. Such action could result in a speedier, more comprehensive, and more acceptable audit. Possibly the attitude of SEA managers will moderate if and when auditors prove themselves through the conduct of meaningful performance audits of State Education Agencies that are a definite aid to SEA management.

BEHAVIORAL CONSIDERATIONS

BACKGROUND REVIEW

Recent research and authoritative opinion indicates a general need for better auditor-auditee relations. Poor relationships are a function of (1) the objective of auditing, discussed earlier, and (2) personal traits of the auditor and the auditee manager. Most writers in this area feel that, since auditing is the auditor's profession, he has the primary responsibility for improving relations. Some suggested ways of doing this are:

1. Have frequent meetings with the auditee.
2. Show a sincere interest in his job and its problems.
3. Try to look at things from the auditee's perspective.
4. Convey the impression that you want to "help" rather than "police." Prove it by your actions.
5. Avoid being secretive — learn to communicate.
6. Try not to carry preconceived notions and attitudes.
7. Do not argue — be a professional.
8. Give praise when it is warranted.
9. Do not present findings as criticisms, but as problems needing solutions.
10. *Learn to listen.*

FINDINGS

Fifty-five SEA managers (from both the interviews and questionnaires) answered, "It is often said that the attitude of management toward auditors and the auditor's attitude regarding management is not of a positive nature. (A) Do you generally agree with this? (B) If so, how may it be changed?"

    (A) A majority (60%) agree.
    (B) The most commonly suggested solution was improved communications, coupled with a better understanding of the other's role.

An interesting discovery was that relations seem to begin as *positive and friendly,* then deteriorate to *cordial* by the end of the audit. Thirty-three SEA managers answered, "(For Federal Audits) What terms best describe the relationship between SEA management and the auditor?"

TABLE 14
MANAGER — AUDITOR RELATIONSHIPS

Response	At the Beginning of the Audit	At the End of the Audit
Positive & Friendly	55%	30%
Cordial	39%	61%
Indifferent	3%	6%
Slightly negative	3%	3%

In general, working relations are better between SEA managers and State auditors than Federal auditors. Forty SEA respondents answered, "Generally, what is the working relationship between the auditor and the SEA staff?"

TABLE 15
MANAGER — AUDITOR WORKING RELATIONSHIP

Response	Federal Auditors	State Auditors
Excellent or Very Good	37%	77%
Good	51%	13%
Fair	9%	8%
Poor	3%	2%

Four SEA managers (10%) indicated fair to poor State Auditor relationships. Two of these stated that they felt the State Audit Agency had enjoyed newspaper publicity at the expense of their State Education Agency.

Finally, our interviews with State Auditors, Federal Auditors, and OE Personnel indicated that a majority also recognized a need for improved auditor - SEA auditee relations.

CONCLUSIONS

It is not surprising that State Auditor-SEA relations are generally better than Federal Auditor-SEA relations. State auditors and SEA managers are both members of State government. Often they are closely and continually associated with each other — sometimes sharing the same office building, and some State auditors are permanently assigned to the State Education Agency.

A majority of SEA managers felt that the attitude of SEA management toward auditors and the auditor's attitude regarding management is not, in general, of a positive nature. Our interviews with State Auditors, Federal Auditors, and OE personnel supported this contention.

Poor auditor-SEA relations can in turn restrict the scope and effectiveness of SEA auditing. For example, poor relations may cause the auditor to meet with resistance in the conduct stage of his audit and the SEA may later resist acceptance and implementation of audit recommendations. It is particularly unfortunate for good audit recommendations to be ignored or restricted by the SEA when the underlying cause is a poor auditor-auditee relationship. But this does happen and we have seen a number of such incidences during the course of this study.

If performance auditing is to have a really significant impact upon SEA management, this relationship must be improved. SEA managers and auditors should make *intentional* efforts in this direction. However, the responsibility for a major effort in this regard rests with the professional auditor. We would like to see all SEA auditors follow the previously listed ten steps toward improved relations.

SEA/LEA AUDIT PROCESSES

BACKGROUND REVIEW

The process of any audit consists of four basic stages: Preparation, Conduct, Reporting, and Settlement. Exact approaches to an audit can vary according to the auditor or audit agency, the nature of the auditee (and audit recipient), and the scope and objective of the audit. The following steps or action categories are general and suggestive only and are certainly not exhaustive. However, exclusion of any of these steps should be intentional, rather than accidental.

SUGGESTED STEPS IN THE AUDIT PROCESS

Preparation

    I.   Decision to Make the Audit
    II.   Selection of the Audit Team
    III.   Pre-engagement Contact
    IV.   Auditor Familiarization
    V.   First Draft of the Audit Plan
    VI.   Audit Entrance Conference
    VII.   The Walk-Through
    VIII.   Revision of the Audit Plan

Conduct

    I.   The Preliminary Survey
    II.   Verification and Evaluation

Reporting

   I. Continuous Reporting to the Auditee
  II. Flash Reports to the Audit Recipient
 III. The Draft Report
 IV. The Audit Exit Conference
  V. The Final Audit Report
 VI. Distribution of the Audit Report

Settlement

   I. Evaluation of Audit Findings and Recommendations
  II. Joint Agreement on a Plan of Action
 III. Audit Recipient Review of Corrective Action
 IV. Audit Agency Follow-Up

FINDINGS

PREPARATION

I. Decision to Make the Audit

HEW Audit Agency develops an annual audit work plan which is prepared in view of available manpower coupled with HEW priorities, such as:

  . . . Sensitivity
  . . . Dollar Amount
  . . . Past Problems
  . . . Interest in Program
  . . . Regional Requests

In addition, audits can be initiated by special requests (such as OE, SEA, or LEA request) complaints from the public, or request from public officials.

Questionnaire responses and SEA interviews indicate that SEA managers are concerned about the frequency of HEWAA audits. In response to the general, open-end question "How could the HEW audit be of greater use in your SEA?" — eleven of twenty-six respondents suggested that HEW audits needed to be more *frequent* and *current*. Furthermore, in response to another open-end question "What do you consider to be most pressing problems relative to audits of your SEA?" — fifteen of thirty-two SEA respondents indicated the *timeliness* of audits.

Several OE officials expressed the same feeling as did several HEWAA auditors. To quote one HEWAA auditor, "We need to be around in the implementation of programs; the army does this — we can do it too!"

HEWAA audits are current in the sense that they do include recent program activities as well as past activities. What the SEA managers apparently object to are those audits that go back four or more years, because:

    . . . The original personnel involved may no longer be with the SEA or LEA.
    . . . Maintenance of old files is a nuisance.
    . . . Old problems may not be particularly significant or appropriate relative to current activities.

On the other hand, more frequent audits may not be worth the added audit cost, because HEWAA cannot increase SEA audit frequency, without sacrifice to other programs, except through additional manpower and increased costs (or by reducing the time on each SEA audit).

GAO audits are initiated in two ways: (1) by congressional request, about ten per cent, or (2) as part of GAO's regular audit program. GAO's Washington headquarters develops a long range (three-year) audit plan; and the specific areas in which GAO auditors will be working is determined every six months.

Ten of the thirteen State audit agencies visited (77%) indicated that they develop annual-biannual audit plans and eight of twenty-six SEA's that reported having an SEA/LEA Audit program indicated that an annual audit plan was prepared. Twenty-six of thirty-four states reporting LEA audits by CPAs (76%) indicated that they are regularly scheduled on a yearly basis.

There does appear, however, to be a need for better audit guidance at the LEA level. OE regulations require that SEAs establish audit guidelines for LEA audits. But fifteen of our sample of forty HEW audits (thirty-eight per cent) mentioned or implied the need for better LEA audit guidance. All four GAO Title I audits implied the same thing.

II. Selection of the Audit Team

SEA questionnaire and interview responses indicate that most SEA audits are conducted by audit teams. Tabulation of these responses reveals that:

    . . . HEWAA, on the average, sends an audit team of three (range one-five).

. . . GAO, on the average, sends an audit team of three (range two-six).

. . . SAA audit team size (forty-three responses).
one — 9% of the time.
two — 47% of the time.
three — 19% of the time.
four or more — 25% of the time.

. . . SEAs and CPAs usually send one man to audit the LEAs (range 1-3).

All of these audit agencies usually designate a team leader — generally the most experienced member.

These audit teams have seldom included educators. In fact, we are aware of only one instance where outside educational specialists were included on a team auditing an SEA. However, HEWAA and GAO have on occasion used experts in their audits in other fields (such as the use of medical doctors on Medicaid audits).

Some audit agencies have developed in-house audit specialists by assigning the same men, when possible, to SEA/LEA audits. For instance, GAO has used some of the same personnel in their several Title I audits. A few of the HEWAA auditors interviewed (not necessarily a representative sample) felt that HEW Audit Agency had not taken full advantage of the possibility of auditor specialization. In this regard, the regionalization of Federal offices, while organizationally sound, does tend to retard auditor specialization. Perhaps auditor specialists could be used inter-regionally. Representatives of the thirteen State Audit Agencies interviewed indicated that, when possible, they assign the same men to SEA/LEA audits.

III. Pre-Engagement Contact

Responses from twenty-three SEA manager and twelve State auditors are presented in Tables 16-19.

TABLE 16
HOW IS INITIAL CONTACT USUALLY MADE
PREPARATORY TO AN AUDIT?

Response Total Number	HEWAA (23)	GAO (3)	State Auditor (12)
Letter	35%	33%	8%
Phone Call	35%	67%	50%
Visitation	13%	—	25%
Combination	17%	—	17%

TABLE 17
WHO IS FIRST CONTACTED?

Responses Total Number	HEWAA (23)	GAO (3)	State Auditor (12)
Chief State School Officer	39%	33%	25%
Associate Superintendent	13%	—	8%
Financial Officer	26%	33%	50%
Program Director	22%	33%	17%

TABLE 18
WHAT PRELIMINARY INFORMATION OR ACTION IS
ASKED FOR AT THIS TIME?

Responses Total Number	HEWAA (23)	GAO (3)	State Auditor (12)
Entrance Conference (scheduled)	17%	—	8%
Contact Official (designated)	22%	33%	—
Financial Statements	43%	67%	—
Guides & Regulations	57%	33%	33%
No Information Requested	35%	33%	67%

TABLE 19
HOW MUCH WARNING (LEAD-TIME) IS
THE SEA GIVEN?

Response Total Number	HEWAA (23)	GAO (3)	State Auditor (12)
1 week	22%	—	—
2 weeks	43%	67%	50%
3 weeks	4%	—	17%
1 month	9%	—	25%
2 months	17%	—	8%
more	4%	33%	—

Table 16 indicates that Federal auditors are more inclined to make formal contact with the SEA (by letter) then are State auditors. However, a phone call appears to be the most common means of initial contact.

Surprisingly, the Chief State School Officer usually is *not* the first SEA official to be contacted. On the surface, at least, this appears to be a break with generally accepted protocol. It may be, however, that some auditors first contact a subordinate official and ask him to arrange a later meeting with the CSSO or, perhaps, a subordinate official has been previously designated to act in behalf of the CSSO for purposes of auditing.

Table 18 reveals that auditors are not taking full advantage of this initial opportunity to (1) ask for a contact official, (2) schedule an entrance conference, or (3) request that preliminary information be readied or forwarded. Thirteen SEA managers indicated in the open-end question, "How do you think the auditor could better prepare for the audit?" that they would appreciate receiving advance notice of auditor needs or desires.

Table 19 shows that audit lead-time (advance warning) is generally one week to a month. Our interviews indicate that SEA managers feel, with some exceptions, that lead-time is usually adequate for their purposes.

IV. Auditor Familiarization, and
V. First Draft of the Audit Plan

Both HEWAA and GAO have developed large libraries of audit guides and programs for use by their auditors. HEWAA, for example, has a collection of general audit guides and programs plus specific guides tailor-made for each HEW program. Also, ten of thirteen state audit agencies visited indicated that they provided some kind of audit guide or guides for their staff. (Not surprisingly, the three agencies with the broadest audit scope — Washington's State Auditor, California's Department of Finance, and California's Auditor General's Office — had the most comprehensive and detailed guides.)

HEWAA's 1966 ESEA Title I Audit Guide states that prior to initiating the audit, the following information should be obtained:

. . State application and budget materials.
. . Financial reports.
. . Prior period audit working papers.
. . Correspondence pertinent to the audit.
. . Information as to administrative review findings which

require audit action.

. . Copies of program guidelines or other information relative to the program prepared by the Program Operations Division, Office of Education.

. . Title I regulations.[25]

GAO officials indicated that auditor familiarization was part of their audit program. "We consult legislation, state plans, regulations, and program guides." Representatives of four of the thirteen state audit agencies interviewed—the four that conducted performance audits—indicated that their auditors also familiarize themselves prior to entering the SEA.

SEA managers were especially critical of HEWAA auditor familiarization with educational programs. Forty-two SEA managers (both questionnaires and interviews) answered the "open end" question: "How do you think HEW auditors could better prepare for the audit?" *Ninety-three per cent* (thirty-nine) felt that HEW auditors were not adequately familiar with educational program matters prior to initiating the audit.

VI. Audit Entrance Conference

Fifty-eight SEA managers (interviews and questionnaires) were asked:

TABLE 20
WHAT TYPE OF ENTRANCE CONFERENCE DOES THE AUDITOR GENERALLY HAVE WITH YOUR SEA?

Responses	HEWAA	GAO	State Auditor
Formal	40%	83%	12%
Informal	57%	17%	36%
Occasional Entrance Conference	3%	—	36%
No Entrance Conference	—	—	16%

(Interviews with SEA managers indicated that SEA/CPA audits of LEAs generally do not include formal entrance conferences, per se.)

Our interviews with GAO officials disclosed that in their entrance conference they generally:

  . . Try to have all interested parties in attendance, including the Chief State School Officer.
  . . Discuss the general nature of the audit.
  . . Make necessary work arrangements, such as obtaining
space and establishing working relationships.

A significant aspect of the entrance conference in need of
strengthening was revealed by the interviews. It seems that most auditors do *not* at this time (or apparently later) ask if the SEA managers
have "any specific areas they would like for the auditor to examine or
if he could be of service in any way as a by-product of his investigation." Of thirty-three total SEA responses, 85% indicated that auditors seldom ask if they can be of assistance (eighty-nine per cent for
HEWAA, fifty per cent for GAO, and seventy-nine per cent for State
audits).

VII. The Walk-Through, and
VIII. Revision of the Audit Plan

We obtained no specific information concerning these steps.
However, these steps are undoubtedly part of some of the audit agencies' preliminary surveys.

CONDUCT

I. The Preliminary Survey

The draft revision of HEWAA's Title I Audit Guide contains a
section concerning the "on-site" preliminary survey. (The current Title I Audit Guide calls for pre-audit "preliminary planning.")

PRELIMINARY SURVEY

Reviews of LEA projects should begin at the SEA. The
auditor should become familiar with the SEA's methods
and procedures for administering the program and
knowledgeable of the types, locations, and scope of projects
throughout the State. He should also review any sources of
information that would provide insight into any problem
that may exist in LEA projects.

Some suggested sources of information follow:

1. Organization and staffing charts and descriptions of staff responsibilities.

2. Approved LEA project applications and related project review documents prepared by the SEA.

3. SEA instructions issued to the LEAs.

4. Written policies and procedures for reviewing LEA project applications and expenditure reports.

5. Written policies and procedures for SEA monitoring of project activities.

6. Project evaluation and expenditure reports submitted by LEAs.

7. Prior audit reports, including those by the General Accounting Office, the SEA, and independent auditors.

8. Correspondence on the results of on-site administrative and management reviews by the SEA and OE.

In those instances where policies and procedures have not been reduced to writing, or the procedures are not clearly defined, the auditor will need to obtain or supplement the above information by interviewing cognizant SEA officials.

After analyzing the information obtained at the SEA, the auditor should be able to make an informed selection of LEAs for detailed audit and should also be alert to problem areas that may be encountered during detailed reviews.[26]

GAO also conducts a preliminary survey "as a means of obtaining familiarity and a working knowledge of the operations and related records being examined." GAO's fourth standard of examination and evaluation states:

An evaluation is to be made of the system of internal control to assess the extent it can be relied upon to insure accurate information, to insure compliance with laws and regulations, and to provide for efficient and effective operations.[27]

However, our interviews with HEW and GAO auditors indicate that they do not use a *standardized* preliminary survey guide or questionnaire.

Only three State audit agencies (out of thirteen) indicated that they require a formal preliminary survey. However, one of these three, the Washington State Auditor's Office, had the most detailed and extensive survey instructions located in the course of our research.

CPAs usually conduct a preliminary survey in order to determine the reliance they will place upon the internal financial control system. The AICPA's second audit standard of field work is:

> There is to be a proper study and evaluation of the existing internal control as a basis for reliance thereon and for the determination of the resultant extent of the tests to which auditing procedures are to be restricted.[28]

II. Verification and Evaluation

Verification and evaluation procedures vary according to audit agency policy and the nature and scope of the audit. For example, HEWAA and GAO are now moving toward a compliance/performance audit. HEWAA has changed its approach considerably in recent years. For purposes of comparison, note that HEWAA's 1966 (still current) ESEA Title I Audit Guide lists and discusses the following areas for audit coverage.

I. Program Administration
II. Financial Administration
    a. General
    b. Salaries and wages
    c. Travel and transportation
    d. Rental of space
    e. Supplies, materials, communications, rental of equipment
    f. Allocation of administrative costs
    g. Equipment[29]

The 1973 draft revision of the same audit guide provides for an audit activity of much broader scope.

I. Preliminary Survey
II. Selected Audit Areas
    a. Selection of target schools and concentration of Title I funds
    b. Design and evaluation of projects
    c. Supplemental use of funds and comparability of services

> d. Procurement of equipment, materials and facilities
> e. Project activities in private schools
> f. Fiscal control and reporting
> g. Follow-up on previously reported findings and recommendations.[30]

Our interviews with GAO personnel indicate that they follow a similar audit approach. Unfortunately, GAO Audit Guides are considered confidential and were not made available to the project.

Federal auditors usually begin their reviews in the SEA with an examination and evaluation of pertinent records, financial statements, and other relevant data coupled with interviews with program managers and accountants. Their audits will usually move to the LEA level and a statistical sample of school districts will be visited. However, some audits — especially those triggered by Congressional or public request — may start at and be directed toward a specific school district.

Of particular concern to many of the Federal Auditors interviewed were those instances of SEA reluctance or outright opposition to Federal on-site reviews at the LEA Level (Four states were mentioned as refusing to allow on-site LEA audits by Federal Auditors). To determine SEA attitudes in this regard, we asked fifty-two SEA managers from forty-five states how they felt about GAO and HEWAA auditors going directly to the LEAs to make audits. In response, fifteen (29%) felt that this was necessary, thirty-seven (71%) were against it.

Federal auditors undoubtedly have the legal authority to conduct LEA reviews. (For instance, see the Intergovernmental Cooperation Act of 1968, the enabling legislation of specific grant programs, and Federal and State "contracts" in the form of "State Plans.") However, they have avoided forcing the issue in those cases where there is clear opposition. But restriction of an auditor's freedom to conduct on-site examinations is a clear and severe compromise of his independence. The reliability of any audit conducted under such circumstances is subject to serious question.

In the course of our interviews with HEWAA and GAO auditors, we discovered that they do not, at the present time, use standardized auditor work papers (fairly detailed, preprinted forms tailor-made for an audit of a specific program or activity). Because of the similarities of educational audits, it would seem that standardized work papers would be particularly effective in the SEA/LEA environment.

We did note an interesting difference in HEWAA and GAO audits: GAO audits take about twice as long. For example, the GAO Illinois ESEA Title I audit took 1,600 man hours; while HEWAA audits, we were told, average 600 to 800 man hours.

We also asked SEA managers what they thought about HEWAA's and GAO's piecemeal — one Federal program at a time — approach to SEA auditing. (To review only one Federal program per audit when an SEA administers many appears to be, on the surface at least, rather uneconomical.) Of fifty-three SEA responses, twenty-five (46%) favored the piecemeal approach, sixteen would rather have multi-program audits, and twelve had no preference. However, OE personnel indicated that multi-program audits were administratively difficult to settle. For instance, an HEWAA audit of seven selected programs conducted in New York's SEA in 1968 was still open several years later.

We also asked, "Does the auditor's examination ever interfere in any way with the routine activities of the SEA?" and "Does the auditor promptly return records and files?" Auditors in all categories scored "high marks" in both regards. Apparently, most auditors are careful to avoid interfering with normal SEA routine.

REPORTING

I. Continuous Reporting to the Auditee

HEWAA's draft revision of the ESEA Title I Audit Guide states:

All audit findings should be discussed with responsible LEA and SEA officials to insure that facts supporting the findings are accurate. The discussion should be held as the findings are developed. At the same time, the auditor should document the official comments on concurrence or nonconcurrence with findings, including corrective measures taken or to be taken, and reasons for non-compliance. Depending upon the nature of the findings and auditor's judgement of circumstances, it may be advantageous to present draft findings in writing and to request that LEA and SEA officials furnish their written responses.[31]

Fifty-seven SEA managers were asked:

TABLE 21
DOES THE AUDITOR GENERALLY DISCUSS PROBLEMS OR AUDIT EXCEPTIONS WITH SEA PERSONNEL AS HE ENCOUNTERS THEM?

Response	HEWAA	GAO	State Auditor
Always	14%	40%	19%
Usually	46%	40%	53%
Occasionally	19%	20%	19%
Seldom	7%	—	—
Never	14%	—	9%

Apparently, most auditors keep SEA management informed of audit developments as they occur. However, HEW's twenty-one per cent "seldom or never" appears high in view of changed approaches reported by HEWAA. Perhaps publication of the revised Title I Guide will clarify HEWAA policies in this regard for its auditors.

II. Flash Reports to the Audit Recipient

We are unaware of any audit agency that, as a matter of regular policy, issues interim reports on matters of immediate interest to an educational audit recipient (OE or SEA recipient).

III. The Draft Report

A recent ESEA Title I memo states with regard to HEWAA's draft audit policy:

> The HEW Audit Agency will issue a draft audit report to the State Educational agency, the appropriate Regional Commissioner and to Office of Education Headquarters, for their information and use in preparing for the audit exit conference. The draft report will be issued in sufficient time prior to the scheduled date of the exit conference, so that those officials who will attend the exit conference may prepare themselves fully for active participation in that conference.[32]

However, SEAs have not always received draft audit reports from

HEW auditors ahead of time. Fifty-one SEA managers answered:

TABLE 22
WHEN DO YOU FIRST SEE A DRAFT OF
THE HEWAA AUDIT REPORT?

Responses	Number	Percent
Before Exit Conference	26	51%
At Exit Conference	6	12%
After Exit Conference	19	37%

Thus, almost half (49%) did not receive a draft audit report prior to the exit conference.

GAO also develops draft audit reports:

> Drafts of reports are usually prepared in the first instance by the audit staffs who made the audits. These drafts are reviewed first in the local regional office and then sent to the appropriate Washington operating division of the General Accounting Office for consideration.[33]

However, we learned from GAO representatives that their auditors do not present a draft report to SEA management prior to the exit conference (or, apparently, after the exit conference). "Our exit conference is for comments only — we do not present the audit report at the exit conference. In other words, SEA management has not as yet seen our comments in writing." Apparently, GAO does not submit draft reports to OE either. Thus, their audit report drafts are for GAO internal use only.

Our interviews with State auditors and SEA managers indicated that State Audit Agencies, SEA external auditors, and CPAs usually do not issue draft reports. However, State auditors often discuss their findings informally with SEA management. To quote a recent study of State legislative auditing practices:

> As a general practice, the Auditor discusses his findings and recommendations with the head of the agency before the report is officially released. This procedure provides for an opportunity to resolve, if possible, any areas of disagreement, controversies or ambiguous situations that may have developed. Some states even allow the agency to implement the Auditor's recommendations before the report is issued.[34]

IV. The Audit Exit Conference

Fifty-four SEA managers were asked:

TABLE 23
HOW DOES THE AUDITOR USUALLY CONCLUDE
THE AUDIT?

Response	HEWAA	GAO	State Auditor
Formal Exit Conference	43%	80%	16%
Informal Exit Conference	22%	—	42%
Both Informal & Formal Exit Conference	31%	20%	—
No Conference	4%	—	42%

Thus, while federal auditors almost always hold an exit conference, forty-two percent of our respondents indicate that their State auditors do not.

SEA managers were also asked:

TABLE 24
IF A (FEDERAL) EXIT CONFERENCE
IS HELD, WHO ATTENDS?

Response	Number	Percent
Chief State School Officer	31	62%
State Program Coordinator	44	88%
State Finance Personnel	33	74%
OE Personnel	16	32%
Other Federal Auditors	23	46%

Noticeably, the Chief State School officer was in attendance only two-thirds of the time, and OE personnel only one-third of the time. OE representatives told us that they would like to attend more exit conferences, but had neither the time nor the money to do so.

Quite possibly, however, there may be greater OE participation in the audit exit conference in the near future. Recent changes in HEW Audit Agency procedures include:

.. Notifying (at least ten days in advance) both Regional and Washington OE Action Officials of the time and place of the exit conference.

.. Furnishing the action officials with a draft report (or with findings and recommendations) prior to the exit conference.

Fifty-three SEA managers (from both the interviews and questionnaires) were asked:

TABLE 25
WHAT IS THE PURPOSE OF THE
(FEDERAL) EXIT CONFERENCE?

Response	Number	Percent
To discuss auditor's findings	53	100%
To explain SEA position	28	53%
To assist auditor in completing audit	19	36%
To work out as many exceptions as possible	24	45%
To aid SEA management	22	42%

Two somewhat surprising observations can be drawn from these responses; (1) only 53% of the SEA managers thought that the purpose of the exit conference was to explain the state position; but (2) some 45% thought that the purpose was to work out audit exceptions. (The objectives of an audit exit conference certainly include explaining the SEA position but, they are not presently conducted for the purpose of working out, at that time, audit exceptions.)

V. The Final Audit Report

For certain significant audit reports, HEW Audit Agency has recently developed a special "Pre-Release Procedure." This will apply to reports:

.. with recommended financial adjustments, prospective savings, or other monetary items of *$100,000* or more; or findings with dollar amounts that are relatively

significant in relation to the total activity
.. which are of a controversial nature or management findings that reflect seriously on the overall efficiency of the
administration of HEW; or precedent type issues.
.. related to the accomplishment of Departmental Operational objectives included by operating agencies in the
Operational Planning System (OPS) and selected for
monitoring by the Secretary.[35]

In such cases, HEW Audit Agency will prepare, following the exit
conference, a "proposed final report" which is submitted to OE for
review and comment. Also submitted are written comments from the
SEA and/or notes made at the exit conference.

OE has *thirty* days in which to respond to the issues in the report.
If OE and HEWAA cannot reach agreement on the issues, either party
may submit the matter for arbitration. They will have five days in
which to request that the Assistant Secretary, Comptroller arbitrate the
differences. Should OE choose not to arbitrate or should they fail to
respond within the 30 day period, the audit report will be issued "as
is."

This "Pre-Release Procedure" has been developed to insure that:

. . . where possible, the recommendations in the
final reports will represent the position not only of the
Audit Agency, but also of the operating agency. Under this
procedure, the auditee will be expected to implement these
recommendations upon receipt of directions from the
operating agencies.

This does not, however, preclude the operating agency
from deviating from the position indicated in the report at a
later date should conditions so warrant.[36]

We asked thirty-eight SEA managers:

TABLE 26
HOW LONG IS IT AFTER THE EXIT CONFERENCE
BEFORE YOU USUALLY RECEIVE A COPY OF
THE FINAL HEWAA AUDIT REPORT?

Response	Number	Percent
One month	6	16%
Two months	9	24%
Three months	10	26%
Four months	4	11%
Six months	5	13%
More than six months	4	11%

Apparently HEW audits are issued fairly promptly (sixty-six per cent in three months or less). However, GAO auditors not only take more man hours in doing the audit, but typically take longer to issue their audit reports than HEW Audit Agency — six months to two years.

Most HEW audit reports have a common format and appearance. Our analysis of forty sample HEWAA reports disclosed:

.. Green outside cover, 100%
.. Cover letter, 75%
.. Table of contents, 87%
.. Introduction, 100%
.. Summary, 72%
.. Status of prior findings, 62%
.. Statement of scope, 87%
.. Exit conference or discussion with SEA officials, 47%
.. Acknowledgements, 17%
.. Tables, 100%
.. Distribution, 82%
.. Signature, 100%
.. Qualification — final determination to be made by OE, 77%

In appearance, these audit reports were rather drab and unattractive. None of the sample contained charts or illustrations, and the type and paper quality was poor. In general, the appearance of the reports failed to reflect the time, effort, and money that went into their preparation (and, as a consequence, they probably had a negative effect on auditee motivation).

Also, as noted earlier in the objective section, only one audit noted any SEA achievements and fourteen used negative words or phrases—such as "important weaknesses," "significant deficiencies," "failure," and "inadequate." In addition, it would be beneficial to the public, the SEA, and others to have stated on the title page of each audit report that it does not purport to contain a complete evaluation of all aspects of the program. (GAO does this in the body of their ESEA Title I reports.)

We also analyzed the format of GAO's four ESEA Title I reports in a manner similar to our analysis of HEWAA's.

.. Blue outside cover, 100%
.. Cover letter, 100%
.. Tear sheet, 100%
.. Table of contents, 100%
.. Digest, 75%

.. Introduction, 100%
.. Scope of review, 100%
.. Persons having responsibility, 100%
.. Audits of Title I activities, 100%
.. Financial tables, 100%
.. Pictures and/or charts, 50%

In general, GAO's audit reports have a better overall appearance than HEWAA's. This is to be expected as they probably take more preparation time and are distributed more widely and to a different audience. But it would seem that HEWAA's report format could be upgraded significantly with relatively little additional cost and effort.

With regard to State Audit Reports, forty-seven SEA managers were asked:

TABLE 27
DOES THE STATE AUDIT AGENCY ISSUE A
FORMAL AUDIT REPORT?

Response	Number	Percent
Yes	43	92%
No	3	6%
Occasionally	1	2%

State audit reports vary from two paragraph opinions on financial statements to reports hundreds of pages in length concerning the needs for operational improvements. All are public documents. Since most LEA audits are financial in scope, the most common LEA audit report is the standard two paragraph attest opinion.

According to our interviews, SEA managers find HEWAA, GAO and State audit reports clear, understandable, and easy to read (95%, nineteen of twenty responses). SEA managers also indicated that there were seldom any surprises in the final audit reports. And they feel that most audit reports adequately incorporate their exit conference comments.

TABLE 28
ARE THERE ANY "SURPRISES" IN THE FINAL REPORT
WHICH WERE NOT NOTED AT THE CONFERENCE?

Responses (total number)	HEWAA (56)	GAO (3)	State Auditor (48)
Always or Usually	7%	—	8%
Occasionally	16%	—	13%
Seldom or Never	77%	100%	79%

TABLE 29
DOES THE FINAL AUDIT REPORT ADEQUATELY AND
ACCURATELY INCORPORATE YOUR
EXIT CONFERENCE COMMENTS?

Response (total number)	HEWAA (49)	GAO (3)	State Auditor (42)
Always or Usually	78%	—	48%
Occasionally	4%	100%	26%
Seldom or Never	18%	—	26%

However, in our sample of audit reports we found that SEA comments were quite frequently followed by *auditor rebuttal.* Several SEA managers indicated that for this reason, they were hesitant to make written comments before issuance of the final report.

VI. Distribution of the Audit Report

HEW Audit Agency includes a distribution schedule on the last page of each audit report. Copies of HEW audit reports are distributed by the Regional Audit Director simultaneously to: (1) The State Education Agency, (2) the appropriate OE Associate Commissioner, (3) OE's Office of Business Management—Audit Liaison and Coordination Staff, (4) HEWAA Headquarters, Division of Audit Coordination, (5) the Regional OE Commissioner, and (6) to other interested parties. An OE memo describes this procedure:

> Copies of the final audit report will be released simultaneously, by the HEW Audit Agency, to the State educational agency, the cognizant Associate Commissioner in Office of Education headquarters, and to the appropriate Regional Commissioner for his information. The letter transmitting the final audit report to the State educational agency will request that agency to forward a response to the audit report to the cognizant Associate Commissioner in Office of Education headquarters within 30 days of the date of the letter of transmittal.[37]

GAO distributes its SEA audit reports simultaneous to Congress, the Office of Management and Budget, the Secretary of HEW, the HEW Controllers Office, the HEW Audit Agency, OE's Audit Liaison and Coordination Staff, and the State Education Agency.

(Some GAO reports, however, are confidential and are not publically distributed.)

Distribution of State Audit Agency reports varies. A 1971 study by the Legislative Research Bureau, Boston, Massachusetts reports:

> The auditor officially files his report with the appropriate legislative committee. In some states, the appropriations committees are entitled to copies at the same time. Next, the report is usually given to the entire legislature and thereafter to the governor and other proper recipients.[38]

LEA audits are distributed to a variety of audit recipients:

TABLE 30
TO WHOM IS THE LEA AUDIT REPORT DIRECTED?

Response	Number	Percent
Local Superintendent of Schools	38	54%
Chief State School Officer	37	53%
Chief State Executive	8	11%
Local Board of Education or Local Government	42	60%
State Audit Agency or Other State Agency	20	29%

A primary weakness of all of these distribution systems is their failure to formally transmit audit findings directly to other SEAs and LEAs where similar conditions might exist. It is unfortunate for such great expenditures of time and effort to benefit only one State or local agency.

It should be noted that audits of SEAs and LEAs are not, as a rule, distributed directly to the press. But audit reports are generally public documents and, therefore, available to anyone upon request. However, the Office of Education periodically issues press releases that refer to or are concerned with SEA/LEA audit reports and audit settlement. The General Accounting Office also issues bulletins that relate to its audit reports and some State Audit Agencies issue press releases on a regular basis.

State Education Agencies and Local Education Agencies, as governmental entities, are publicly accountable for their activities. Thus, they should (and do) expect the occasional "glare" of newspaper publicity as a result of audit findings. Unfortunately, some journalists may try to sensationalize an audit report and, by so doing, possibly exaggerate or misinterpret audit recommendations. Some audit agencies are also guilty of occasional sensationalism for public consumption and political gain.

During the course of our interviews, SEA managers frequently mentioned the "problem" of unfavorable newspaper publicity of audit findings. Some of their comments and suggestions that warrant mention are:

. . SEAs and LEAs should be informed in advance of the date of public release of an audit report.
. . They should be given enough advance warning to enable adequate preparation of their own public statements and comments. (HEWAA gives fourteen days).
. . Auditors and other representatives of audit agencies should conduct themselves at all times in an ethical and professional manner. Inflammatory statements and comments to the press and public constitute unethical behavior. An audit report should "speak for itself."
. . Audit reports should have a clear statement of scope, including whether or not they represent a complete evaluation of the SEA/LEA program or programs.
. . Audit reports should clearly state, when applicable, that final determination and settlement is to be made by the appropriate higher authority/audit recipient.

SETTLEMENT

I. Evaluation of Audit Findings and Recommendations

When a State Education Agency receives a Federal audit report, containing findings of a financial or program nature, it has thirty days in which to reply to the appropriate Associate Commissioner in the U.S. Office of Education.

SEA managers were asked:

TABLE 31
DOES YOUR FIRST WRITTEN RESPONSE TO THE AUDIT EVER TAKE MORE THAN 30 DAYS?

Response	Number	Percent
Never	4	13%
Seldom	10	31%
Occasionally	11	34%
Usually	7	23%
Always	0	—

Interview responses indicated that the SEA program director or coordinator is generally responsible for preparing the official reply to the audit report.

TABLE 32
WHAT SEA OFFICIAL IS RESPONSIBLE FOR WORKING WITH THE OFFICE OF EDUCATION RELATIVE TO AUDIT RECONCILIATION?

Response	Number	Percent
Chief State School Officer	2	10%
Finance Director	5	24%
Program Director or Coordinator	9	43%
Other	5	24%

Interestingly, over one-third of the SEAs seek OE assistance in preparing their reply to OE.

TABLE 33
DO YOU SEEK OE ASSISTANCE IN THE PREPARATION OF YOUR RESPONSE?

Response	Number	Percent
Yes	11	34%
No	21	66%

In recent years, the Office of Education's settlement process has generally begun as follows:

Thirty days after the expiration of the 30-day period given the State Educational Agency to respond to the final audit report, the appropriate Division will prepare a letter of preliminary audit determinations to be sent to the State Educational Agency. This letter will take into consideration any comments which the State Educational Agency has provided concerning the final audit report. The letter will offer the State Educational Agency the opportunity to meet with Office of Education staff to discuss the preliminary determinations and to present additional information within a 30-day period. It will inform the State Educational Agency that a final determination letter will be issued, taking into consideration the information obtained through the meeting and in writing, and will inform the State Educational Agency of the opportunity for hearing on the matters contained in the final determination letter. The preliminary determination letter will be signed by the Associate Commissioner after concurrence by the Deputy Commissioner for School Systems.[39]

However, the new "Prerelease Procedures" are supposed to eliminate these steps in the majority of cases. Instead, the *final* audit report is intended to represent the position of both HEW Audit Agency *and the Office of Education;* thereby eliminating the need for a determination letter. This allows the Office of Education to move directly toward resolution of audit findings.

If a State Education Agency disagrees with OE's position relative to an audit finding, the SEA may wish to request an appeal. HEW has recently established two *appeal* systems that will apply to Federal audits of State and Local Education Agencies. They are (1) the Grant Appeals Board, and (2) The Title I Audit Hearing Board.

The Grant Appeals Board

The Grant Appeals Board was established recently for the purpose of reviewing and providing hearings for disputes between Grantee's and HEW Operating Agencies. This would include *audit settlement disputes* between SEAs and the Office of Education.

The Board as it is now formed is composed of 18 to 19 members from both within and outside of HEW. For operating purposes, the chairman of the Board will usually appoint a panel of three or more Board members to review each dispute. Application for review is made by the grantee (SEA).

Such application must be made by the SEA within *30 days* following written receipt of the disputed OE decision (determination). However, the arbitrated decision of the Grant Appeals Board may be later modified or reversed by OE's Commissioner of Education. Although this appeal system is available for most programs administered by SEAs, some programs are not covered. For example, ESEA Title I programs are excluded because there exists a separate appeal procedure called the Title I Audit Hearing Board.

The Title I Audit Hearing Board

If an SEA does not accept or agree with a final determination made by OE with respect to a Title I audit, they can request a hearing by the Title I Audit Hearing Board.

The State's request for a hearing must indicate the grounds on which the hearing is requested, i.e., whether the State is raising issues of fact or of law or both. In those cases in which the State raises issues of fact, or of law or both an evidentiary hearing before a hearing tribunal will be held. If the State merely raises questions of law (i.e., questions the Office of Education's interpretation of the statute, regulations or guidelines) an evidentiary hearing will not be arranged, but the State may submit a formal argument by brief or other written document for consideration by a hearing tribunal. The hearing tribunal may permit the State to present oral arguments if it feels that such would be in the interest of justice.

The hearing will be conducted by the hearing tribunal.

Recommendations will be made to OE's Commissioner by the hearing tribunal.

The Commissioner will then notify the State Education Agency of his final determinations.[40]

Settlement continues in a cyclic fashion until the Office of Education is satisfied with SEA action. At that point, the audit file is closed and a closing letter is transmitted to the State Education Agency. At the same time, the Audit Liaison and Coordination Staff is informed that the audit has been closed. ALCS, which may already be involved in the settlement process, informs HEW Audit Agency Headquarters (and through them, the Secretary of HEW via the "Stewardship Report") that the audit is now closed. HEWAA headquarters then informs the Regional Audit Office. If it is a GAO report, GAO is informed of settlement status every six months.

This settlement process may take a long time.

TABLE 34
IN GENERAL, HOW LONG DOES IT USUALLY
TAKE TO SETTLE AN HEW AUDIT?

Response	Number	Percent
1 - 6 Months	8	24%
6 Months to 1 Year	9	27%
1 - 2 Years	9	27%
2 Years or More	2	6%
Varies	5	15%

In fact, the Office of Education has been criticized by the General Accounting Office for taking too long in resolving some ESEA Title I audits.

HEW Audit Agency records show that, during the 4-year period from March 1967 through February 1971, 55 reports were issued on the Title I program in 41 States and the District of Columbia. As of June 30, 1971, findings involving about $37 million in Title I funds in 27 of the reports on 24 States had not been resolved. Findings in 11 of the reports had been unresolved from 2 to 4 years.[41]

However, OE's Audit Liaison and Coordination Staff reports recent progress in the reduction of (1) overall settlement time and (2) the number of unresolved audits — six months or older.

Large Dollar Audit Findings

An important problem with regard to audit settlement concerns large-dollar audit findings. As of July 1972, HEW Audit Agency had challenged the spending of $39.4 million of ESEA Title I funds in 42 states. By the end of the year, the U.S. Office of Education had formally asked 18 States to refund $19.5 million. Indications are, however, that in some cases restitution may be difficult to achieve.

SEA "charge-backs" of large amounts of allegedly misspent funds (usually compliance violations) is a critical problem that has not yet been resolved statisfactorily. The difficulty is that State Education Agencies find it almost impossible to comply with refund requests.

The original funds, although spent in possible violation of Federal compliance rules, have never-the-less been spent. Few SEAs have surpluses or discretionary funds available in any great amounts. Thus to pay a large "charge-back," a State Education Agency must either take from the current program or some other program (which is inequitable and, possibly, illegal) or request special funding from its Legislature. To ask a Legislature for an appropriation to pay an audit finding is embarrassing to the SEA and the Legislature may, in any case, refuse the request.

A related issue concerns the possibility of joint blame between USOE and the State Agencies for compliance violations. In some cases, Federal regulations and guidelines may have been unclear and/or the SEA may have received direct or tacit approval from OE for activities that HEW Audit Agency later found exception to. Thus, some States may object to the repayment of funds in those cases were such joint blame exists.

If a State does not make restitution, the U.S. Office of Education is also faced with some difficult alternatives. The cutting-off of other Federal aid and/or court action to force repayment are both *politically* unsound solutions.

To gain some insight into this difficult problem, we asked our respondents

TABLE 35
WHAT HAS BEEN THE SOURCE OF FUNDS FOR SEA RETURNS RESULTING FROM AUDIT EXCEPTIONS?

Response	Number	Percent
Other Programs	3	8%
Special Appropriations	3	8%
Surpluses	6	16%
Cut-back on Current Program	7	19%
State Transfer of Public Funds	6	16%
None Settled	12	32%

Interestingly, the most frequent response was "none settled." However, in the course of our interviews, SEA managers did suggest some possible alternative solutions.

1. Take from future Federal appropriations.
2. Give the SEA credit against future administrative costs.
3. Take from unclaimed Federal funds to which the State is entitled.
4. Use money set aside for matching funds.

With regard to this problem, the National Advisory Council on the Education of Disadvantaged Children recommends:

. . . that the states be required to spend from their own funds an amount equivalent to the audit exception, on Title I eligible children according to Title I regulations, in the LEA's where the questionable expenditures occurred.

The Council suggests that this is a better alternative, since Title I eligible children will be served in the "year of compliance."[42]

The Office of Education has announced that this approach will be an acceptable settlement procedure for certain ESEA Title I exceptions. However, this is still a significant problem area that has not yet been fully resolved.

With regard to the settlement of State audits, SEA managers were asked:

TABLE 36
WHAT RECOURSES HAVE YOU FOLLOWED IN THE
SETTLEMENT OF STATE AUDIT FINDINGS?

Response	Number	Percent
Negotiate	22	65%
Refuse to Comply	1	3%
No Recourse	3	9%
Comply in Part	8	24%

Our interviews indicate that State Auditors seldom ask for monetary refunds from SEAs and LEAs. When they do, such refunds — except in cases of fraud — are usually minor in nature.

State Education Agencies generally review LEA audits. Often these audits contain no audit exceptions (typical financial statement attestations). When they do contain exceptions, the State Education Agency contacts the LEA and they work together to make appropriate adjustments.

II. Joint Agreement on a Plan of Action

When an audit recommends changes of an operational nature, such recommendations should be reviewed and the audit recipient should develop, in conjunction with the auditee, a management plan of action — including interim progress deadlines. This generally is not done, however, although SEA managers are receptive to the idea.

TABLE 37
WOULD YOU LIKE TO SEE THE DEVELOPMENT OF A UNIFORM
IMPLEMENTATION PLAN FOR MANAGEMENT IMPROVEMENT
BASED ON AUDIT FINDINGS?

Response	Number	Percent
Yes	21	61%
No	7	14%
Maybe	13	25%

III. Audit Recipient Review of Corrective Action

When a management plan of action has been agreed upon, a formal review of SEA/LEA corrective action should be made by the audit recipient. For the most part, the Office of Education has relied upon SEA assurances that corrective action had or would soon be made. To some extent, OE has relied upon Title I Reviews and the State Management Review Program. Our interviews with OE and HEWAA personnel indicate that these review programs are not tailor-made for following up audit findings and recommendations. Hence, OE's review of corrective action at the SEA/LEA level needs to be strengthened.

IV. Audit Agency Follow-Up

HEWAA auditors usually review the status of prior audit findings during the course of SEA audits. HEWAA also conducts special follow-up reviews on occasion. The General Accounting Office does not audit frequently enough to require follow-ups — but asks OE for biannual status reports on open audits. Finally, interviews with State auditors indicate that they also follow-up on past audit findings and recommendations (eleven of thirteen, 85%).

CONCLUSIONS

In the last section of this chapter, we have examined the processes and procedures of the auditors of State and Local Education Agencies. In the course of discussion, a number of issues and areas in need of improvement have been identified. Following is a summarization of those matters contained in this section which we feel are of particular importance.

.. SEA managers feel that audits of Federal Programs need to be more frequent and timely.
.. There is an apparent need for better audit guidance at the LEA level.
.. Audit teams for SEA/LEA audits seldom include educators.
.. HEW Audit Agency has not taken full advantage of auditor specialization.
.. SEA managers ask for advance notice of auditor infor-

mation and facility needs.

. . A majority of SEA managers feel that HEW auditors are not adequately familar with educational program matters.

. . State auditors frequently fail to hold entrance and exit conferences.

. . Auditors usually do not ask if they can be of any service to SEA management as a byproduct of their examination.

. . Federal auditors are not utilizing standardized survey guides and questionnaires.

. . There has been occasional SEA reluctance to on-site reviews at the LEA level.

. . Federal auditors are not using standardized work papers for SEA audits.

. . Auditors of SEAs generally do not issue Flash Reports.

. . State Audit Agencies, SEA external auditors, and CPAs usually do not issue draft reports.

. . Draft Federal audit reports frequently have been unavailable prior to and at the time of the exit conference.

. . Chief State School Officers and OE Representatives are often absent from the audit exit conference.

. . The appearance of HEWAA's audit reports could be significantly upgraded with relatively little additional cost and effort.

. . SEA comments when included in audit reports are frequently followed by auditor rebuttal.

. . SEA audit reports and findings are generally not distributed to other SEAs and LEAs.

. . SEA managers feel that auditors should be sensitive to potential newspaper abuses.

. . A significant and unresolved problem concerns the settlement of large dollar, Federal compliance exceptions.

. . OE/SEA/LEA Managers usually do not develop a *formal* "plan of action" for the disposition of audit findings.

. . OE's on-site review of SEA/LEA corrective action needs to be strengthened.

FOOTNOTES

Chapter V

[1]U.S. Department of Health, Education, and Welfare, *1970 Annual Report,* (Washington: U.S. Government Printing Office, 1971), p. 30. The Annual Report has since been discontinued.

[2]HEW Audit Agency, *Audit Guide, Elementary and Secondary Education Act of 1965, Title I,* Interim Audit Instruction C-10, (Washington: HEWAA, 1966), p. 2.

[3]HEW Audit Agency, *Audit Guide for Review of Local Education Agency Programs Under Title I of the Elementary and Secondary Education Act of 1965,* (Unpublished Draft, HEWAA, 1973), p. 4.

[4]HEW Audit Agency, Region I, *Follow-up Review of Audit Report 90110-01, ESEA Title V, State of Connecticut,* Audit Control No. 10086-01, (Boston: HEWAA, December 4, 1970), pp. 2, 3, 4.

[5]U.S. General Accounting Office, *GAO: Purposes, Functions, and Services,* (Washington: GAO, May, 1969), p. 1.

[6]U.S. General Accounting Office, *GAO,* (Washington: GAO, November, 1970), p. 1.

[7]*Congressional Record,* (April 13, 1970), p. H2861.

[8]United States General Accounting Office, The Comptroller General, *Standards for Audit of Governmental Organizations, Programs, Activities, and Functions,* (Washington: GAO, 1972), p. 8.

[9]HEW Audit agency, Region I, *Report on Review of Grants Awarded to the Commonwealth of Massachusetts Under Title V Elementary and Secondary Act of 1965,* Audit Control No. 00015-1, (Boston, HEWAA, December 1969).

[10]HEW Audit Agency, *1973 Draft Title I Audit Guide,* p. 4.

[11]Office of Washington State Auditor, Division of Departmental Audits, *Report of Examination: Superintendent of Public Instruction,* (Olympia, Washington: Auditor of State, 1968).

[12]Legislative Auditor of the State of Hawaii, *Management Audit of the State Department of Education,* Audit Report No. 73-1, (Honolulu: Legislative Auditor, 1973).

[13]Kentucky Department of Education, Bureau of Administration and Finance, *Administrative Survey: Bowling Green Independent School District,* (Frankfort, Ky.: Department of Education, 1971).

[14]Burton D. Friedman and Laird J. Dunbar, *Grants Management in Education: Federal Impact on State Agencies,* (Chicago: Public Administration Service, 1971), pp. 86-87.

[15]Hawaii Department of Education, Management Audit and Review Branch, *A Staff Report of an Organizational Review of the*

Department of Education, (Honolulu: Department of Education, 1969).

[16]United States General Accounting Office, *Internal Auditing in Federal Agencies,* (Washington: GAO, 1968), p. 1.

[17]U.S. Bureau of the Budget, *Audit of Federal Grants-in-Aid to State and Local Governments,* Circular Number A-73, (Washington: BOB, 1965).

[18]Comptroller General Elmer B. Staats, *Progress in the Financial Management of Federal Grant-in-Aid Programs,* (Address to the Joint State-Federal Financial Management Conference, Washington, D.C., October 9, 1970).

[19]GAO, *Standards.*

[20]Robert B. Brown and Edward W. Stepnick, "What's Ahead in the Field of Auditing?," *Footnote,* II (Summer, 1970), pp. 21-23.

[21]U.S. Civil Service Commission, *Questions and Answers on the Intergovernmental Personnel Act of 1970,* (News Release for Afternoon Newspapers, January 18, 1971), pp. 1-2.

[22]GAO, *Standards.*

[23]HEW Audit Agency, *Report on Auditor Intern Program Survey,* (Unpublished Report, HEWAA, September, 1969).

[24]GAO, *Standards.*

[25]HEW Audit Agency, *1966 Title I Audit Guide,* p. 2.

[26]HEW Audit Agency, *1973 Draft Title I Audit Guide,* pp. 10-11.

[27]GAO, *Standards,* p. 7.

[28]American Institute of Certified Public Accountants, Committee on Auditing Procedures, *Statement on Auditing Standards: Codification of Auditing Standards and Procedures Number One,* (New York: AICPA, 1973), p. 13.

[29]HEW Audit Agency, *1966 Title I Audit Guide,* p. ii.

[30]HEW Audit Agency, *1973 Draft Title I Audit Guide,* pp. i-ii.

[31]*Ibid.,* p. 6.

[32]Department of Health, Education, and Welfare, Office of Education, *Memorandum to Chief State School Officers, April 21, 1972,* (Washington: OE, 1972) p. 1.

[33] United State General Accounting Office, *Audits of Government Contracts,* Washington: U.S. Government Printing Office, 1967), p. 17.

[34]The Commonwealth of Massachusetts, Legislative Research Bureau, *Report Relative to Legislative Post Audit,* (Boston: Legislative Research Bureau, February 17, 1971), p. 66.

[35]HEW Audit Agency, *Procedures Handbook, Part III, Prerelease Procedures,* (Washington: HEWAA, 1973), p. 3.

[36]*Ibid.,* p. 1.

[37]HEW, Office of Education, *Memorandum,* p. 2.

[38]Massachusetts Legislative Research Bureau, *Audit Report,* p. 66.

[39]HEW, Office of Education, *Memorandum,* p. 2.

[40]*Ibid.,* p. 3.

[41]U.S. General Accounting Office, The Comptroller General, *Report to the Congress: The Federal Program of Aid to Educationally Deprived Children in Illinois Can be Strengthened,* B-164031 (1), (Washington: GAO, June 22, 1972), p. 56.

[42]National Advisory Council on the Education of Disadvantaged Children, *Educating the Disadvantaged Child: Where We Stand,* Annual Report to the President and Congress, 1972, (Washington: U.S. Government Printing Office, 1972), p. 10.

CHAPTER VI

FUTURE DIRECTIONS
AND RECOMMENDATIONS

This chapter concludes our study of SEA/LEA auditing. The discussion has ranged from matters of a broad philosophical nature to very specific issues — such as the need for standardized audit work papers. It should now be apparent to the reader that a "revolution" is taking place in the field of auditing. The *milestones* of this revolution include:

- . . an expansion of the scope of auditing — to encompass matters of a management or performance nature.
- . . a growing concern with regard to the objective of auditing — should it be policing, helping, or something in between.
- . . a realization that internal auditing can be used as a highly effective management tool.
- . . an immediate need for an integrated, coordinated, and cooperative Federal-State-Local audit network.
- . . a growing desire for improved auditor-auditee relations.
- . . a widespread interest in improving and modernizing auditor training and audit techniques.

The issues which have been presented have not been intended as criticisms but as challenges. They represent the growing pains of a new era in auditing.

Within the next decade, the trends — so recently established — should become permanent features of the audit environment. Following these projections to their most likely conclusion suggests the following "Future Directions."

FUTURE DIRECTIONS

AUDIT PHILOSOPHY

It is likely that in the near future auditors will be giving much closer consideration to the subject of audit philosophy. To date, most auditors have operated under the assumption that "everyone knows what an audit is and why it is conducted." But auditing is clearly changing, and auditors must now decide where they stand with regard to the evolving concepts.

AUDIT TERMINOLOGY

Auditing terms will probably continue to be somewhat confusing. For example, broad scope audits are referred to, depending upon the source, as:

Operational Audits	Performance Audits
Mission Audits	Management Audits
Efficiency Audits	Functional Audits
Program Audits	Status Audits
Total Audits	Substantive Audits
Depth Audits	Effectiveness Audits
System Audits	Comprehensive Audits

etc., etc., etc.

This proliferation of terms is due, in part, to the fact that auditing is not a closely organized and coordinated profession. Actually, there are three basic, overlapping areas of auditing:

1. Internal Auditing
2. Governmental Auditing
3. CPA Auditing

INTERNAL AUDITING

There is good reason to expect continuing and significant advancement in the field of Internal Auditing with regard to (1) extension of audit scope, (2) modification of audit objectives, (3) improvement of behavioral relations, and (4) development of auditing techniques. In fact, it is quite possible that internal auditors will be the trend setters for innovative auditing in the coming decade. This projection is based upon some of the following factors.

Traditional Leadership Role

The term "operational auditing" was coined by internal auditors and internal auditors were the first to extend the scope of auditing to encompass management matters. In recent years, internal auditors were first to become concerned with audit objectives and behavioral considerations. They have also made major contributions with regard to operational auditing procedures and techniques.

The Institute of Internal Auditors

The fact that internal auditing has made such progress to date is due in large part to the existence of the Institute of Internal Auditors. Since 1941, the Institute has sponsored professional activities, research studies, training programs, technical publications, and, recently, an auditor certification program. Thus, the Institute has served as a medium for communication and coordination of effort and has stimulated the development and advancement of auditing theory and technique.

Environmental Pressures

The environment of internal auditing is particularly conducive to extension of the traditional boundaries of auditing. Internal auditors are often encouraged in this regard by both their top management audit recipients and their lower management auditees.

Top management needs reliable and confidential information concerning the economy, efficiency, and effectiveness of operations. Therefore, the internal auditors in many organizations have been encouraged by top management to extend the scope of their audit activities.

Often, the auditor's report is treated as simply an additional source of information for the benefit of both top and middle management. When the auditee manager realizes that the audit is to be treated as confidential and is not intended as criticism but rather as a tool for his benefit; he also encourages the auditor to expand the scope of his examination.

GOVERNMENTAL AUDITING

It is quite likely that within the next decade broad scope auditing will become relatively common in the governmental environment. This will probably be on a descending scale, with such auditing being quite common in the Federal Government, common in State Government, and fairly common in Local Government. Also, the development of more sophisticated auditing techniques will undoubtedly take place. Modification of audit objectives and improved behavioral relations will probably take place but not as rapidly as in the field of internal auditing. This conclusion is based upon some of the following factors.

Governmental Audit Standards

The issuance by the Comptroller General of *Standards for Audit of Governmental Organizations, Programs, Activities and Functions* filled a pressing need in the governmental audit environment. The lack of uniform audit standards had seriously retarded the progress of governmental auditing.

The new standards encourage a broad scope audit concept and, in some respects, a more cooperative audit approach. It is also significant that the standards are considered applicable to all levels of government. These auditing standards will undoubtedly strongly influence the future evolution of auditing in the governmental sector.

Professional Associations

Progress in governmental auditing has and continues to be hampered to some extent by the fact that there is no one central professional association for governmental auditors. While there are several professional associations to which governmental auditors can belong, none of them are devoted exclusively to auditing or to all levels of government. Those associations include:

Federal Auditing
>The Federal Government Accountants Association

State Auditing
>The National Legislative Conference
>The National Association of State Auditors, Controllers, and Treasurers

Local Auditing
>Municipal Finance Officers Association

Many of these associations have encouraged auditing research, professional activities, and advancement of audit concepts. But the present lack of one strong, central professional association devoted exclusively to governmental auditing has tended to (1) encourage segmentation of the levels of governmental auditing, (2) retard communication and cooperation between auditors, and (3) generally hamper the progress and development of auditing theory and techniques.

Recently, the General Accounting Office, as a by-product of their Audit Standards Program, has helped to organize a National Intergovernmental Audit Forum and several Regional Forums. The National Forum includes the chief auditor of each Federal agency and representatives from State and Local auditor associations. The Regional Forums include State Auditors, Regional Audit Directors of Federal Agencies, and their staffs. The Forums are not, as of yet, open to Local Auditors and State Internal Auditors, but their membership is under consideration. Perhaps, these Forums will in time develop into the strong professional association that is so needed.

Environmental Pressures

Governmental auditors are frequently encouraged by legislative and/or executive audit recipients to expand the scope of their audit activities. They are not often encouraged in this regard by auditees. Congress, State Legislatures, Governors, and Local Governments need information on the economy, efficiency, and effectiveness of governmental programs. The auditor is already "out in the field," is independent and competent, and is a natural choice as a reliable source for such information.

However, high level audit recipients because of their traditional "oversight" role often tend to reinforce the "watchdog" concept of auditing. Also, governmental audits are almost always public documents. Thus, governmental auditees tend to resist extension of the audit function.

CPA AUDITING

CPAs have been moving slowly and cautiously into management auditing. It is likely that many CPAs will extend the scope of their audit activities within the next decade to encompass some matters of a performance nature. Initially, however, they will probably be conducting a greater number of compliance audits, with performance audit effort developing more slowly.

Behavioral relations should continue to be a matter of concern to CPAs, and they should continue to make significant contributions with regard to auditing procedures and techniques. This conclusion is based upon several factors.

Traditional Role

The CPA's traditional and primary audit function has been that of attesting to the fairness of the financial statements of private firms. (Government has been a poor market for CPA services.) The CPA carefully gathers evidence, documents it, and satisfies himself that the accounting statements of the organization fairly reflect the firm's financial position and results of operation. If the CPA should make a significant error in his examination he may be liable for damages. Therefore, the CPA views extension of the scope of auditing with a certain amount of distrust.

. . He questions whether broad scope "audits" are in fact "audits." (They are certainly not in the traditional *financial* sence of the word.)

. . He wonders if involvement in management matters may later compromise his independence to conduct financial audits.

. . He is concerned about the fact that evidence concerning management conditions often is not as clear-cut and objective as is accounting data.

. . He wonders if his statements concerning management conditions may subject him to possible legal liabilities.

. . He often feels that he is already providing this kind of service but in a different form.

(1) During a financial audit the CPA often provides

auditee management with an informal "management letter" that discusses matters of a financial and administrative control nature.

(2) Many CPAs can provide "management reviews" for the benefit of their client firms. This is a management service activity conducted quite seperately from the financial audit — and often by a separate staff.

The American Institute of Certified Public Accountants

The CPA is represented by a strong professional organization — the AICPA. The Institute sponsors an extensive amount of professional activities including development and grading of CPA examinations, training and educational programs, conferences and seminars, research studies and activities, technical publications, and official pronouncement on accounting and auditing procedures.

The AICPA's Committee on Relations with the General Accounting Office recently issued *Auditing Standards Established by the GAO: Their Meaning and Significance for CPAs.* Some of the conclusions and recommendations of this report include:

> Independent public accountants should be encouraged to participate in audits of the types contemplated by the GAO standards but should be cautioned to define carefully, in an engagement agreement, the scope of each engagement and the method of reporting. The profession should work to further define standards for performing such audits.

. . . .

> The members of this Committee agree with the philosophy and objectives advocated by the GAO in its standards and believe that the GAO's broadened definition of auditing is a logical and worthwhile continuation of the evolution and growth of the auditing discipline.

This strong statement of approval from a committee of the American Institute of CPAs should significantly influence CPAs to expand the scope of their governmental audits.

Environmental Pressures

The CPA has received relatively little pressure from the financial community to expand the scope of his audits to the extent that they encompass performance matters. (He has been encouraged to give opinions upon business forecasts and to make other sophisticated financial analyses.)

The auditee managers of firms in the public sector have not pushed for extension of audit scope because in part they may want to minimize audit costs and/or would not like for such information to be made public. The CPA is encouraged to promote good behavioral relations because he is usually engaged by the auditee on behalf of the audit recipient. However, the CPA has received pressure from governmental recipients to extend the scope of his audit — particularly to encompass matters of a compliance nature.

THE FEDERAL-STATE-LOCAL AUDIT NETWORK

The Federal-State-Local audit network should become much more of a reality within the next decade. This conclusion is based upon the following factors.

Auditor Workloads

Auditor workloads have reached the point where Federal auditors can no longer adequately survey all Federal programs; nor can State auditors adequately survey many State and Local programs. Thus, they must now — through necessity — rely when possible upon the work of each other and upon audits by CPAs, internal auditors, and local government auditors.

Revenue Sharing

Federal Revenue Sharing significantly increases the need for auditor cooperation and co-reliance. Because of the extent of Revenue Sharing, the Federal Government will have to increasingly rely upon State and Local audits.

Environmental Pressures

Federal Audit Agencies are actively promoting the audit network concept. In addition, proposed Federal legislation and official policy encourage and require Federal reliance upon State, Local, and Independent auditors.

Keys to Success

There are two major keys to success with regard to a *viable* Federal-State-Local audit network.

(1) Audit Standards
    For a workable audit network to be achieved, uniform audit standards must be followed by the many different audit agencies. Therefore, widespread acceptance and adoption of the Comptroller General's *Standards for Audit of Governmental Organizations, Programs, Activities, and Functions* is essential.

(2) Federal Acceptance
    Although Federal Audit Agencies have promoted the concept of an audit network, some have in turn shown hesitancy on occasion to accept the work of other auditors. Lack of uniform standards has undoubtedly been a principal cause of this reluctance. However, a feeling that is common to us all, "That work will be up to *our* standards only if *we* do it ourselves," has sometimes existed. This reluctance will have to moderate if a successful audit network is to be achieved.

AUDITOR COMPETENCIES

Auditor expertise and sophistication should continue to advance at a rapid rate — particularly in the governmental environment. Entry into the auditing profession now generally requires a college degree in accounting; and college accounting curriculums increasingly include courses in management and behavior theory. Audit agencies have also increased their commitments to in-house training programs. Professional auditing associations and educational firms are now offering more continuing education programs than ever before and the trends in this direction are clearly upward.

The growth of auditor competency is especially apparent in the governmental environment. For many years, private businesses and public accounting firms had acquired the "best" of the accounting graduates. Now, more competitive salaries, increasing numbers of accounting graduates, and growing interest in governmental affairs are bringing greater numbers of qualifed people into governmental auditing. These trends are expected to continue.

AUDITING PROCEDURES

Auditing techniques will undoubtedly continue to advance. It is expected that there will be increased standardization of auditing tools and procedures. As auditor expertise continues to grow, there should be a related increase in the use of mathematics, quantitative methods, statistics, and greater utilization of the computer as an audit tool.

There should also be greater utilization of sophisticated audit approaches such as simulation, discriminate analysis, and audits that build on previous work. Growth will also come about because there will be a larger body of source material upon which to rely. In addition, auditing settlement procedures are expected to become more sophisticated and auditees should expect increased follow-up by both audit recipients and auditors.

SOME SUGGESTIONS AND CONSIDERATIONS FOR AUDITORS AND EDUCATIONAL MANAGERS

The AIDE Project would like to make some suggestions and considerations, based upon the findings in this study — that could make the future more of a reality today.

FOR LEA/SEA/OE MANAGERS

1. We recommend that State Education Agencies give priority attention to the establishment of vigorous, broad scope, management oriented, internal audit staffs. The functions of such internal audit staffs could include:

   . . Coordination and communication between SEA and State and Federal auditors.

   . . Conduct of operational and management type audits of SEA activities.

   . . Guidance and review of LEA audit activities.

2. We would like to see SEA and LEA managers adopt the positive attitude of "How can I best take advantage of the new audit approaches for the benefit of my own programs and operations?"

3. We feel that SEA and LEA managers should make a concerted effort to maintain frequent and close communication with auditors.

4. If at all possible, the Chief State School Officer should attend both entrance and exit audit conferences.

5. We suggest that in order to achieve a reliable independent audit, Federal auditors should always be allowed to visit Local Educa-

tion Agencies on a sample basis for review of Federal programs.

6. All SEAs should provide comprehensive audit assistance and guidance at the LEA level.

7. We suggest that the Office of Education in cooperation with several State Education Agencies consider developing a model LEA Audit Handbook.

8. We recommend that State Education Agencies investigate the possibilities of utilizing the assistance made available through the Intergovernmental Personnel Act.

9. It would be beneficial to all parties concerned if a representative of the Office of Education could attend HEWAA and GAO exit conferences.

10. We suggest that consideration be given to greater involvement of regional OE personnel in HEW's audit settlement process.

11. We fully endorse the development of HEW's "Audit Courts" (The Grant Appeals Board and The Title I Audit Hearing Board). We suggest that State Education Agencies fully acquaint themselves with these opportunities for audit appeals.

12. We recommend that the Office of Education make a practice of developing, with the cooperation of the SEA, a management plan of action for audit recommendations—including interim progress deadlines. The Office of Education should also have a formal follow-up program for on-site review of SEA corrective action.

13. We suggest the development of a department-wide policy manual on audit settlement for the Office of Education.

14. We propose that SEA audit exceptions resulting from OE administrative error not be charged against the State Education Agency.

15. We recommend that a publisher be encouraged to develop a comprehensive summary and interpretations service covering educational legislation, regulations, and guidelines.

16. We suggest that the Office of Education and/or State Education Agencies give consideration to the development of SEA management standards—which would facilitate management audits of SEAs.

FOR LOCAL/STATE/FEDERAL AUDITORS

17. We encourage all auditors to adopt a positive audit approach and to promote positive auditor-auditee relations.

18. We endorse broad-scope audits of SEAs and LEAs, if the objectives of such audits are oriented toward "helping" rather than "policing."

19. We feel that consideration should be given to developing new Federal legislation that more clearly describes the scope of the word "audit."

20. We recommend that Federal auditors conduct, at least on an experimental basis, educational audits that are of a "general performance" nature rather than a "compliance/performance" nature.

21. We would like to see a clear public statement of audit philosophy from each audit agency. This should also be incorporated into their audit guides and manuals and should include:

    . . The audit objectives of the agency.

    . . The scope of the agency's audits.

    . . Auditor-auditee behavioral considerations.

    . . Rationale for basic audit processes and procedures.

22. We endorse Federal efforts to develop a viable Federal-State-Local audit network. We suggest that consideration be given to the development of Federal Assistance and Cost Sharing Programs specifically designed to aid State and Local audit agencies.

23. We recommend that State and Local audit agencies investigate the possibility of utilizing the assistance made available through the Intergovernmental Personnel Act.

24. We encourage rapid and widespread adoption of the Comptroller General's *Standards for Audit of Governmental Organizations, Programs, Activities, and Functions.*

25. We suggest that experimental programs be implemented to test the feasibility and potential of (1) auditor specialization in educational audits and (2) audit teams which include professional educators.

26. We recommend that training programs for educational auditors include:

    . . Educational philosophy and program matters.

    . . Management techniques and controls.

    . . Concepts of behavior and communication.

27. Audits should be conducted on as current a basis as possible. If audit agencies are unable to conduct audits on a relatively current basis, they should actively attempt to expand their audit staff and/or reduce their audit workload, carefully examine their audit scheduling and efficiency, and utilize, when possible, the work and services of other auditors.

28. We recommend that auditors (1) ask in advance for a contact official, (2) schedule in advance an entrance conference, and (3) request in advance that preliminary information be provided.

29. We suggest that State Auditors consider the possibility of increased utilization of entrance and exit conferences.

30. We encourage auditors to ask, during the entrance conference, "If they can be of any assistance to management as a by-product of their examination."

31. Audit agencies should give consideration to the standardization of auditor working papers and survey guides.

32. We feel that auditors should make a concerted effort to maintain frequent and close communication with auditee management.

33. We recommend that SEA comments be included in State and Federal audit reports without rebuttal.

34. We suggest that auditors clearly state (in the introduction of their reports) the objectives, scope, and limitations of their audits and whether or not their examination represents a complete evaluation of the administration of that particular program.

35. We recommend that educational audit findings and recommendations be circulated to other SEAs and LEAs for consideration with regard to their own program activities.

APPENDIXES

APPENDIX A

SEA QUESTIONNAIRE AND INTERVIEW GUIDE

STATE _____

DATE _____

NAME _____

POSITION _____

PHONE _____

SEA AUDIT QUESTIONNAIRE

FOR

THE AIDE PROJECT

INSTRUMENT PREPARED BY
P.L. McMICKLE, MA, CPA
M.E. ELROD, ED.D.
ASSOCIATE DIRECTORS

AUDITING IN DEPARTMENTS OF EDUCATION

(THE AIDE PROJECT)

INTRODUCTION

PURPOSE: THE PURPOSE OF THE AIDE PROJECT IS TO EXAMINE IN DEPTH THE AUDIT ENVIRONMENT OF STATE EDUCATION AGENCIES IN ORDER TO:

1. BRING ABOUT A BETTER UNDERSTANDING ON THE PART OF SEA & OE MANAGEMENT CONCERNING THE PURPOSE AND PRESENT STATUS OF AUDITING AND FUTURE DIRECTIONS.

2. RECOMMEND WAYS IN WHICH TO MAKE INTERNAL AND EXTERNAL AUDITING MORE BENEFICIAL TO SEA & OE MANAGEMENT.

SCOPE: SPECIFICALLY, THE PROJECT IS CONDUCTING THE FOLLOWING ACTIVITIES:

1. CONTINUING AND EXTENSIVE RESEARCH INCLUDING THE DEVELOPMENT OF A MODEL OR CONCEPTUAL FRAMEWORK OF AUDITING IN THE GOVERNMENTAL ENVIRONMENT.

2. AN INDEPTH REVIEW OF AUDIT GUIDES, DIRECTIVES, AND REPORTS.

3. INTERVIEWS OF PERTINENT FEDERAL AGENCY PERSONNEL.

4. INTERVIEWS AT A SELECTED SAMPLE OF STATE EDUCATION AGENCIES.

5. THE DEVELOPMENT AND DISTRIBUTION OF A QUESTIONNAIRE TO BE COMPLETED BY ALL STATE EDUCATION AGENCIES.

AFTER AN OBJECTIVE INTERPRETATION OF THE DATA GENERATED BY THE ABOVE ACTIVITIES, THE PROJECT WILL DEVELOP A FINAL REPORT TO BE DISTRIBUTED TO ALL INTERESTED PARTIES. IN ADDITION, REGIONAL CONFERENCES OF SEA, OE, SAA, HEWAA, AND GAO PERSONNEL WILL BE HELD TO REVIEW THE FINDINGS AND SUGGEST FUTURE ACTIONS TO BE TAKEN.

QUESTIONNAIRE OBJECTIVE

THE OBJECTIVE OF THIS QUESTIONNAIRE IS TO ANALYZE IN DETAIL THE AUDIT ENVIRONMENT OF YOUR STATE EDUCATION AGENCY (ALL TYPES OF AUDITS) AND IN SO DOING, OBTAIN YOUR VIEWPOINTS, BOTH SUBJECTIVE AND OBJECTIVE.

THE QUESTIONNAIRE FORMAT DEALS SPECIFICALLY WITH THE FOLLOWING:

(1) HEW AUDIT AGENCY

(2) THE GENERAL ACCOUNTING OFFICE

(3) STATE AUDITORS

(4) INTERNAL AUDITORS

(5) INDEPENDENT AUDITORS (CPA'S AND PUBLIC ACCOUNTANTS)

(6) LOCAL EDUCATION AGENCY AUDITS, AND

(7) ATTITUDES AND FUTURE TRENDS.

THE QUESTIONNAIRE INCLUDES ALL PHASES OF AUDITING, BEGINNING WITH THE AUDIT PREPARATION AND TRACING ITS PROGRESS THROUGH THE SETTLEMENT PROCESS. THIS INSTRUMENT GIVES YOU AN OPPORTUNITY TO EXPRESS YOUR VIEWS ON AUDITING OF SEA'S AND TO ASSIST IN CORRECTING AUDIT PROBLEMS THAT YOU MAY HAVE ENCOUNTERED.

2

QUESTIONNAIRE INSTRUCTIONS

(IMPORTANT - PLEASE READ)

1. IN MANY OF THE QUESTIONS, WE FACE THE DIFFICULT PROBLEM OF TRYING TO GENERALIZE ABOUT A PROCESS THAT IS OFTEN INDIVIDUALISTIC. THROUGHOUT THE QUESTIONNAIRE, WE OFTEN REFER TO "THE AUDITOR". WE REALIZE THAT THERE IS NO "THE AUDITOR". PLEASE KEEP THIS IN MIND IN RESPONDING TO THE QUESTIONS. IF YOU FIND THAT YOUR ANSWER WOULD VARY DEPENDING UPON YOUR EXPERIENCES WITH VARIOUS AUDITORS, PLEASE INDICATE THIS DIFFERENCE.

2. PLEASE ANSWER EACH QUESTION THAT IS APPLICABLE TO YOUR STATE EDUCATION AGENCY. IN THE EVENT THAT SOME SECTIONS OR QUESTIONS DO NOT APPLY TO YOUR STATE, PLEASE SIGNIFY THIS BY PLACING NA (NOT APPLICABLE) BY THE SECTION OR QUESTIONS.

3. AT ANY POINT, FEEL FREE TO ADD YOUR COMMENTS ON ANY QUESTION.

4. IF YOU SHOULD NEED ADDITIONAL SPACE, YOU MAY WRITE IN THE MARGIN OR USE THE BLANK PAGE AT THE END OF THE QUESTIONNAIRE.

5. SOME QUESTIONS MAY REQUIRE MORE THAN ONE RESPONSE.

6. SECTION THREE, SAA: SINCE YOUR STATE MAY HAVE MORE THAN ONE STATE AGENCY RESPONSIBLE FOR REVIEWING OR AUDITING SOME OR ALL OF THE ACTIVITIES OF YOUR SEA--MULTIPLE COLUMNS HAVE BEEN PROVIDED.

7. SECTION SIX, LEA'S: SINCE YOUR STATE MAY HAVE MORE THAN ONE AGENCY OR CATEGORY OF AUDITOR RESPONSIBLE FOR REVIEWING OR AUDITING SOME OR ALL OF THE ACTIVITIES OF YOUR LEA'S--MULTIPLE COLUMNS HAVE BEEN PROVIDED.

8. FOR YOUR CONVENIENCE AND TO ASSIST YOU IN RESPONDING TO THE QUESTIONS, WE HAVE INCLUDED A GLOSSARY AND A LIST OF ACRONYMS.

GLOSSARY

1. FISCAL OR FINANCIAL AUDIT — CONCENTRATES ON FINANCIAL ACCOUNTING AND REPORTING.

2. FEDERAL COMPLIANCE AUDIT — CONCERNS COMPLIANCE WITH FEDERAL LEGISLATION, REGULATIONS, GUIDELINES, AND RULES.

3. STATE COMPLIANCE AUDIT — CONCERNS COMPLIANCE WITH STATE LEGISLATION, REGULATIONS, GUIDELINES, AND RULES.

4. PERFORMANCE AUDIT — ALSO CALLED PROGRAM AUDIT, OPERATIONAL AUDIT, OR MANAGEMENT AUDIT. IT CONCENTRATES ON MANAGEMENT SYSTEMS, CONTROL TECHNIQUES, AND PROCEDURES--FOR THE PURPOSE OF AIDING MANAGEMENT TO DO A MORE ECONOMICAL, EFFICIENT, AND EFFECTIVE JOB.

5. INTERNAL AUDIT — AN AUDIT ACTIVITY CONDUCTED BY EMPLOYEES OF THE AGENCY BEING AUDITED (EX., STATE EDUCATION AGENCY AUDITORS REVIEWING STATE EDUCATION AGENCY ACTIVITIES AND/OR ACCOUNTS).

6. PRE-AUDIT — BEFORE THE FACT AUDIT, A REVIEW MADE BEFORE TRANSACTIONS OR ACTIVITIES ARE COMPLETED.

7. POST-AUDIT — AFTER THE FACT AUDIT, A REVIEW MADE AFTER TRANSACTIONS OR ACTIVITIES ARE COMPLETED.

8. AUDIT RECONCILIATION OR SETTLEMENT — MEDIATING PROCESS USED TO SETTLE OR RECONCIL AUDIT EXCEPTIONS.

9. ENTRANCE CONFERENCE — A BEFORE THE AUDIT CONFERENCE OF AUDITORS AND MANAGEMENT.

10. EXIT CONFERENCE — AN AFTER THE AUDIT CONFERENCE OF AUDITORS AND MANAGEMENT.

ACRONYMS USED IN THIS QUESTIONNAIRE

1.	GAO	GENERAL ACCOUNTING OFFICE	6.	CSSO	CHIEF STATE SCHOOL OFFICER
2.	HEWAA	HEALTH, EDUCATION, AND WELFARE AUDIT AGENCY	7.	SEA	STATE EDUCATION AGENCY
3.	SAA	STATE AUDIT AGENCY	8.	LEA	LOCAL EDUCATION AGENCY
4.	SA	STATE AUDITOR	9.	OE	U. S. OFFICE OF EDUCATION
5.	CPA	CERTIFIED PUBLIC ACCOUNTANT			

3

(Blank Page)

I.

HEW AUDIT AGENCY
(HEWAA)

A. GENERAL:

1. LIST THE PROGRAMS OR ACTIVITIES OF YOUR SEA AUDITED BY HEWAA IN THE FOLLOWING YEARS:

	PROGRAM PERIOD COVERED		PROGRAM PERIOD COVERED		PROGRAM PERIOD COVERED
A. IN 1971		C. IN 1969		E. IN 1967	
B. IN 1970		D. IN 1968		F. IN 1966	

2. DID THE AUDITORS USUALLY: (CHECK ONE OR MORE)

A.___CONDUCT A FINANCIAL AUDIT?   C.___CONDUCT A STATE COMPLIANCE AUDIT?   E.___OTHER (PLEASE SPECIFY)

B.___CONDUCT A FEDERAL COMPLIANCE? D.___CONDUCT A PERFORMANCE AUDIT?
      AUDIT

B. PREPARATION:

1. CHECK THE TYPE OF ENTRANCE CONFERENCE THAT THE AUDITOR GENERALLY HAS WITH YOUR SEA PERSONNEL.

_____ FORMAL   _____ INFORMAL   _____ NO ENTRANCE CONFERENCE

2. DOES THE AUDITOR ASK IF YOU HAVE ANY SPECIFIC AREAS YOU WOULD LIKE FOR HIM TO EXAMINE OR IF HE COULD BE OF SERVICE TO YOU AS A BY-PRODUCT OF HIS INVESTIGATION?

A.___ALWAYS   C.___OCCASIONALLY   E.___NEVER

B.___USUALLY   D.___SELDOM

3. WHICH TERMS BEST DESCRIBE YOUR INITIAL RELATIONSHIP WITH THE AUDITOR?

A.___POSITIVE AND FRIENDLY   C.___INDIFFERENT   E.___NEGATIVE AND UNFRIENDLY

B.___CORDIAL   D.___SLIGHTLY NEGATIVE   F.___OTHER

4. HOW DO YOU THINK THE AUDITOR COULD BETTER PREPARE FOR THE AUDIT?

_____

_____

_____

C. CONDUCT:

1. HOW WOULD YOU RATE THE COMMUNICATION THAT EXISTS BETWEEN SEA OFFICIALS AND THE AUDITOR?

A.___EXCELLENT   C.___GOOD   E.___POOR

B.___VERY GOOD   D.___FAIR   F.___OTHER

2. GENERALLY, WHAT IS THE WORKING RELATIONSHIP BETWEEN THE AUDITOR AND THE SEA STAFF?

A.___POSITIVE AND FRIENDLY   C.___INDIFFERENT   E.___NEGATIVE AND UNFRIENDLY

B.___CORDIAL   D.___SLIGHTLY NEGATIVE   F.___OTHER

3. DOES THE AUDITOR PROMPTLY RETURN RECORDS AND FILES?

A.___ALWAYS   C.___OCCASIONALLY   E.___NEVER

B.___USUALLY   D.___SELDOM

4. ARE THEY IN THE SAME CONDITION IN WHICH HE RECEIVED THEM?

A.___ALWAYS   C.___OCCASIONALLY   E.___NEVER

B.___USUALLY   D.___SELDOM

5. DOES THE AUDITOR GENERALLY DISCUSS PROBLEMS OR AUDIT EXCEPTIONS WITH THE STATE PERSONNEL AS HE ENCOUNTERS THEM?

A.___ALWAYS   C.___OCCASIONALLY   E.___NEVER

B.___USUALLY   D.___SELDOM

HEW AUDIT AGENCY (CON'T)

6. WHICH TERM BEST DESCRIBES THE AUDITOR'S COMPETENCE TO CONDUCT FISCAL AUDITS?

A. ___ EXCELLENT   C. ___ GOOD   E. ___ POOR

B. ___ VERY GOOD   D. ___ FAIR   F. ___ OTHER _____

7. WHICH TERM BEST DESCRIBES THE AUDITOR'S COMPETENCE IN EDUCATIONAL PROGRAM MATTERS (REGULATIONS, GUIDELINES, OBJECTIVES, ETC.)?

A. ___ EXCELLENT   C. ___ GOOD   E. ___ POOR

B. ___ VERY GOOD   D. ___ FAIR   F. ___ OTHER _____

8. DOES THE AUDITOR'S EXAMINATION EVER INTERFERE IN ANY WAY WITH THE ROUTINE ACTIVITIES OF THE SEA?

A. ___ ALWAYS   C. ___ OCCASIONALLY   E. ___ NEVER

B. ___ USUALLY   D. ___ SELDOM

9. (A) DOES THE AUDITOR APPEAR WELL PREPARED?

A. ___ ALWAYS   B. ___ USUALLY   C. ___ OCCASIONALLY   D. ___ SELDOM   E. ___ NEVER

9. (B) DOES HE APPEAR TO FOLLOW A PLANNED APPROACH?

A. ___ ALWAYS   B. ___ USUALLY   C. ___ OCCASIONALLY   D. ___ SELDOM   E. ___ NEVER

10. TO YOUR KNOWLEDGE, DOES THE HEW AUDITOR EVER RELY ON INAPPROPRIATE RULES, REGULATIONS, OR ACCOUNTING PROCEDURES?

A. ___ ALWAYS   B. ___ USUALLY   C. ___ OCCASIONALLY   D. ___ SELDOM   E. ___ NEVER

11. IN YOUR OPINION, DOES THE AUDITOR TRY TO ASSIST OR FIND SOMETHING WRONG?

A. ___ ASSIST   B. ___ FAULT FINDING   C. ___ IMPARTIAL

12. WHAT WAYS WOULD YOU SUGGEST FOR IMPROVING THE CONDUCT OF THE AUDIT?

_____

_____

_____

_____

D. REPORTING:

1. DOES THE AUDITOR CONCLUDE THE AUDIT WITH A:

A. ___ FORMAL EXIT CONFERENCE?   C. ___ BOTH INFORMAL AND FORMAL EXIT CONFERENCES?   E. ___ OTHER _____

B. ___ INFORMAL EXIT CONFERENCE?   D. ___ NO CONFERENCE?

2. IF AN EXIT CONFERENCE IS HELD, WHO ATTENDS? (CHECK ONE OR MORE)

A. ___ CHIEF STATE SCHOOL OFFICER   C. ___ STATE FINANCE OFFICER   E. ___ OTHER HEW REGIONAL AUDITORS

B. ___ STATE PROGRAM COORDINATOR   D. ___ OE PERSONNEL   F. ___ OTHER _____

3. WHAT IS THE PURPOSE OF THE EXIT CONFERENCE? (CHECK ONE OR MORE)

A. ___ TO DISCUSS AUDITORS FINDINGS   D. ___ TO WORK OUT AS MANY EXCEPTIONS AS POSSIBLE

B. ___ TO EXPLAIN THE STATE'S POSITION   E. ___ TO AID SEA MANAGEMENT

C. ___ TO ASSIST AUDITOR IN COMPLETING AUDIT   F. ___ OTHER _____

4. WHAT TERMS BEST DESCRIBE THE RELATIONSHIP BETWEEN SEA MANAGEMENT AND THE AUDITORS AT THE EXIT CONFERENCE?

A. ___ POSITIVE AND FRIENDLY   C. ___ INDIFFERENT   F. ___ OTHER _____

B. ___ CORDIAL   D. ___ SLIGHTLY NEGATIVE

6

HEW AUDIT AGENCY (CON'T)

5. WHEN DO YOU FIRST SEE A COPY OF THE DRAFT AUDIT REPORT?

A.___ BEFORE EXIT CONFERENCE   B.___ AT EXIT CONFERENCE   C.___ AFTER EXIT CONFERENCE

6. HOW LONG IS IT AFTER THE EXIT CONFERENCE BEFORE YOU USUALLY RECEIVE A COPY OF THE FINAL AUDIT REPORT?

7. IS THE FINAL AUDIT REPORT STILL RELEVANT BY THE TIME YOU GET THE REPORT?

_____ YES _____ NO _____ PARTIALLY

8. DOES THE FINAL AUDIT REPORT ADEQUATELY AND ACCURATELY INCORPORATE YOUR EXIT CONFERENCE COMMENTS?

A.___ ALWAYS   B.___ USUALLY   C.___ OCCASIONALLY   D.___ SELDOM   E.___ NEVER   F.___ OTHER _____

9. ARE THERE ANY "SURPRISES" IN THE FINAL REPORT WHICH WERE NOT NOTED AT THE CONFERENCE?

A.___ ALWAYS   B.___ USUALLY   C.___ OCCASIONALLY   D.___ SELDOM   E.___ NEVER   F.___ OTHER _____

10. DOES THE AUDITOR NOTE POSITIVE AS WELL AS NEGATIVE ASPECTS?

A.___ ALWAYS   B.___ USUALLY   C.___ OCCASIONALLY   D.___ SELDOM   E.___ NEVER   F.___ OTHER_____

11. HOW WOULD YOU IMPROVE THE EXIT CONFERENCE?

_____

_____

_____

12. HOW WOULD YOU IMPROVE THE AUDITORS' REPORTING PROCEDURES AND THE AUDIT REPORT ITSELF?

_____

_____

_____

13. PLEASE IDENTIFY WHAT YOU CONSIDER THE MOST POSITIVE OR OUTSTANDING ASPECTS OF THE HEW AUDIT OR AUDITOR.

_____

_____

_____

_____

E. RECONCILIATION (SETTLEMENT):

1. DOES YOUR FIRST WRITTEN RESPONSE TO THE AUDIT REPORT EVER TAKE MORE THAN 30 DAYS?

A.___ NEVER   D.___ USUALLY

B.___ SELDOM   E.___ ALWAYS (PLEASE EXPLAIN)

C.___ OCCASIONALLY

2. (A) DO YOU SEEK OR ASSISTANCE IN THE PREPARATION OF YOUR RESPONSE?

_____ YES ___ NO

2. (B) IF SO, IS THEIR ASSISTANCE ADEQUATE?

_____ YES _____ NO (PLEASE EXPLAIN)

7

3. HOW LONG DOES IT USUALLY TAKE OE TO ANSWER YOUR RESPONSE? _____

4. WHAT IS THE NATURE AND TONE OF OE's ANSWER? _____

A.___ POSITIVE AND PRACTICAL   C.___ NEGATIVE AND CRITICAL   E.___ OTHER _____

B.___ IMPARTIAL AND OBJECTIVE   D.___ NO POSITION EXPRESSED

5. IN GENERAL, HOW LONG DOES IT USUALLY TAKE TO SETTLE AN HEW AUDIT?

A.___ 1-6 MONTHS   C.___ 1-2 YEARS   E.___ OTHER

B.___ 6 MOS. - 1 YEAR   D.___ 2 YEARS

6. IN GENERAL, ARE AUDIT FINDINGS RECONCILED AS EXPEDITIOUSLY AS POSSIBLE?

A.___ ALWAYS   C.___ OCCASIONALLY   E.___ NEVER

B.___ USUALLY   D.___ SELDOM   F.___ OTHER _____

7. CHECK THE RECOURSE YOU HAVE FOLLOWED IN AUDIT EXCEPTIONS WITH WHICH YOU DISAGREED.   (CHECK ONE OR MORE)

A.___ CONTINUE NEGOTIATION WITH OE   C.___ NO RECOURSE   E.___ OBTAIN POLITICAL ACTION   G.___ OTHER _____

B.___ REFUSE TO COMPLY   D.___ COMPLY IN PART   F.___ SEEK JUDICIAL REVIEW

8. WHAT IS THE SOURCE OF FUNDS FOR SEA RETURNS RESULTING FROM AUDIT EXCEPTIONS?   (CHECK ONE OR MORE)

A.___ OTHER PROGRAMS   C.___ SURPLUSES   E.___ OTHER _____

B.___ SPECIAL APPROPRIATIONS   D.___ CUT-BACK IN CURRENT PROGRAM

9. CHECK THE WAYS IN WHICH YOUR SEA USES THE HEWAA REPORT?   (CHECK ONE OR MORE)

A.___ AS A MANAGEMENT TOOL   D.___ TO IMPROVE COMPLIANCE WITH FEDERAL LAWS & REGULATIONS

B.___ TO IMPROVE FINANCIAL CONTROLS   E.___ TO IMPROVE PROGRAM PERFORMANCE

C.___ TO IMPROVE COMPLIANCE WITH STATE LAWS & REGULATIONS   F.___ OTHER _____

10. WHAT SPECIFIC PROBLEMS HAVE YOU ENCOUNTERED IN THE AUDIT RECONCILIATION PROCESS? _____

_____

_____

11. HOW WOULD YOU IMPROVE THE AUDIT RECONCILIATION PROCEDURES? _____

_____

_____

12. WHAT CHANGES, IF ANY, HAVE YOU NOTED IN HEW AUDITS IN RECENT YEARS? _____

_____

_____

13. HOW COULD THE HEW AUDIT BE OF GREATER USE TO YOUR SEA? _____

_____

_____

14. ARE THERE ANY OTHER COMMENTS OR EXPERIENCES THAT YOU WOULD LIKE TO DISCUSS REGARDING HEW AUDITS OF SEA'S?

_____

_____

_____

_____

8

II.

THE GENERAL ACCOUNTING OFFICE
(GAO)

A. GENERAL:

1. IN RECENT YEARS, THE GENERAL ACCOUNTING OFFICE HAS INCREASED THE FREQUENCY OF SEA AUDITS. SPECIFICALLY, WHEN AND WHAT PROGRAMS HAVE BEEN AUDITED IN YOUR SEA IN THE FOLLOWING YEARS?

PROGRAM	PERIOD COVERED		PROGRAM	PERIOD COVERED	(IF NO GAO AUDITS SINCE 1965, SKIP

A. IN 1971 _____ _____   D. IN 1968 _____ _____   (IF NO GAO AUDITS SINCE 1965, SKIP THIS SECTION AND GO TO THE NEXT SECTION--STATE AUDIT AGENCY.)

B. IN 1970 _____ _____   E. IN 1967 _____ _____

C. IN 1969 _____ _____   F. IN 1966 _____ _____

2. DID THE AUDITORS USUALLY: (CHECK ONE OR MORE)

A. ____ CONDUCT A FINANCIAL AUDIT?   C. ____ CONDUCT A STATE COMPLIANCE AUDIT?   E. ____ OTHER (PLEASE SPECIFY)

B. ____ CONDUCT A FEDERAL COMPLIANCE AUDIT?   D. ____ CONDUCT A PERFORMANCE AUDIT?

B. PREPARATION:

1. CHECK THE TYPE OF ENTRANCE CONFERENCE THAT THE AUDITOR GENERALLY HAS WITH YOUR SEA PERSONNEL.

_____ FORMAL   _____ INFORMAL   _____ NO ENTRANCE CONFERENCE

2. DOES THE AUDITOR ASK IF YOU HAVE ANY SPECIFIC AREAS YOU WOULD LIKE FOR HIM TO EXAMINE OR IF HE COULD BE OF SERVICE TO YOU AS A BY-PRODUCT OF HIS INVESTIGATION?

A. ____ ALWAYS   C. ____ OCCASIONALLY   E. ____ NEVER

B. ____ USUALLY   D. ____ SELDOM

3. WHICH TERMS BEST DESCRIBE YOUR INITIAL RELATIONSHIP WITH THE AUDITOR?

A. ____ POSITIVE AND FRIENDLY   C. ____ INDIFFERENT   E. ____ NEGATIVE AND UNFRIENDLY

B. ____ CORDIAL   D. ____ SLIGHTLY NEGATIVE   F. ____ OTHER _____

4. HOW DO YOU THINK THE AUDITOR COULD BETTER PREPARE FOR THE AUDIT?

_____
_____
_____
_____
_____

C. CONDUCT:

1. HOW WOULD YOU RATE THE COMMUNICATION THAT EXISTS BETWEEN SEA OFFICIALS AND THE AUDITOR?

A. ____ EXCELLENT   C. ____ GOOD   E. ____ POOR

B. ____ VERY GOOD   D. ____ FAIR   F. ____ OTHER _____

2. GENERALLY, WHAT IS THE WORKING RELATIONSHIP BETWEEN THE AUDITOR AND THE SEA STAFF?

A. ____ POSITIVE AND FRIENDLY   C. ____ INDIFFERENT   E. ____ NEGATIVE AND UNFRIENDLY

B. ____ CORDIAL   D. ____ SLIGHTLY NEGATIVE   F. ____ OTHER _____

3. DOES THE AUDITOR PROMPTLY RETURN RECORDS AND FILES?

A. ____ ALWAYS   C. ____ OCCASIONALLY   E. ____ NEVER

B. ____ USUALLY   D. ____ SELDOM

4. ARE THEY IN THE SAME CONDITION IN WHICH HE RECEIVED THEM?

A. ____ ALWAYS   C. ____ OCCASIONALLY   E. ____ NEVER

B. ____ USUALLY   D. ____ SELDOM

5. DOES THE AUDITOR GENERALLY DISCUSS PROBLEMS OR AUDIT EXCEPTIONS WITH THE STATE PERSONNEL AS HE ENCOUNTERS THEM?

A. ____ ALWAYS   C. ____ OCCASIONALLY   E. ____ NEVER

B. ____ USUALLY   D. ____ SELDOM

9

GAO (CON'T)

6. WHICH TERM BEST DESCRIBES THE AUDITOR'S COMPETENCE TO CONDUCT FISCAL AUDITS?

A. ___ EXCELLENT   C. ___ GOOD   E. ___ POOR

B. ___ VERY GOOD   D. ___ FAIR   F. ___ OTHER _____

7. WHICH TERM BEST DESCRIBES THE AUDITOR'S COMPETENCE IN EDUCATIONAL PROGRAM MATTERS (REGULATIONS, GUIDELINES, OBJECTIVES, ETC.)?

A. ___ EXCELLENT   C. ___ GOOD   E. ___ POOR

B. ___ VERY GOOD   D. ___ FAIR   F. ___ OTHER _____

8. DOES THE AUDITOR'S EXAMINATION EVER INTERFERE IN ANY WAY WITH THE ROUTINE ACTIVITIES OF THE SEA?

A. ___ ALWAYS   C. ___ OCCASIONALLY   E. ___ NEVER

B. ___ USUALLY   D. ___ SELDOM

9. (A) DOES THE AUDITOR APPEAR WELL PREPARED?

A. ___ ALWAYS   C. ___ OCCASIONALLY   E. ___ NEVER

B. ___ USUALLY   D. ___ SELDOM

9. (B) DOES HE APPEAR TO FOLLOW A PLANNED APPROACH?

A. ___ ALWAYS   C. ___ OCCASIONALLY   E. ___ NEVER

B. ___ USUALLY   D. ___ SELDOM

10. TO YOUR KNOWLEDGE, DOES THE GAO AUDITOR EVER RELY ON INAPPROPRIATE RULES, REGULATIONS, OR ACCOUNTING PROCEDURES?

A. ___ ALWAYS   C. ___ OCCASIONALLY   E. ___ NEVER

B. ___ USUALLY   D. ___ SELDOM

11. IN YOUR OPINION, DOES THE AUDITOR TRY TO ASSIST OR FIND SOMETHING WRONG?

A. ___ ASSIST   B. ___ FAULT FINDING   C. ___ IMPARTIAL

12. WHAT WAYS WOULD YOU SUGGEST FOR IMPROVING THE CONDUCT OF THE AUDIT?

_____
_____
_____
_____
_____

D. REPORTING:

1. DOES THE AUDITOR CONCLUDE THE AUDIT WITH A:

A. ___ FORMAL EXIT CONFERENCE?   C. ___ BOTH INFORMAL AND FORMAL EXIT CONFERENCES?   E. ___ OTHER _____

B. ___ INFORMAL EXIT CONFERENCE?   D. ___ NO CONFERENCE?

2. IF AN EXIT CONFERENCE IS HELD, WHO ATTENDS? (CHECK ONE OR MORE)

A. ___ CHIEF STATE SCHOOL OFFICER   C. ___ STATE FINANCE OFFICER   E. ___ OTHER GAO REGIONAL AUDITORS

B. ___ STATE PROGRAM COORDINATOR   D. ___ OE PERSONNEL   F. ___ OTHER_____

3. WHAT IS THE PURPOSE OF THE EXIT CONFERENCE? (CHECK ONE OR MORE)

A. ___ TO DISCUSS AUDITORS FINDINGS   D. ___ TO WORK OUT AS MANY EXCEPTIONS AS POSSIBLE

B. ___ TO EXPLAIN THE STATE'S POSITION   E. ___ TO AID SEA MANAGEMENT

C. ___ TO ASSIST AUDITOR IN COMPLETING AUDIT   F. ___ OTHER_____

4. WHAT TERMS BEST DESCRIBE THE RELATIONSHIP BETWEEN SEA MANAGEMENT AND THE AUDITORS AT THE EXIT CONFERENCE?

A. ___ POSITIVE AND FRIENDLY   C. ___ INDIFFERENT   E. ___ OTHER _____

B. ___ CORDIAL   D. ___ SLIGHTLY NEGATIVE

GAO (CON'T)

5. WHEN DO YOU FIRST SEE A COPY OF THE DRAFT AUDIT REPORT?

A. ___ BEFORE EXIT CONFERENCE   B. ___ AT EXIT CONFERENCE   C. ___ AFTER EXIT CONFERENCE

6. HOW LONG IS IT AFTER THE EXIT CONFERENCE BEFORE YOU USUALLY RECEIVE A COPY OF THE FINAL AUDIT REPORT?

7. IS THE FINAL AUDIT REPORT STILL RELEVANT BY THE TIME YOU GET THE REPORT?

___ YES   ___ NO   ___ PARTIALLY

8. DOES THE FINAL AUDIT REPORT ADEQUATELY AND ACCURATELY INCORPORATE YOUR EXIT CONFERENCE COMMENTS?

A. ___ ALWAYS   C. ___ OCCASIONALLY   D. ___ NEVER

B. ___ USUALLY   D. ___ SELDOM   E. ___ OTHER _____

9. ARE THERE ANY "SURPRISES" IN THE FINAL REPORT WHICH WERE NOT NOTED AT THE CONFERENCE?

A. ___ ALWAYS   C. ___ OCCASIONALLY   E. ___ NEVER

B. ___ USUALLY   D. ___ SELDOM   F. ___ OTHER _____

10. DOES THE AUDITOR NOTE POSITIVE AS WELL AS NEGATIVE ASPECTS?

A. ___ ALWAYS   C. ___ OCCASIONALLY   E. ___ NEVER

B. ___ USUALLY   D. ___ SELDOM

11. HOW WOULD YOU IMPROVE THE EXIT CONFERENCE(S)?

_____
_____
_____
_____

12. HOW WOULD YOU IMPROVE THE AUDITORS' REPORTING PROCEDURES AND THE AUDIT REPORT ITSELF?

_____
_____
_____
_____

13. PLEASE IDENTIFY WHAT YOU CONSIDER THE MOST POSITIVE OR OUTSTANDING ASPECTS OF THE GAO AUDIT OR AUDITOR.

_____
_____

E. RECONCILIATION (SETTLEMENT):

1. DOES OE'S RECONCILIATION OR SETTLEMENT OF GAO REPORTS DIFFER IN ANY WAY FROM THE SETTLEMENT FOR HEW AUDIT REPORTS? (PLEASE EXPLAIN)

_____
_____
_____

2. WHAT SPECIFIC PROBLEMS HAVE YOU ENCOUNTERED IN THE AUDIT RECONCILIATION PROCESS FOR GAO REPORTS?

_____
_____
_____

GAO (CON'T)

3. HOW WOULD YOU IMPROVE THE AUDIT RECONCILIATION PROCEDURE FOR GAO REPORTS? (PLEASE EXPLAIN)

4. CHECK THE WAYS IN WHICH YOUR SEA USES THE GAO REPORT? (CHECK ONE OR MORE)

A.____ AS A MANAGEMENT TOOL

B.____ TO IMPROVE FINANCIAL CONTROLS

C.____ TO IMPROVE COMPLIANCE WITH STATE LAWS & REGULATIONS

D.____ TO IMPROVE COMPLIANCE WITH FEDERAL LAWS AND REGULATIONS

E.____ TO IMPROVE PROGRAM PERFORMANCE

F.____ OTHER _____

5. ARE THERE ANY OTHER COMMENTS OR EXPERIENCES THAT YOU WOULD LIKE TO DISCUSS REGARDING GAO AUDITS?

6. HOW COULD THE GAO AUDIT BE OF GREATER USE TO YOUR SEA? (PLEASE DISCUSS)

III.

STATE AUDIT AGENCY (SAA)   (PLEASE SEE INSTRUCTION # 6)

	STATE AUDITOR # 1	STATE AUDITOR # 2	STATE AUDITOR #3
1. WHAT IS THE TITLE OF THE STATE AGENCY OR AGENCIES RESPONSIBLE FOR AUDITING YOUR SEA?			
2. HOW IS THE STATE AUDITOR SELECTED?			
A. ELECTED BY PEOPLE			
B. APPOINTED BY GOVERNOR			
C. ELECTED BY LEGISLATURE (AS A WHOLE)			
D. APPOINTED BY A LEGISLATIVE COUNCIL OR COMMITTEE			
E. OTHER (PLEASE EXPLAIN)			
3. WHAT IS THE LEGAL AUTHORITY UNDER WHICH THE STATE AUDIT AGENCY OPERATES?			
A. CONSTITUTIONAL MANDATE			
B. LEGISLATIVE STATUTE			
C. EXECUTIVE ORDER			
D. OTHER (PLEASE SPECIFY)			
4. WHAT IS THE APPROXIMATE SIZE OF THE STATE AUDIT STAFF?			
A. PROFESSIONAL AUDITORS			
B. NON-PROFESSIONAL AUDITORS			

12

STATE AUDIT AGENCY (CON'T)

	STATE AUDITOR # 1	STATE AUDITOR #2	STATE AUDITOR # 3
5. WHAT ARE THE QUALIFICATIONS OF THE STATE AUDIT STAFF? (CHECK ONE OR MORE)			
A. CPA CERTIFICATION			
B. ACCOUNTING DEGREE			
C. STATE EXAMINATION			
D. NO REQUIREMENTS			
E. OTHER (PLEASE DISCUSS)			
6. WHEN DOES THE STATE AUDIT AGENCY AUDIT YOUR SEA?			
A. CONTINUOUSLY			
B. YEARLY			
C. EVERY TWO YEARS			
D. OTHER (PLEASE SPECIFY)			
7. DOES THE MANDATE OF SAA SPECIFICALLY REQUIRE ANY OF THE FOLLOWING POST AUDITS? (CHECK ONE OR MORE)			
A. FISCAL POST-AUDITS			
B. LEGAL COMPLIANCE POST-AUDITS			
C. PERFORMANCE POST-AUDITS			
D. NO POST-AUDIT FUNCTIONS MANDATED			
E. OTHER (PLEASE SPECIFY)			
8. DOES THE STATE AUDITOR IN ACTUALITY (CHECK ONE OR MORE)			
A. CONDUCT A FISCAL AUDIT?			
B. CONDUCT A FEDERAL COMPLIANCE AUDIT?			
C. CONDUCT A STATE COMPLIANCE AUDIT?			
D. CONDUCT A PERFORMANCE AUDIT?			
E. OTHER (PLEASE SPECIFY)			
9. HOW MANY AUDITORS ARE INVOLVED IN THE ON-SITE AUDIT?			
A. ONE			
B. TWO			
C. THREE			
D. FOUR OR MORE			
0. DOES THE SAA HOLD AN AUDIT ENTRANCE CONFERENCE WITH THE SEA?			
A. YES			
B. NO			
C. OCCASIONALLY			

13

STATE AUDIT AGENCY (CON'T)

	STATE AUDITOR # 1	STATE AUDITOR # 2	STATE AUDITOR # 3
11. DOES THE STATE AUDIT AGENCY CONDUCT A PRE-AUDIT OF SEA TRANSACTIONS?			
A. YES			
B. NO			
12. DOES THE AUDITOR's EXAMINATION INTERFERE IN ANY WAY WITH THE ROUTINE ACTIVITIES OF THE SEA?			
A. ALWAYS			
B. USUALLY			
C. OCCASIONALLY			
D. SELDOM			
E. NEVER			
13. DOES THE STATE AUDITOR ASK IF YOU HAVE ANY SPECIFIC AREAS YOU WOULD LIKE HIM TO EXAMINE OR IF HE COULD BE OF SERVICE TO YOU AS A BY-PRODUCT OF HIS INVESTIGATION?			
A. ALWAYS			
B. USUALLY			
C. OCCASIONALLY			
D. SELDOM			
E. NEVER			
14. DOES THE AUDITOR DISCUSS PROBLEMS OR AUDIT EXCEPTIONS AS HE ENCOUNTERS THEM WITH STATE PERSONNEL?			
A. YES			
B. NO			
C. OCCASIONALLY			
15. WHAT IS THE WORKING RELATIONSHIP BETWEEN THE SEA AND THE SAA?			
A. EXCELLENT			
B. VERY GOOD			
C. GOOD			
D. FAIR			
E. POOR			
16. WHICH TERM BEST DESCRIBES THE AUDITOR'S COMPETENCE TO CONDUCT FISCAL AUDITS?			
A. EXCELLENT			
B. VERY GOOD			
C. GOOD			
D. FAIR			
E. POOR			
F. OTHER _____			

14

STATE AUDIT AGENCY (CON'T)

	STATE AUDITOR # 1	STATE AUDITOR # 2	STATE AUDITOR # 3
17. WHICH TERM BEST DESCRIBES THE AUDITOR'S COMPETENCE IN EDUCATIONAL PROGRAM MATTERS (REGULATIONS, GUIDELINES, OBJECTIVES, ETC.)?			
A. EXCELLENT			
B. VERY GOOD			
C. GOOD			
D. FAIR			
E. POOR			
F. OTHER _____			
18. DOES THE AUDITOR HOLD A FORMAL EXIT CONFERENCE?			
A. YES			
B. NO			
C. OCCASIONALLY			
19. DOES THE SAA ISSUE A FORMAL AUDIT REPORT?			
A. YES			
B. NO			
C. OCCASIONALLY			
20. DO AUDIT REPORTS OF SAA INCLUDE DATA ON: (CHECK ONE OR MORE)			
A. EXPENDITURE OF FEDERAL FUNDS BY THE SEA's?			
B. COMPLIANCE WITH FEDERAL REGULATIONS GOVERNING USE OF THESE FUNDS?			
C. PROGRAM OPERATIONS IN TERMS OF THE ESTABLISHED FEDERAL OBJECTIVES OF THE PROGRAM?			
D. NONE OF THE ABOVE?			
E. SOME COMBINATION OF THE ABOVE?			
21. DOES THE FINAL AUDIT REPORT ADEQUATELY AND ACCURATELY INCORPORATE YOUR COMMENTS?			
A. ALWAYS			
B. USUALLY			
C. OCCASIONALLY			
D. SELDOM			
E. NEVER			
22. ARE THERE EVER ANY "SURPRISES" IN THE FINAL AUDIT REPORT WHICH WERE NOT NOTED AT THE EXIT CONFERENCE?			
A. ALWAYS			
B. USUALLY			
C. OCCASIONALLY			
D. SELDOM			
E. NEVER			

15

STATE AUDIT AGENCY (CON'T)

	STATE AUDITOR # 1	STATE AUDITOR # 2	STATE AUDITOR # 3
23. DOES THE AUDITOR NOTE POSITIVE AS WELL AS NEGATIVE ASPECTS?			
A. ALWAYS			
B. USUALLY			
C. OCCASIONALLY			
D. SELDOM			
E. NEVER			
24. ARE ALL AUDITS CONDUCTED BY YOUR SAA PUBLIC DOCUMENTS?			
A. YES			
B. NO			
25. WHAT RECOURSES HAVE YOU FOLLOWED IN THE SETTLEMENT OF SAA FINDINGS? (CHECK ONE OR MORE)			
A. NEGOTIATE			
B. REFUSE TO COMPLY			
C. NO RECOURSE			
D. COMPLY IN PART			
E. OBTAIN POLITICAL INTERVENTION			
F. OTHER _____			
26. HOW DOES YOUR SEA USE THE SAA REPORT? (CHECK ONE OR MORE)			
A. AS A MANAGEMENT TOOL			
B. TO IMPROVE FINANCIAL CONTROLS			
C. TO IMPROVE COMPLIANCE WITH STATE LAWS AND REGULATIONS			
D. TO IMPROVE COMPLIANCE WITH FEDERAL LAWS AND REGULATIONS			
E. TO IMPROVE PROGRAM PERFORMANCE			
F. OTHER _____			

27. IN WHAT AREAS CAN THIS STATE IMPROVE THE OVERALL EFFECTIVENESS OF THE STATE AUDIT SYSTEM CONSIDERING SUCH FACTORS AS AUDIT APPROACH, REPORTING PROCEDURES, SALARIES, NUMBERS OF EMPLOYEES, EDUCATION, LEGAL STATUS, AUTHORITY OF THE AGENCIES, ETC.? (DISCUSS BY AGENCY)

_____

_____

_____

_____

_____

_____

_____

_____

_____

_____

IV.   INTERNAL AUDITORS
                                            (IA)

1.   DO YOU HAVE AN INTERNAL AUDIT STAFF (DO NOT INCLUDE BOOKKEEPERS)?   ___YES ___NO. (IF YES, PLEASE ANSWER
     THIS SECTION.)

2.   WHAT IS THE SIZE OF THE INTERNAL AUDIT STAFF?   _____

3.   ARE THERE ANY EDUCATIONAL OR OTHER REQUIREMENTS FOR THE STAFF?   (CHECK ONE OR MORE)

A.__CPA CERTIFICATION   C.__STATE EXAMINATION   E.__OTHER
                                                             (PLEASE EXPLAIN)
B.__ACCOUNTING DEGREE   D.__NO REQUIREMENTS

4.   WHAT TYPE AUDIT IS CONDUCTED?   (CHECK ONE OR MORE)

A.__PRE-AUDIT   C.__FISCAL AUDIT   E.__PERFORMANCE AUDIT

B.__POST-AUDIT   D.__COMPLIANCE AUDIT   F.__OTHER
                                                             (PLEASE EXPLAIN)

5.   (A) TO WHOM IS THE CHIEF AUDITOR RESPONSIBLE?   _____

     (B) DO YOU PROVIDE OR SUPPORT PROFESSIONAL TRAINING PROGRAMS OR COURSES? ____YES ____NO

6.   WHAT AREAS OF THE SEA ARE AUDITED?   (CHECK ONE OR MORE)

A.__ACCOUNTING AND BOOKKEEPING   C.__PROJECT ADMINISTRATION   E.__PERSONNEL MANAGEMENT   G.__OTHER
                                                                                              (PLEASE EXPLAIN)
B.__GENERAL ADMINISTRATION   D.__FINANCIAL MANAGEMENT   F.__MANAGEMENT INFORMATION

7.   DO THEY AUDIT THE LEA'S?   ____YES ____NO

8.   DOES THE AUDIT STAFF ISSUE A FORMAL AUDIT REPORT?   ____YES ____NO

9.   HOW FREQUENTLY DO THEY ISSUE A REPORT?

A.__ANNUALLY   C.__QUARTERLY   E.__OTHER

B.__SEMI-ANNUALLY   D.__VARIES WITH AUDIT

10. TO WHOM ARE THE RESULTS OF THEIR AUDITS DIRECTED?   (CHECK ONE OR MORE)

A.__STATE LEGISLATURE   C.__STATE AUDIT AGENCY   E.__OTHER OR SOME COMBINATION OF THE ABOVE
                                                              (PLEASE SPECIFY)
B.__CHIEF STATE EXECUTIVE   D.__CHIEF STATE SCHOOL OFFICER

11. ARE THEIR FINDINGS FOR INTERNAL USE ONLY?   ____YES ____NO

12. IS THEIR AUDIT FUNCTION PARTICULARLY USEFUL IN IMPROVING SEA MANAGEMENT?   ____YES ____NO

V.   AUDITS BY INDEPENDENT PUBLIC ACCOUNTANTS (CPA's AND PUBLIC ACCOUNTANTS)

1.   IS YOUR SEA AUDITED BY INDEPENDENT AUDITORS (CPA'S, ETC.) THAT ARE NOT EMPLOYEES OF YOUR SEA OR MEMBERS OF A
     SPECIFIC AUDIT AGENCY OF THE STATE OR FEDERAL GOVERNMENT?   (ANSWER YES OR NO)

          _____CPA   ___PUBLIC ACCOUNTANT   ____OTHER, PLEASE EXPLAIN

     IF YES, PLEASE ANSWER THIS SECTION. IF NECESSARY, STRUCTURE YOUR ANSWERS TO INDICATE APPROPRIATE AUDITOR
     E.G. CPA, PUBLIC ACCOUNTANT, OTHER).

2.   WHAT IS THE PURPOSE OR REASON FOR THIS INDEPENDENT AUDIT?

INDEPENDENT PUBLIC ACCOUNTANT (CON'T)

3. HOW FREQUENTLY IS THE INDEPENDENT AUDIT MADE?

A.___ CONTINUOUSLY   C.___ BI-ANNUALLY   E.___ OTHER

B.___ ANNUALLY   D.___ SPECIAL ENGAGEMENT

4. TO WHOM IS THE INDEPENDENT AUDIT REPORT DIRECTED?

A.___ STATE LEGISLATURE   C.___ STATE AUDIT AGENCY   E.___ OFFICE OF EDUCATION

B.___ CHIEF STATE EXECUTIVE   D.___ CHIEF STATE SCHOOL OFFICER   F.___ OTHER _____

5. (A) HOW IS THE AUDITOR SELECTED? (B) IN GENERAL, WHAT ARE THE TERMS OF THE ENGAGEMENT CONTRACT?

_____
_____
_____
_____
_____

6. WHAT TYPE OF AUDIT IS CONDUCTED?

A.___ FISCAL AUDIT (EXAMINATION OF   C.___ STATE COMPLIANCE AUDIT (ABIDING   E.___ OTHER, OR SOME COMBINATION
       ACCOUNTING RECORDS)   BY STATE RULES AND REGULATIONS)   (PLEASE SPECIFY)

B.___ FEDERAL COMPLIANCE AUDIT (ABIDING   D.___ PERFORMANCE AUDIT
       BY FEDERAL RULES AND REGULATIONS)

7. HOW COULD INDEPENDENT PUBLIC ACCOUNTANTS' AUDITS OF YOUR SEA BE IMPROVED? (PLEASE EXPLAIN)

_____
_____
_____
_____

VI.   LOCAL EDUCATION AGENCIES   (PLEASE SEE INSTRUCTION # 7)
                               (LEA)

1. PLEASE IDENTIFY AND EXPLAIN WHO AUDITS THE LOCAL EDUCATION AGENCIES IN YOUR STATE.

(EXAMPLE) (1) STATE AUDITOR AUDITS COUNTY DISTRICTS, (2) SEA AUDITS LUNCH PROGRAMS IN ALL DISTRICTS,
           (3) CPA's AUDIT CITY OR INDEPENDENT DISTRICTS, ETC.

AUDIT AGENCY	TYPE OF LEA AUDITED		AUDIT AGENCY	TYPE OF LEA AUDITED
1._____	_____	3.	_____	_____
2._____	_____	4.	_____	_____

	AGENCY # 1	AGENCY # 2	AGENCY # 3	AGENCY # 4
2. WHAT TYPE OR TYPES OF AUDITS ARE CONDUCTED BY THE AGENCIES LISTED IN QUESTION # 1?				
A. FISCAL AUDIT				
B. FEDERAL COMPLIANCE AUDIT				
C. STATE COMPLIANCE AUDIT				
D. PERFORMANCE AUDIT				
E. PRE-AUDIT				
F. AUDIT ONLY OF SPECIFIC PROGRAMS				
G. OTHER _____				

18

LOCAL EDUCATION AGENCIES (CON'T)

	AGENCY # 1	AGENCY # 2	AGENCY # 3	AGENCY # 4
3. HOW FREQUENTLY ARE THE AUDITS CONDUCTED? (CHECK ONE OR MORE)				
A. CONTINUOUSLY				
B. YEARLY				
C. EVERY TWO YEARS				
D. SPECIAL ENGAGEMENT				
E. OTHER _____				
4. TO WHOM IS THE LEA AUDIT REPORT DIRECTED? (CHECK ONE OR MORE)				
A. LOCAL SUPERINTENDENT OF SCHOOLS				
B. CHIEF STATE SCHOOL OFFICER				
C. CHIEF STATE EXECUTIVE				
D. LOCAL BOARD OF EDUCATION				
E. STATE AUDIT AGENCY				
F. OTHER _____				
5. WHAT IS YOUR GENERAL OPINION OF THE QUALITY OF AUDITS? (CHECK ONE OR MORE)				
A. EXCELLENT				
B. VERY GOOD				
C. GOOD				
D. FAIR				
E. POOR				

6. WHO NEGOTIATES LEA AUDIT SETTLEMENTS IN YOUR STATE? (PLEASE DISCUSS)

_____

_____

_____

_____

7. HOW DOES YOUR SEA USE LEA AUDITS? (PLEASE DISCUSS BY AGENCY)

_____

_____

_____

_____

8. HOW MIGHT THE AUDITS OF LEA'S BE IMPROVED? (PLEASE DISCUSS BY AGENCY)

_____

_____

_____

_____

_____

19

VII. _____ ATTITUDES AND FUTURE TRENDS _____

NOTE: THESE QUESTIONS WHICH DEAL WITH AUDITING IN GENERAL ARE MOST IMPORTANT TO THE SUCCESS OF THIS PROJECT. PLEASE GIVE THEM SPECIAL ATTENTION.

1. IT IS OFTEN SAID THAT THE ATTITUDE OF MANAGEMENT TOWARD AUDITORS AND THE AUDITORS' ATTITUDE REGARDING MANAGEMENT IS NOT OF A POSITIVE NATURE. (A) DO YOU GENERALLY AGREE WITH THIS? (B) IF SO, HOW MAY IT BE CHANGED? (PLEASE ELABORATE)

2. WHAT DO YOU CONSIDER TO BE THE MOST PRESSING PROBLEMS RELATIVE TO AUDITS OF YOUR SEA? (PLEASE EXPLAIN FULLY BY AGENCY)

3. HAVE YOU EXPERIENCED ANY PARTICULAR DIFFICULTY OR PROBLEM WITH ANY AUDIT AGENCY? (PLEASE ELABORATE)

4. WHICH OF THE FOLLOWING AUDITS ARE MOST BENEFICIAL TO YOUR SEA MANAGEMENT? (LIST IN ORDER OF IMPORTANCE, 1 MOST BENEFICIAL, 5 LEAST BENEFICIAL)

____ HEWAA AUDITS   ____ STATE AGENCY AUDITS   ____ CPA AUDITS

____ GAO AUDITS   ____ INTERNAL AUDITS   ____ OTHER _____

5. WHICH AUDITORS SEEM TO BE THE BEST QUALIFIED AND MOST COMPETENT? (LIST IN ORDER WITH 1 BEST QUALIFIED AND 5 LEAST QUALIFIED)

	FISCAL MATTERS	EDUCATION PROGRAM MATTERS		FISCAL MATTERS	EDUCATION PROGRAM MATTERS
HEWAA			INTERNAL AUDITORS		
GAO			CPA's		
STATE AUDIT AGENCY			OTHER		

6. WHAT IS YOUR OPINION OF THE USEFULNESS AND PRACTICALITY OF PERFORMANCE AUDITING?

A. ____ EXCELLENT   D. ____ NO VALUE

B. ____ VERY HELPFUL

C. ____ SOME VALUE

7. IN YOUR OPINION IN WHICH OF THE FOLLOWING AREAS ARE AUDITORS (IN GENERAL) PRESENTLY QUALIFIED TO CONDUCT AUDITS?

A. FISCAL AUDITS ____ HIGHLY QUALIFIED ____ QUALIFIED ____ FAIRLY QUALIFIED ____ NOT QUALIFIED

B. COMPLIANCE AUDIT ____ HIGHLY QUALIFIED ____ QUALIFIED ____ FAIRLY QUALIFIED ____ NOT QUALIFIED

C. PERFORMANCE AUDITS ____ HIGHLY QUALIFIED ____ QUALIFIED ____ FAIRLY QUALIFIED ____ NOT QUALIFIED

ATTITUDES AND FUTURE TRENDS (CON'T)

8. WHAT WOULD BE YOUR REACTION TO A TEAM APPROACH TO AUDITING? (E.G. OE PROGRAM PEOPLE WORKING WITH THE HEW AUDITORS?)

9. WHAT WOULD BE YOUR REACTION TO FEDERAL AUDITORS <u>SPECIALIZING</u> IN EDUCATIONAL AUDITS? (AT THE PRESENT TIME THEIR ASSIGNMENTS USUALLY VARY QUITE WIDELY)

10. IN YOUR OPINION, ARE THERE ANY ADDITIONAL TRAINING OR COMPETENCIES NEEDED BY THE AUDITOR TO CONDUCT A PERFORMANCE AUDIT?

11. HAVE ANY OF THE FOLLOWING REVIEWS OR AUDITS BEEN CONDUCTED IN YOUR STATE? (CHECK ONE OR MORE)

A.____ HEWAA FOLLOW-UP AUDIT REVIEW   D.____ OE STATE MANAGEMENT REVIEW

B.____ TITLE I, ESEA REVIEW   E.____ HEWAA QUALITY MANAGEMENT PROGRAM REVIEW

C.____ EDUCATIONAL PROGRAM AUDIT   F.____ OTHER SPECIAL REVIEW OR AUDITS

12. (A) WHICH REVIEWS AND AUDITS WERE BENEFICIAL AND IN WHAT WAY?

____ (B) WHICH WERE NOT BENEFICIAL?

13. CAN THE AUDITOR BE BOTH A "WATCHDOG" AND AN AID TO MANAGEMENT?

14. WHAT IS YOUR OPINION OF THE WAY HEWAA APPROACHES THE AUDIT? IN OTHER WORDS, WOULD YOU RATHER THEY TOOK A PIECEMEAL APPROACH (AUDIT ONE PROGRAM AT A TIME) OR A TOTAL COMPREHENSIVE APPROACH? (DISCUSS ADVANTAGES AND DISADVANTAGES)

21

ATTITUDES AND FUTURE TRENDS (CON'T)

15. PLEASE DISCUSS WHAT YOU ENVISION AS MAJOR PROBLEMS IN A PROGRAM THAT WOULD ALLOW FEDERAL RELIANCE ON AUDITS CONDUCTED BY THE STATE AUDIT AGENCY? (INCLUDING ACCESSABILITY OF WORKING PAPERS, UNIFORM STANDARDS, AND GUIDELINES, ETC.)

16. WHY DO MANY OF THE SAME AUDIT EXCEPTIONS CONTINUE TO RECUR YEAR AFTER YEAR?

17. WOULD YOU LIKE TO SEE THE DEVELOPMENT OF A UNIFORM IMPLEMENTATION PLAN FOR MANAGEMENT IMPROVEMENT BASED ON AUDIT FINDINGS? (IT WOULD INCLUDE OBJECTIVES, ACTIVITIES, TIMELINES, RESOURCES, ETC.) PLEASE DISCUSS.

18. DO YOU FEEL THAT CRITERIA SHOULD BE ESTABLISHED FOR THE SETTLEMENT OF FINDINGS? IF SO, WHAT SHOULD THEY BE? (FOR EXAMPLE, EXCUSE ADMINISTRATIVE ERROR, DEMONSTRATE IMPROVEMENT PLANS, SHOW IMPROVEMENTS NOW UNDERWAY, SET A SERIES OF DEADLINES, ETC.)

19. IF YOU WERE IN AN OE POSITION, HOW WOULD YOU RESOLVE FINDINGS? (DISCUSS SPECIFIC EXAMPLES)

20. HOW DO YOU FEEL ABOUT GAO AND HEW GOING DIRECTLY TO THE LOCALS TO MAKE AUDITS? WOULD YOUR SEA RATHER OBTAIN INFORMATION FOR THEM?

21. DO YOU CONTACT HEWAA BETWEEN AUDITS FOR ASSISTANCE? IF YOU DO NOT RECEIVE ASSISTANCE FROM THE HEWAA, WHERE DO YOU OBTAIN INFORMATION?

ATTITUDES AND FUTURE TRENDS (CON'T)

22. HAVE YOU EVER REQUESTED AN AUDIT? WHY AND FROM WHAT AGENCY?

23. IN YOUR OPINION, DO AUDITORS FEEL THAT THEY HAVE TO MAKE A FINDING OF SOME KIND?

24. HAVE ANY OF THE AUDITS OF YOUR SEA IDENTIFIED IMPORTANT MANAGEMENT PROBLEMS? WHICH PROBLEMS?

25. WHAT PERCENT OF EDUCATION ACTIVITIES IN YOUR STATE ARE AUDITED BY SOMEONE? (INDICATE ANY GAPS IN COVERAGE)

26. (A) WHAT SHOULD BE THE FUTURE ROLE OF AUDITING IN SEA's? (B) HOW CAN IT BE ACCOMPLISHED?

27. CONSIDERING THAT THIS STUDY IS CONCERNED WITH IMPROVING THE AUDIT PROCESS AND MAKING AUDITS MORE MEANINGFUL TO SEA MANAGEMENT, ARE THERE ANY OTHER COMMENTS WHICH YOU WOULD LIKE TO MAKE OF EITHER A GENERAL OR SPECIFIC NATURE?

28. IN MOST STUDIES OF THIS TYPE, INDIVIDUALS ARE NOT GIVEN AN OPPORTUNITY TO EXPRESS HOW THEY WOULD APPROACH THE PROBLEM OF MAKING THE AUDIT MORE MEANINGFUL TO SEA MANAGEMENT. THE PROJECT STAFF WOULD WELCOME YOUR IDEAS ON THIS SUBJECT. PLEASE USE THE FOLLOWING SPACE TO PRESENT YOUR SUGGESTIONS CONCERNING THE DIRECTIONS OR APPROACHES THIS PROJECT SHOULD TAKE TO BRING ABOUT POSITIVE CHANGES IN AUDITING OF SEA's.

APPENDIX B

INTERVIEW AND QUESTIONNAIRE RESPONDENTS

The AIDE Project would like to thank the following individuals and their Agencies for taking time out of their busy schedules to participate in our interviews or respond to our questionnaires.

State Education Agency
Questionnaire Respondents

State	*Respondent*
Alaska	Nathaniel Cole Director, Administrative Services
Arizona	John M. George Director, Business and Financial Services
Arkansas	Joe L. Hudson Associate Director for Finance
Connecticut	Marion F. Kennedy Assistant Chief, Division of Administration

Delaware	William Corkle Title I Coordinator
Georgia	Bert K. Adams Assistant State Superintendent of Schools
Hawaii	Clarence N. Masumotoya Director, Federal Programs
Indiana	Robert D. Gadsberry Director of Accounting
Iowa	Earl R. Linden Budget Coordinator
Kansas	Leonard N. Moore Director, Auditing & Finance
Louisiana	George B. Benton, Jr. Assistant Superintendent in Charge of Administration & Finance
Maine	P. R. Dumont Assistant Director of Education Administrative Services
Michigan	R. Hornberger Department Services Division
Minnesota	Ronald J. Laliberte Administrative Services Director
Mississippi	W. S. Griffin, Director Division of Administration & Finance
Missouri	William J. Wasson Associate Commissioner
Montana	William J. Cunneen Assistant Superintendent
Nebraska	Robert E. Dyke Deputy Assistant Commissioner
Nevada	L. W. Liston Associate Superintendent
New Mexico	Orlando J. Giron Director, Budgets & Finance
New York	August E. Cerrito Supervisor of School Business Management

North Carolina J. A. Porter, Jr.
Director, Division of Auditing and Accounting

North Dakota   Lowell L. Jensen
Director, Program Planning & Evaluation

Oklahoma   Marion Patrick
Director, Budgets & Audits

Oregon   James F. Collins
Coordinator - Internal Fiscal Service

Pennsylvania   John J. Windish
Assistant Comptroller

Rhode Island   Robert C. Whitaker
Coordinator of Administrative Services

South Carolina R. W. Burnette
Director, Office of Finance

South Dakota   Grace M. Ashmore
Comptroller

Tennessee   T. B. Webb
Assistant Commissioner

Utah   Bernarr S. Furse
Administrative Assistant

Vermont   Leslie S. White
Business Manager

Virginia   T. J. Bise
Director, Division of Finance

West Virginia   B. G. Pauley
Assistant State Superintendent

Wisconsin   Donald Dimick
Assistant Superintendent, Administrative Services

Wyoming   Clyde Gerrard
Director, Fiscal Services

State Education Agency
Interviews

ALABAMA

LeRoy Brown   Nell R. Haynes, Accountant
Superintendent of Education   Title I and IV

W. H. Kimbrough, Director
Administration & Finance

Gladys Stokley
Accountant III

T. L Faulkner, Director
Vocational Education

William E. Mellown, Jr.
State Coordinator, Title I,
III, and V

Roy T. Alverson, Coordinator
Food Services, Local Accounting,
and Auditing

CALIFORNIA

Wilson Riles, Superintendent
Public Instruction and
Director of Education

Alvin J. Schmidt, Assistant
Superintendent, Administration

Ernest Lehr, Acting Chief
Compensatory Education
Fiscal Management

Wesley Smith, Director
Vocational Education

Leo Lopez, Director
Compensatory Education

Weynard Bailey, Consultant
Secondary Education

Warren C. Coffey, Coordinator
Program Planning & Development

FLORIDA

John W. Seay
Deputy Commissioner

James T. Campbell
Associate Commissioner
Administration

Herman O. Myers, Associate
Commissioner for Budgeting,
Planning, and Development

Jon L. Stapleton,
Administrator, Office
Federal-State Relations

Charlie N. Fagan, Chief
Accountant, Research and
Development

Hal Lewis
ESEA Title I Coordinator

George D. Jacobs
Assistant Comptroller

Howard M. Blomberg, Accounting
Specialist—Cost Benefit Analysis

Bob Watson, Accountant
ESEA I, II III

Philip S. Shaw
Comptroller

KENTUCKY

Wendell P. Butler
Superintendent of
Public Instruction

Fred Johnson, Assistant
Director, Division of
Finance

Jim Melton, Assistant
Superintendent, Administration
and Finance

William Coakley, Assistant
Director, Department of
Finance and Services

John Bruce, Director
ESEA Title I

C. E. Salyer
Budget Analyst

MARYLAND

Quentin L. Earhart
Deputy Superintendent

Percy V. Williams, Assistant
Superintendent, Division of
Compensatory, Urban and
Supplementary Programs

James E. Reter, Auditor
School Systems

Brian Fleming, Specialist
Federal Programs

McComb Nichols, Assistant
Director, Fiscal Management
and Services

Frances S. Meginnis
Assistant Director
ESEA Title III

MASSACHUSETTS

Everett G. Thistle, Assistant
Commissioner, State and
Federal Assistance

James J. McGrath,
Administrative
Assistant in Auditing

Robert F. Nolan, Director
Surplus Property

Frank Calahan,
Chief Accountant
Federal Programs

G. F. Lambert
Business Manager

J. C. Bradley, Director
Program Assistance

Joe Yannaci
Title I Accountant

Gerry McGovern
Semi-senior Field Accountant

OHIO

Martin W. Essex
Superintendent of Public
Instruction

R. A. Horn, Director
Division of Federal
Assistance

John G. Oldgers, Former
Director, Division of Guidance
and Testing now with Ohio State
University

Byrl R. Shoemaker, Director
Division of Vocational
Education

Clayton Corke, Chief
Services, Title I Section

Jack Brown, Chief
Title II Section

Arlie Cox, Chief Programs
Title I Section

James Miller, Chief Special
Programs, Title I Section

Robert Chandler,
Coordinator, NDEA Title III
Section

Kenneth W. Richards, Director
Division of Guidance & Testing

Bob Barb, Accountant
Division of Vocational
Education

Samuel J. Bonham, Director
Division of Special Education

Charles Galey
Business Manager

Harold J. Bowers
Deputy Superintendent

TEXAS

J. W. Edgar
Commissioner of Education

Leon Graham, Assistant
Commissioner, Administration

R. E. Slayton, Director
Funds Management

John K. Taylor
Junior Field Auditor

Edward E. Randall, Director
Division of School Audits

William H. Van Horn, Jr
Business Agent

WASHINGTON

H. Louis Bruno, State
Superintendent of Public
Instruction

Thomas Deering
Administrative Assistant

Rich Boyd, Coordinator
Federal Title III Programs

Twila Brassfield, Fiscal Officer
Budgeting and Accounting

James Oechsner, Budget
Administrator
for Federal Programs

Melvin Collart
Supervisor, School Financial
Services

Keith Bigelow, Staff Member,
School Financial Services

James Click, Supervisor
Migrant Education

Robert Lindemuth
Federal Liaison Officer

Newton Buker, Institutional
Education Liaison

State Audit Office
Interviews

ALABAMA

A. W. Steineker, Chief
Examiner of Public Accounts

William W. Dillard
Supervisor of County Audits
Examiners of Public Accounts

Melba Till Allen
State Auditor

CALIFORNIA

Robert L. Hamric
Senior Management Auditor
State Department of Finance

Richard K. Piper, Auditor
State Department of Finance

Walter J. Quinn, Audit
Manager, Office of Auditor
General

Richard Brandsma
Legislative Analysts Office

FLORIDA

Sid Torbet, Auditor
Florida Office of the Auditor General

KENTUCKY

Mary Louise Foust, Auditor
of Public Accounts

James E. Truempy
Legislative Research Auditor

MARYLAND

Pierce J. Lambdin
Legislative Auditor

MASSACHUSETTS

Peter Gavrilles, Director
State Audits

John Dimetrakis

Ben A. Ciailone

OHIO

Robert Millisor, Assistant Deputy Inspector
Bureau of Inspection and Supervision of
Public Office

TEXAS

George McNeil
State Auditor

WASHINGTON

Robert Graham
State Auditor

Jim Cornett
Chief Assistant Auditor

APPENDIX C

SELECTED

BIBLIOGRAPHY

The following selected bibliography lists those books and articles which The AIDE Project found to be particularly helpful and informative.

BOOKS AND MONOGRAPHS

American Accounting Association, Committee on Accounting Practices for Not-for-Profit Organizations. Robert J. Freeman, Chairman. *Accounting for Not-for-Profit Organizations.* New York: The American Accounting Association, 1970.

_____, Committee on Basic Auditing Concepts. *A Statement of Basic Auditing Concepts.* Studies in Accounting Research, Number VI. Sarasota, Florida: AAA, 1973.

American Institute of Certified Public Accountants. *Audits of State and Local Governmental Units.* Industry Audit Guide. New York: AICPA, 1974.

_____. *Code of Professional Ethics.* New York: AICPA, 1972.

_____, Committee on Auditing for Federal Agencies (1970-71). *Suggested Guidelines for the Structure and Content of Audit Guides Prepared by Federal Agencies for Use by CPAs.* New York: AICPA, 1972.

_____, Committee on Audit Procedure. *Statement on Auditing Standards.* Codification of Auditing Standards and Procedures, Number I. New York: AICPA, 1973.

_____, Committee on Relations with the General Accounting Office. *Auditing Standards Established by the GAO: Their Meaning and Significance for CPAs.* New York: AICPA, 1973.

American Institute of Industrial Engineers, Inc. *Criteria for Evaluating Company Performance.* New York: American Institute of Industrial Engineers, Inc., 1962.

Anthony, Robert N. *Planning and Control Systems: A Framework for Analysis.* Boston, Mass.: Harvard University, 1965.

Brink, Victor Z. *Internal Auditing: Its Nature and Function and Methods of Procedure.* New York: The Ronald Press Company, 1941.

_____, et al. *Modern Internal Auditing: An Operational Approach.* 3rd ed. New York: The Ronald Press Company, 1973.

Brown, Richard E. *The GAO: Untapped Source of Congressional Power.* Knoxville, Tennessee: The University of Tennessee Press, 1970.

Cadmus, Bradford. *Operational Auditing Handbook.* New York: The Institute of Internal Auditors, Inc., 1964.

Carmichael, D. R. *The Auditor's Reporting Obligation: The Meaning and Implementation of the Fourth Standard of Reporting.* Auditing Research Monograph, Number I. New York: American Institute of Certified Public Accountants, 1972.

Cashin, James A. *Handbook for Auditors.* New York: McGraw-Hill Book Company, 1971.

The Council of State Governments. *The Book of the States, 1972-1973.* Lexington, Kentucky: The Council of State Governments, 1972.

Faucett, Philip M. *Management Audit for Small Manufacturers.* Washington, D.C.: Small Business Administration, 1963.

Federal Government Accountants Association. *Bibliography on Federal Accounting, Auditing, Budgeting, and Reporting, 1900-1970.* Arlington, Virginia: FGAA, 1971.

_____, Northern Virginia Chapter. *Auditing: A Compendium.* Washington, D.C.: The Joint OMB/CSC/GAO Project on Improving Federal Productivity, 1972.

_____, Washington Chapter. *Sophisticated Auditing Techniques.* Washington, D.C.: FGAA, 1973.

Friedman, Burton D. *State Government and Education: Management in the State Education Agency.* Chicago: Public Administration Service, 1971.
_____. *The Quest for Accountability.* Chicago: Public Administration Service, 1973.

_____, and Laird, Dunbar J. *Grants Management in Education: Federal Impact on State Agencies.* Chicago: Public Administration Service, 1971.

George, Claude S., Jr. *The History of Management Thought.* Englewood Cliffs, N. J.: Prentice-Hall, Inc., 1968.

Harris, Sam P. *State Departments of Education, State Boards of Education, and Chief State School Officers.* Department of Health, Education, and Welfare Publication No. (OE) 73-07400. Washington, D.C.: U.S. Government Printing Office, 1973.

The Institute of Internal Auditors. *Behavioral Patterns in Internal Audit Relationships.* Research Committee Report 17. Frederic E. Mints, Project Researcher. New York: IIA, 1972.

_____. *Bibliography of Internal Auditing, 1950-1965.* New York: The Institute of Internal Auditors, 1967.

_____. *Bibliography of Internal Auditing, Supplement 1966-1968.* New York: The Institute of Internal Auditors, 1969.

_____. *Capsule Course in Internal Auditing.* New York: The Institute of Internal Auditors, Inc., 1965.

_____. *Code of Ethics.* New York: The Institute of Internal Auditors, Inc., 1968.

_____. *Statement of the Responsibilities of the Internal Auditor.* New York: The Institute of Internal Auditors, Inc., 1971.

_____. *A Guide to Organization and Administration of an Internal Auditing Department.* New York: The Institute of Internal Auditors, Inc., 1962.

_____. *Survey of Internal Auditing.* New York: The Institute of Internal Auditors, Inc., 1969.

Knighton, Lennis M. *Internal Auditing in State Government.* Orlando, Florida: The Institute of Internal Auditors, 1973.

_____. *The Performance Post Audit in State Government.* East Lansing, Mich.: Michigan State University, Bureau of Business and Economic Research, 1967.

Leonard, William P. *Management Audit: An Appraisal of Management Methods and Performance.* Englewood Cliffs, N. J.: Prentice-Hall, Inc., 1962.

Lindberg, Roy A. and Cohn, Theodore. *Operations Auditing.* New York: American Management Association, 1972.

Martindell, Jackson. *The Scientific Appraisal of Management.* New York: Harper and Brothers, 1950.

Massachusetts Legislative Research Bureau. *Report Relative to Legislative Post Audit.* Boston: Legislative Research Bureau, 1971.

Mautz, R. K. and Sharaf, Hussein A. *The Philosophy of Auditing.* American Accounting Association Monograph No. 6. Madison, Wisconsin: American Accounting Association, 1961.

McGregor, Douglas. *The Human Side of Enterprise.* New York: McGraw-Hill Book Company, 1960.

Morin, Alfred J. *Handbook for Educational Program Audit.* Washington, D.C.: Alfred J. Morin and Associates, 1971.

National Committee on Governmental Accounting. *Governmental Accounting, Auditing and Financial Reporting.* Chicago, Illinois: Municipal Finance Officers Association, 1968.

Norbeck, Edward F., *et al. Operational Auditing for Management Control.* New York: American Management Association, 1969.

Normanton, E. L. *The Accountability and Audit of Governments: A Comparative Study.* New York: Frederic A. Praeger, Inc., 1966.

Rose, T. G. *The Management Audit.* 3rd ed. London: Gee and Company, 1961.

Roy, Robert H. and MacNeill, James H. *Horizons for a Profession.* New York: American Institute of Certified Public Accountants, 1967.

Sawyer, Lawrence B. *The Practice of Modern Internal Auditing: Ap-*

praising Operations for Management. New York: The Institute of Internal Auditors, 1973.

Schein, Edgar H. *Process Consultation: Its Role in Organization Development.* Reading, Massachusetts: Addison-Wesley, 1969.

Stenner, A Jackson and Webster, William J. *Educational Program Audit Handbook.* Arlington, Virginia: The Institute for The Development of Educational Auditing, 1971.

Stettler, Howard F. *Systems Based Independent Audits.* Englewood Cliffs, New Jersey: Prentice-Hall, 1967.

U.S. Bureau of the Budget. *Audit of Federal Grants-In-Aid to State and Local Governments.* Circular Number A-73. Washington, D.C.: BOB, 1965.

U.S. Department of Health, Education, and Welfare. *A Program for Improving the Quality of Grantee Management: Financially Independent Organizations,* Vol I. Washington, D.C.: HEW, 1970.

_____. *A Program for Improving the Quality of Grantee Management: Financially Dependent Organization,* Vol II. Washington, D.C.: HEW, 1970.

_____, HEW Audit Agency. *Audit Guide , Elementary and Secondary Education Act of 1965, Title I.* Interim Audit Instruction C-10. Washington, D.C.: HEWAA, 1966.

_____. *Audit Guide for Review of Local Education Agency Programs Under Title I of the Elementary and Secondary Education Act of 1965.* (Unpublished Draft). HEWAA, 1973.

_____. *Procedures Handbook, Part III, Prerelease Procedures.* Washington, D.C.: HEWAA, 1973.

U.S. General Accounting Office. *Audits of Government Contracts.* Washington, D.C.: U.S. Government Printing Office, 1967.

_____. *Internal Auditing in Federal Agencies.* Washington, D.C.: GAO, 1968.

_____, The Comptroller General. *Auditors-Agents for Good Government.* Washington, D.C.: GAO, 1973.

_____. *Case Study: Illinois' Use of Public Accountants For Auditing State Activities.* Washington, D.C.: GAO, 1973.

_____. *Examples of Findings from Governmental Audits.* Washington, D.C.: GAO, 1973.

_____. *Standards for Audit of Governmental Organizations,*

Programs, Activities, and Functions. Washington, D.C.: GAO, 1972.

_____. *What GAO is Doing to Improve Governmental Auditing Standards.* Washington, D.C.: GAO, 1973.

U.S. General Services Administration, Office of Federal Management Policy. *Federal Management Circular 73-2: Audit of Federal Operations and Programs by Executive Branch Agencies.* Washington, D.C.: GSA, 1973.

Wingate, John W. *Management Audit for Small Retailers.* Washington, D.C.: Small Business Administration, 1964.

PERIODICALS AND PAPERS

Allen, J. R. "Managing the Operational Audit Function." *The Internal Auditor,* XXIII (Fall, 1966), pp. 21-29.

Ard, James H. "The Problem with Operational Auditing." *The Federal Accountant,* XXII (March, 1973), pp. 41-46.

Arrowood, H. S. "The Modern Concept of Internal Auditing." *The Internal Auditor,* XX (Summer, 1963), pp. 12-24.

Beale, F. A. "The Changing Role of the Internal Auditor." *The Internal Auditor,* XXII (Winter, 1965), pp. 34-38.

Bhushan, B. S. N. "The Internal Auditor in Industry and His Role in Management." *The Internal Auditor,* XX (Summer, 1963), pp. 48-53.

Brown, Robert B. and Stepnick, Edward W. "What's Ahead in the Field of Auditing?" *Footnote,* II (Summer, 1970), pp. 21-23.

Buckley, J. W. "Operational Audits by Public Accountants." *Abacus,* II (December, 1966), pp. 159-71.

Butler, John J. "Human Relations in Auditing." *The Internal Auditor,* XX (Spring, 1963), pp. 61-71.

Cadmus, Bradford. "Eyes and Ears of Management." *The Accountant,* CXLVII (October 13, 1962), pp. 466-68.

_____. "A Quarter Century of Internal Auditing." *The Internal Auditor,* XV (December, 1958), pp. 59-63.

Campfield, William L. "Education for Management Auditing." *The Federal Accountant,* XV (Spring, 1966), pp. 30-40.

_____. "Independence in Internal Auditing — Fact or Fiction?" *The Internal Auditor,* XXII (Fall, 1965), pp. 20-23.

Carlson, R. E. "Specialization — A New Approach in Staffing an Internal Auditing Function." *The Internal Auditor,* XXII (Winter, 1965), pp. 23-33.

Carmichael, Douglas R. "Some Hard Questions on Management Audits." *The Journal of Accountancy,* CXXIX (February, 1970), pp. 72-74.

Carolus, Roger N. "Some Challenges of Operational Auditing." *The Internal Auditor,* XXVI (November-December, 1969), pp. 12-27.

_____. "The Who's , Why's, What's and How's of Operational Auditing." *The Internal Auditor,* XXV (July-August, 1968), pp. 27-36.

Cato, Wilbur M. "Developing Teamwork for the Audit Organization." *U. S. Army Audit Agency Bulletin,* 465-18 (Fall, 1969), pp. 23-27.

Cayton, Roy S. "Management Audits: Systems and Procedures Personnel or Internal Auditors?" *The Internal Auditor,* XIX (Spring, 1962), pp. 47-48.

Choi, J. T. "Operational Auditing: Part I." *The Internal Auditor,* XXVIII (March/April, 1971), pp. 6-26.

_____. "Operational Auditing: Part II." *The Internal Auditor,* XXVIII (May/June, 1971), pp. 37-55.

Churchill, Neil C. and Cyert, Richard M. "An Experiment in Management Auditing." *The Journal of Accountancy,* CXXI (February, 1966), pp. 39-43.

Cloutier, Paul. "The Management Audit." *The Canadian Chartered Accountant,* XXCIX (September, 1966), pp. 178-81.

Davis, Paul M. "The Management Audit and the Need for a Managerial Efficiency Attest Function." *The Illinois CPA,* XXI (Autumn, 1968), pp. 18-24.

DeZerne, Wilbur R. "Management Controls and the Auditor." *The Virginia Accountant,* XVII (Winter, 1965), pp. 13-20.

Dittenhofer, Mortimer A. "The Case for Standards and Guidelines for State Audits." *The Internal Auditor,* XXVII (July-August, 1970), pp. 61-69.

_____. "Federal Performance Auditing: Its Application to

State Audit Effort." *The Federal Accountant,* XIX (March, 1970), pp. 60-72.

Dodwell, Joseph W. "Operational Auditing." *Management Controls,* (January, 1961), pp. 3-6.

_____. "Operational Auditing: A Part of the Basic Audit." *The Journal of Accountancy,* CXXI (June, 1966), pp. 31-39.

_____. "Operations Auditing." *The Internal Auditor,* XVIII (Fall, 1961), pp. 71-81.

Dooley, D.C. "Gradual Change in Internal Auditing." *The Office,* LIX (January, 1964), pp. 88, 249-52.

_____. "Nothing New Under the Sun?" *The Internal Auditor,* XXII (Summer, 1965), pp. 8-15.

Elliott, Norman J., ed. "Audit of Management." *The Journal of Accountancy,* CXIII (May, 1962), pp. 85-86.

Estes, O'Ferrell. "Audit of Operations." *The Internal Auditor,* XIII (December, 1956), pp. 6-10.

Evans, E. R. "Approach — the Key to Operational Auditing." *The Internal Auditor,* XXIII (Spring, 1966), pp. 29-36.

_____. "Audit Technique." *The Internal Auditor,* XX (Winter, 1963), pp. 66-71.

_____. "Managing the Internal Audit Function." *The Internal Auditor,* XXVII (January-February, 1970), pp. 12-18.

Evans, James R. "Operational Auditing in Practice." *NAA Bulletin,* XLV (June, 1964), pp. 16-18.

Ford, Robert W. "The Interview as an Audit Technique." *The GAO Review,* (Fall, 1968), pp. 39-44.

Forsstrom, Borje. "Auditing the Management." *The Accountant,* CXXVIII (May 24, 1958), pp. 620-22.

Freeman, Robert J. "Aspects of Performance Auditing." Paper presented at the 3rd Annual Series of U.S. General Accounting Office Regional Workshops for State Auditors, Boston, Mass., 1972.

"The General Accounting Office and Its Functions — A Brief Historical Outline." *The GAO Review,* (Summer, 1971), pp. 1-15.

Goldstein, Louis L. "Some Problems of State, Local and Federal Relationships." *The Federal Accountant,* XIX (September, 1970), pp. 29-36.

Goodwin, E. S. L. "Control: A Brief Excursion on the Meaning of A Word." *The Michigan Business Review,* VIII (January, 1960), pp. 13-17, 28.

Graese, C. E. "Managerial Auditing and the Independent Accountant." *Management Controls,* XII (April, 1965), pp. 60-63.

Grubel, Frederick. "Role of the Management Audit." *Hospital Accounting,* XXI (April , 1967), pp. 4-5.

Harrison, Horace H. "Improved Operations through Operational Auditing." *Auditgram,* XLII (August, 1966), pp. 8-12.

Higgins, J. A. C. "The Effective Audit Report — Our Most Important Product." *The Internal Auditor,* XXX (May/June, 1973), pp. 44-49.

Holt, Dean W. "An Audit for Management." *U. S. Army Audit Agency Bulletin,* 465-23 (Winter, 1967), pp. 35-38.

"How to Get Ready for a Management Audit." *Nation's Schools,* LXVIII (September, 1966), pp. 66-68.

Howard, Leslie R. "The Management Audit — I." *Accountancy,* XXC (October, 1969), pp. 772-74.

_____. "The Management Audit — II." *Accountancy,* XXC (November, 1969), pp. 835-38.

Inman, Charles N. "Managerial Auditing of Operations." *The Internal Auditor,* XV (June, 1958), pp. 42-50.

"The Institute of Internal Auditors — 25 Years of Progress." *The Internal Auditor,* XXIII (Summer, 1966), pp. 50-56.

"Is the Term 'Audit' Too Loosely Used?" *The Journal of Accountancy,* XCV (May, 1953), pp. 551-52.

Ives, Martin. "Operational Auditing in State Government." *The Internal Auditor,* XXV (May-June, 1968), pp. 51-57.

Joplin, H. Bruce. "Internal Auditing: Management vs. Financial." *The Oklahoma CPA,* IV (October, 1965), pp. 13-18.

Keating, Stephen F. "How Honeywell Management Views Operational Auditing." *The Internal Auditor,* XXVI (September-October, 1969), pp. 43-51.

Kelly, James F. "Grant Administration, Federal-State Relationships." *The Federal Accountant,* XVI (October, 1967), pp. 19-22.

Kent, Arthur H. "Audits of Operations." *The Internal Auditor,* V (March, 1948), pp. 11-20.

Knighton, Lennis M. "Improving the Audit of Federal/State/Local Programs." *The Federal Accountant,* XVII (December, 1968), pp. 31-43.

_____. "Improving Internal Auditing in State Agencies." *The Internal Auditor,* XXIX (November/December, 1972), pp. 72-74.

_____. "An Integrated Framework for Conceptualizing Alternative Approaches to State Audit Programs." *The Federal Accountant,* XX (March, 1971), pp. 6-23.

_____. "Performance Auditing: A New Dimension in State Auditing." *The Illinois CPA,* XXX (Winter, 1967), pp. 1-9.

_____. "Public Sector Audits by CPA Firms: Challenge and Opportunity." *Texas CPA,* XLII (October, 1969), pp. 15-28.

_____. and Graham, R. V. "Is Auditing a Fourth Power?" *State Government,* XXX (Autumn, 1970), pp. 258-270.

Kropatkin, Philip. "How to Write an Audit Finding." *Footnote,* I (Fall, 1969), pp. 20-24.

Langenderfer, Harold Q. and Robertson, Jack C. "A Theoretical Structure for Independent Audits of Management." *The Accounting Review,* XLIV (October, 1969), pp. 777-87.

Lee, T. A. "The Nature of Auditing and Its Objectives." *Accountancy,* LXXXI (April, 1970), pp. 292-96.

Levitt, Arthur. "Operational Auditing in New York State." *The New York Certified Public Accountant,* XXXIV (May, 1964), pp. 337-41.

Lindberg, Roy A. "Operations Auditing: What It Is, What It Isn't." *Management Review,* LVIII (December, 1969), pp. 2-10.

Lindsey, Allen F. "The Internal Audit — Service to Management." *The Internal Auditor,* XXVI (May-June, 1969), pp. 64-71.

Lissenden, H. Jack. "Management Audits: Systems and Procedures Personnel or Internal Auditors?" *The Internal Auditor,* XIX (Spring, 1962), pp. 56-60.

Lordan, John J. "Federal Auditing — A Look at Some Changes From the Top." *Journal of Accountancy,* CXXXVI (December, 1973), pp. 29-34.

Lowe, E. A. "The Audit of Management Efficiency." *The Internal Auditor,* XXIII (Winter, 1966), pp. 45-52.

Lowery, Joseph M. "Governmental Accounting, Auditing, and Financial Reporting." *Municipal Finance,* XL (February, 1968), pp. 111-16.

Lynn, Bernard B. "Army Operational Auditing." *The Internal Auditor,* XXII (Fall, 1965), pp. 37-43.

Matthews, K. B., ed. "Audit of an Operating Department." *The Internal Auditor,* XXIV (Summer, 1967), p. 83.

_____, "Defining Operational Auditing." *The Internal Auditor,* XXIII (Winter, 1966), p. 87.

_____. "Functional Areas — Measuring Performance." *The Internal Auditor,* XXIII (Fall, 1966), p. 85.

_____. "Scope of Operational Audits." *The Internal Auditor,* XXV (January-February, 1968), p. 74.

Maxwell, Joe E. "Conducting a Management Audit." *Association Management,* XIX (December, 1967), pp. 38-40, 45.

McClung, G. L. "History and Background of the Internal Auditing Profession." *The Internal Auditor,* XVI (June, 1959), pp. 78-79.

McGhee, Archie. "Salesmanship for Auditors." *The Internal Auditor,* XXVIII (January/February, 1971), pp. 28-32.

"Meaning of 'Audit.' " *The Journal of Accountancy,* CIX (May, 1960), pp. 34-35.

Miller, John R., and Ostrow, Harry. "Road to Professionalizing a State Audit Organization." *The Federal Accountant,* XXIII (March, 1974), pp. 10-18.

Mints, Frederic E. "Operational Auditing." *The Internal Auditor,* XI (June, 1954), pp. 32-45.

Morse, Ellsworth H., Jr. "Auditing Federal Grant Programs." *The Federal Accountant,* XVIII (June, 1969), pp. 4-21.

_____. "Auditing Government Operations." *The Internal Auditor,* XXX (July/August, 1973), pp. 10-19.

_____. "GAO Audits of Management Performance." *The Journal of Accountancy,* CXII (October, 1961), pp. 42-48.

_____. "Internal Auditing Principles and Concepts for Federal Agencies." *The Federal Accountant,* XIX (March, 1970), pp. 34-50.

Newman, William A., Jr. "Broad Horizon of Auditing." *The Federal Accountant,* XI (March, 1962), pp. 67-79.

_____. "Evolutionary Changes in Auditing in the Federal Government." *The Federal Accountant,* VIII (December, 1958), pp. 41-55.

Norgaard, Corine T. "Extending the Boundaries of the Attest Function." *The Accounting Review,* XLVII (July, 1972), pp. 433-42.

_____. "The Professional Accountant's View of Operational Auditing." *The Journal of Accountancy,* CXXVIII (December, 1969), pp. 45-48.

Nurnberg, Hugh. "The Independent Auditor's Attest Function: Its Prospects for Extension." *The New York Certified Public Accountant,* XLI (October, 1971), pp. 727-32.

Osborne, Richard W. "Practical Aspects of an Operational Audit." *The Internal Auditor,* XVII (Winter, 1960), pp. 28-38.

Pinkelman, Franklin C. "Development of Performance Auditing in Michigan." *The Florida CPA,* VII (May, 1967), pp. 10-19.

Protheroe, J. H. "The Modern Concept of Internal Audit." *The Accountant,* CLII (April, 1965), pp. 469-71.

Pyhrr, Peter A. "Operational Auditing: New Profit Tool for Top Management." *Business Management,* XXXIV (September, 1968), pp. 87-92.

_____. "Operational Auditing: A Run for Daylight." *Financial Executive,* XXXVII (May, 1969), pp. 19-20.

Raffensperger, O. E. "The Human Element in Auditing." *The Internal Auditor,* XXIX (January/February, 1972), pp. 9-17.

Ratcliff, E. F. "Auditing for Operations." *The Internal Auditor,* XIV (December, 1957), pp. 6-12.

_____. "Extending Auditing into Operations." *The Internal Auditor,* XI (September, 1954), pp. 7-15.

"Responsibilities of Auditor — King County, Washington." *The GAO Review,* (Summer, 1972), pp. 73-74.

Rigg, F. J. "The Management Audit." *The Internal Auditor,* XXV (May-June, 1968), pp. 21-28.

Robinson, B. F. "Management Report Writing." *U. S. Army Audit Agency Bulletin,* 465-12 (March, 1965), pp. 18-26.

Robinson, H. N. "Management Audits: Internal Auditors or Systems and Procedures Personnel?" *The Internal Auditor,* XIX (Spring, 1962), pp. 49-55.

Sawyer, Lawrence B. "Just What Is Management Auditing?" *The Internal Auditor,* XXX (March/April, 1973), pp. 10-21.

Scantlebury, D. L. "The Structure of a Management Audit Finding." *The Internal Auditor,* XXIX (March/April, 1972), pp. 10-22.

Seiler, Robert E. "The Operational Audit: An Extension of Management Controls." *The Internal Auditor,* XXIII (Summer, 1966), pp. 72-79.

Simonetti, Gilbert, Jr. "Auditing Standards Published by the GAO." *Journal of Accountancy,* CXXXVII (January, 1974), pp. 33-39.

Smith, Charles H., *et al.* "The Need for and Scope of the Audit of Management: A Survey of Attitudes." *The Accounting Review,* XLVII (April, 1972), pp. 270-283.

Smith, Stancil M. "What's Going on in Government Auditing?" *U. S. Army Audit Agency Bulletin,* 465-15 (December, 1965), pp. 17-30.

Staats, Elmer B. "The Growing Importance of Internal Auditing in the Federal Government." *The Internal Auditor,* XXV (January-February, 1968), pp. 8-16.

_____. "Management or Operational Auditing." *The GAO Review,* (Winter, 1972), pp. 25-35.

_____. "The Nation's Interest in Improving State and Local Government." Address to the Regional Conference of the American Society of Public Administrators, Topeka, Kansas, October 23, 1970.

_____. "Progress in the Financial Management of Federal Grant-In-Aid Programs." Address to the Joint State-Federal Financial Management Conference, Washington, D.C., October 9, 1970.

_____. "The Role of the General Accounting Office in Reviewing the Results of Federal Programs." *The GAO Review,* (Summer, 1971), pp. 74-82.

Staerkel, William M. "How a School Management Audit Works." *Nation's Schools,* LXVVI (December, 1965), pp. 33-36.

Stanley, E. D., Jr. "Internal Audit in the Navy." *Armed Forces Controller,* IX (September, 1964), pp. 9-13.

Stepnick, Edward W. "Audit Findings — Their Nature and Development." *Footnote,* (Fall, 1969), pp. 16-19.

_____. "Federal-State Audit Partnership." Address to the Effective Governmental Auditing Course of the Intergency Auditor Training Center, Department of Commerce, Washington, D.C., (April 20, 1971).

Stettler, H. F. "Current Trends in Auditing." *The Cooperative Accountant,* XX (Fall, 1967), pp. 2-7.

Stone, Willard E. "Auditing Management Efficiency." *The Australian Accountant,* XXXVII (March, 1967), pp. 155-60.

_____. "Depth Auditing: Appraisal of Management Performance." *The New York Certified Public Accountant,* XXXI (August, 1961), pp. 521-28.

Swann, William K. "On-the-Job Training of New Auditors." *U. S. Army Audit Agency Bulletin,* 465-12 (March, 1965), pp. 35-37.

Thompson, Raymond L. "History, Uses and Potential of the Management Audit." *The Florida Certified Public Accountant,* VII (May, 1967), pp. 1-9.

Towers, Elwood. "Aspects of Operational Auditing and Internal Control." *The Internal Auditor,* XX (Winter, 1963), pp. 55-63.

U. S. General Accounting Office. "Internal Auditing: A Statement of Basic Principles and Concepts." *The Internal Auditor,* XV (March, 1958), pp. 13-25.

Walsh, Francis J., Jr. "Trends in Audit Management." *U. S. Army Audit Agency Bulletin,* 465-15 (December, 1965), pp. 7-15.

Watt, M. Laird. "The Accountant Looks at Operational Auditing." *The Canadian Chartered Accountant,* XXC (April, 1962), pp. 352-56.

Wilson, Arthur P. "Management Audit Comes of Age." *The Controller,* XVIII (September, 1950), pp. 411-12, 414-16.

Wilson, Reginald. "'Efficiency Audit' — a Misleading and Dangerous Term." *The Accountant,* CXXVIII (January 31, 1953), pp. 116-19.

Zimmerman, Robert R. "Auditing the Organization Structure." *The Internal Auditor,* XXII (Fall, 1965), pp. 58-70.